FORBIDDEN
RELATIVES

The American Myth of Cousin Marriage

MARTIN OTTENHEIMER

University of Illinois Press   Urbana and Chicago

Library of Congress Cataloging-in-Publication Data
Ottenheimer, Martin
    Forbidden relatives : the American myth of cousin marriage /
Martin Ottenheimer.
        p.   cm.
    Includes bibliographical references and index.
    ISBN 0-252-02239-4 (acid-free paper).—ISBN 0-252-06540-9 (pbk. :
acid-free paper)
    1. Cross-cousin marriage—United States. 2. Cross-cousin
marriage—Europe. 3. United States—Social life and customs.
4. Europe—Social life and customs. I. Title.
GN560.U6O77   1996
306.8—dc20   95-41800
                                                                CIP

Contents

Introduction   1

1
U.S. Laws Prohibiting the Marriage
of Relatives   19

2
The Reasons for U.S. Laws against
First Cousin Marriage   42

3
European Laws Prohibiting the Marriage
of Relatives   61

4
European Views of Cousin Marriage   79

5
The Evolutionary Factor   94

6
Biogenetics and First Cousin Marriage   116

7
Culture and Cousin Marriage   134

Bibliography   155

Index   169

Acknowledgments

There are a number of people who have helped make this publication possible. From the gathering of information to the final copy, I have been aided by librarians, lawyers, anthropologists, biologist, writers, editors, and historians. Their support, contributions, and even their criticisms have been much appreciated. While it is impossible for me to mention everyone involved in the production of this work, I want to thank the following: Alan Bittles, University of London; Kathy Coleman, Kansas State University; Nelda Elder, Kansas State University; Jack Glazier, Oberlin College; Jack Holl, Kansas State University; Lynn B. Jorde, University of Utah; Robert Littrell, Manhattan; Marianne Mason, Indiana University; Bunny McBride, Manhattan; John McCulloh, Kansas State University; Berkeley Miller, Santa Cruz; Jane Mohraz, University of Illinois Press; Michael Poulson, New Mexico Law Library; Harald Prins, Kansas State University; Dwight Read, University of California, Los Angeles; Orlando Romeo, New Mexico Museum of History; Fritz Snyder, Kansas University; and my partner in life, Harriet Ottenheimer, Kansas State University. Of course, not all agree with what I have done with the materials they provided or the advice they offered. The responsibility for what is said in this book lies solely with me.

Introduction

Sally's in de garden siftin' sand,
And all she want is a honey man.
De reason why I wouldn't marry,
Because she was my cousin
O, row de boat ashore, hey, hey,
Sally's in de garden siftin' sand.

—Allen Parker, *Recollections
of Slavery Times*

Why does the United States have laws against marriage between first cousins? Many assume these statutes exist to protect us from the genetic risks of inbreeding. Many fear that close relatives who wed may produce offspring with physical defects or disabilities. Zoologists recognize advantages as well as disadvantages among inbred animals, but few would apply this insight to homo sapiens. As one animal scientist points out, "In humans, it is believed that children from the marriage of first cousins are doomed to be deformed physically or mentally, and this belief is so strong that we have certain moral and legal laws which prohibit the marriage of close relatives" (Lasley 1970:199). The belief that children of close kin marriages are doomed has been linked to the recognition in the field of population genetics that the mating of relatives can increase the probability of homozygosity for recessive genes. It is likely, says M. M. Green (1975), that "this is the empirical reason underlying both religious and secular prohibitions against marriages between relatives since often the homologous recessive genotype determines an undesirable trait" (68).

Some human biologists and legal reformers, however, see no great risk to first cousin marriage. They believe laws prohibiting it serve no useful purpose and should be dropped (Bittles et al. 1991; Commissioners on Uniform State Laws 1970). This book describes the major cultural factors in the development of laws against first cousin marriage in the United States and suggests that these laws need to be reconsidered.

In 1974 the American Bar Association approved the Uniform Marriage and Divorce Act recommended by the National Conference of Commissioners on Uniform State Laws (Glendon 1989:39, note 11). The Uniform Marriage and Divorce Act was designed as a model for all states and allows first cousin marriage. Yet no state with a cousin marriage proscription has accepted this idea, and one state has even enacted legislation against first cousin marriage since the approval of the act.

Although there is serious doubt that the physical dangers to offspring of first cousin marriage justify legislation, the injunctions in the United States have been enacted on the basis of a belief that such a serious risk exists. Why? The answer lies, at least in part, in a myth.

All societies have myths—deeply held assumptions about the nature of the world—which underlie and rationalize social regulations affecting members' behavior. These beliefs are sometimes maintained in spite of contradictory evidence. The American myth of cousin marriage is a case in point. It perpetuates the idea that procreation between first cousins carries an intolerable biological hazard for offspring. This myth first appeared in the United States over two hundred years ago. Beginning in the middle of the nineteenth century it found its way into our legislation system, and a majority of states passed laws against first cousin marriage that remain on the books to this day. Almost invariably, challenging this myth evinces a strong emotional reaction among Americans.

Several important facts counter the myth. First, physical evidence from modern human biological research does not substantiate the exaggerated fears about the possible genetic dangers of cousin marriage (see chapter 6 for details). Second, prohibitions against cousins' marrying predate modern genetics by centuries and have rarely reflected biological concerns. Two thousand years of documentation provides evidence for some form of ban against the marriage of cousins in Europe (Bratt 1984; Goody 1983). For most of their history the injunctions have dealt primarily with social issues. Only relatively recently have people become concerned that the offspring of cousins would inherit defects. The American myth of cousin marriage appears to be a modern rationalization of an ancient custom rather than a conclusion derived from empirical biological research or genetic theory.

This basis for the myth is reflected in the legislation against first cousin marriage in the United States. Today thirty-one states have prohibitions against this practice (including North Carolina, which only prohibits double first cousin marriage—marriage between two individuals if their first cousin relationship is through both their mothers and fathers). Several of these states enacted their statutes in the nineteenth century before the re-discovery of Mendelian genetics, and most passed their laws before the development of modern population genetics in the 1950s. Only one state, Maine, has recently (1985) legislated a prohibition, and it permits first cousin marriage if the couple has had genetic counseling.

A third challenge to the myth is the fact that cousin marriage proscriptions in the Western world fall within a set of marital regulations that do not lend themselves to a biological explanation. Restrictions on the union of close kin include injunctions against in-laws and, in some religious groups, even spiritual kin (see chapters 1 and 2 for details). These regulations are an integral part of the complex of marriage prohibitions among relatives. They must be considered along with the injunctions against con-sanguineal kin in any thorough investigation of the laws forbidding cousin marriage.

Finally, the myth ignores the fact that nineteen states have no laws against matrimony between first cousins. How does the belief in the genetic dangers of close kin marriage relate to the number of states that allow cousin marriage? There is no evidence that these states have more genetically fit individuals with less chance of producing at-risk offspring than do those that have prohibitions.

Clearly, when it comes to the laws banning cousin marriage in the United States, there must be more to the issue than genetics. Furthermore, if cousin marriage really posed a health threat, one would expect all Western countries would recognize the potential hazards and prohibit it. An examination of marital laws outside of the United States, however, reveals that cousin marriage is permitted in every country in Europe.

In England first cousin unions have been legal for several centuries and have been undertaken by a significant number of people. The list includes many famous individuals, such as Charles Darwin, who produced normal and, in some cases, exceptional offspring. The myth of cousin marriage tends to ignore this fact, however. It focuses instead, in a process of self-confirmation, on the family of Queen Victoria. A number of her children and grandchildren married European royalty and suffered from hemophilia. Many Americans, linking this to the general practice of intermarriage among European royalty, mistakenly associate hemophilia with cousin marriage (see chapter 6).

If we broaden the discussion of cousin marriage to include peoples beyond Western societies, it becomes very clear that proscriptions are not rooted in biology. Some societies rule out unions between certain kinds of first cousins, while permitting (and sometimes even encouraging) marriage between other kinds. For example, in some societies one's mother's brother's daughter is a preferred spouse, while one's mother's sister's daughter is forbidden. Since the different cousins in these cases are not distinguishable by consanguineal distance, consanguinity has no apparent application to the prohibitions in these societies.

For those who may wonder if worldwide data have any relevance to the historical development of the prohibitions in the United States, it is worth pointing out that an adequate theory of cousin marriage and its prohibitions should be universally applicable. The U.S. case should fit within the purview of a general theory of the regulation of the marriage of relatives.

Given these considerations, it should be evident that the American myth of cousin marriage does not account for the development of the laws banning first cousin marriage in the United States and cannot have arisen in response to a discovery of significant genetic risks because of procreation among close relatives. If first cousin marriage prohibitions in the United States, part of the general proscriptions against marriages of relatives, cannot be explained simply by reference to potential genetic risks, why were they enacted? And why did the myth of cousin marriage become such a general part of the American cultural landscape? Some contend that "there is no simple explanation of the basis for the current legal regulation of marriages between persons related in various ways" (Glendon 1989:57). I disagree.

Marriage lies at the nexus of biological and social factors of human life and is strongly influenced by culture. An investigation of inbreeding in Finland, for example, concludes that cultural factors are the best predictors of consanguinity at the first cousin level (Jorde and Pitkänen 1991). The authors note that the "evaluation of cultural variables can provide a greatly enriched interpretation of complex biosocial phenomena such as inbreeding" (Jorde and Pitkänen 1991:127). To understand the development of the laws forbidding cousin marriage in the United States, it is particularly important to understand the origin and cultural significance of the American myth of cousin marriage.

The federal government of the United States prohibits polygamy, and its courts have done away with miscegenation laws. Although the states conform to these aspects of marital law, there is no countrywide guideline for legislation governing the marriage of relatives. All fifty states and the

District of Columbia regulate the marriage of relatives, but each state has its own rules.

Just a cursory glance at the statutes is sure to amuse or perhaps confuse the reader. Second cousins, for example, were prohibited from marrying until recently in Oklahoma, while in some states it was legal to marry a half sibling. Colorado prohibited first cousins from marrying for a period during the nineteenth century but now permits it, while Maine permitted them to marry until this past decade but now prohibits it. At one time, a man in Georgia could legally marry his daughter but not his sister-in-law. In Massachusetts a woman is forbidden to marry her daughter's husband but not her husband's father. Women are prohibited from marrying their sons-in-law in several states, while men can marry their nieces in others.

This state of affairs appears to make little sense. One type of marriage relationship is recognized as legal in some states but not in others. Citizens of some states are prohibited from marrying affinal relatives, while others are permitted to marry consanguineal relatives who are no more distantly related. Furthermore, close consanguineal relatives may wed in some states, while in others more distantly related kin may not.

The situation in the United States today can be compared with that of early nineteenth-century Switzerland. There, each canton was responsible for its own set of regulations. This produced a patchwork of approximately two dozen different systems governing marriage in the country. Some were based on popular law, others on French law, Austrian law, Roman Catholic canon law, or Protestant common law. What was legal in one canton could be illegal in a neighboring one. First cousin marriage, in particular, was permitted in some cantons but prohibited in others. This complex mixture of marriage statutes ended in 1876 with the adoption of the Swiss federal law regulating civil status and marriage (Wright 1889:1062–65). The federal law provided a single code for all Swiss cantons, including a statute permitting the marriage of first cousins throughout the country. This statute reflected the general thinking in Europe at that time about the civil regulation of the marriage of relatives. Since the time of the Protestant Reformation and the secularization of marriage regulation, most European countries have not included cousins in the laws prohibiting marriages between relatives.

Regulation of marriage between relatives has a long history in the Western world. Prohibitions against the marriage of first cousins were initiated in the early Roman Catholic church under conditions that are somewhat puzzling (see chapter 3 for details). They have been maintained since then for reasons that are still not clear. A provocative work recently published argues that cousin marriage prohibitions in the Catholic church were instituted and maintained for profit (Goody 1983). Whether this was the motive behind the church's regulations, profit—or *lucre,* the sixteenth-century critics' word—does not pertain in any meaningful way to the development of the laws in the United States.

A distaste for cousin marriage arrived in the United States with the Puritans, Quakers, and other early European immigrant groups, but it was not until the second half of the nineteenth century that first cousin marriage was prohibited under civil law. At this time, statutes disallowing the wedding of first cousins began to be introduced on a state-by-state basis. By the end of the first quarter of the twentieth century a majority of states had enacted legislation against first cousin marriage (see chapter 2 for details). These statutes, part of the states' regulations governing the marriage of relatives, reflect a change in the United States in basic assumptions about marriage.

In the nineteenth century, scholars searching for a rational basis for marital statutes debated over natural laws governing the family and proposed different theories of social relationships. In Europe the discussion and debate focusing on the nature of the family and marriage did not lead to any consensus about precisely which relatives should be excluded from the pool of potential partners, but civil laws emerged permitting first cousins to marry. A similar discussion and debate occurred in the United States but with a different result. The states adopted a variety of statutes governing the marriage of relatives, without any agreement about the propriety of first cousin marriage.

Before the middle of the nineteenth century no state had prohibited the marriage of first cousins (Adam 1865). During this period the family was understood to be a crucial social unit responsible for maintaining morality and civil obedience by properly enculturating its members. Anything that interfered with these functions of the family was a threat to society and deserved to be banned. This was one reason a controversy raged about the legitimacy of marriage between a man and his sister-in-law. Antagonists argued that it was incestuous and dangerous and should be prohibited. They believed it threatened the ability of the family to preserve morality, for if a wife's sister were permitted to marry the widower, the man might take this as a license to have conjugal relations with the sister before the demise of his wife, which would threaten the sanctity of the conjugal unit and its ability to maintain morality. Proponents thought marriage between a widower and his wife's sister was a natural union, given the social conditions of the times. Families frequently had a wife's unmarried sister living with them; upon the death of the wife her sister was often seen as the most sensible individual to take up her responsibilities legally. The argument was never decided. It became moot before the end of the century with the emergence of a new view of the family in the United States. In this newer framework the family became primarily a breeding unit, and the health of offspring rather than family morality became the major concern of lawmakers. For reasons discussed later, this change was accompanied by a shift in the focus on the relatives prohibited from marrying. Cousins, rather than in-laws, became the primary concern of the new laws. By 1890 thirteen states, almost a third of those in the Union, had passed statutes against first cousin marriage (Wright 1889). The number of states with this form of legislation has continued to grow during the twentieth century. Today thirty-one states (62 percent) prohibit first cousin marriage.

The search for rational marital legislation based on natural law led legal scholars to the comparative analysis of marriage systems (Adam 1865:711). Publications appeared around the middle of the nineteenth century that utilized worldwide cross-cultural data in discussions of the nature of marriage. Many of the authors of these studies were lawyers: Johann Jakob Bachofen, Josef Köhler, Henry Sumner Maine, John Ferguson McLennan, Lewis Henry Morgan, and C. Staniland Wake, for example. At the same time, comparative social organization became central to the newly emerging field of cultural anthropology. Two pioneering nineteenth-century comparative evolutionary anthropologists and social analysts, Lewis Henry Morgan and Edward Tylor, expended considerable effort collecting data from around the world, analyzing the differences in marriage systems, and proposing functions for the regulation of marriage. Their common framework for examining data was the newly developed theory of evolution, but there was a significant difference in the way each interpreted evolution. Tylor accepted a form of Darwinian evolution, while Morgan was Spencerian. The critical difference here is how each approach treats the ends or aims of evolution. In the Darwinian approach, a system (organic or superorganic) responds to its environment, and as the environment changes, different forms within the system flourish. A process of "natural selection" is at work, in which different forms of organization prosper according to the environmental conditions. No overall goal or form of organization or organism is superior in absolute terms. In Spencer's evolutionary formulation, there is, in addition to a process of natural selection, an end toward which the process proceeds. There is progress; a process of directional change toward some long-range valued end. In other words, there are certain forms that are better suited for long-term existence. This is manifested by Herbert Spencer's phrase "the survival of the fittest." It implied some superior type of organization or organism would emerge through struggle or conflict. This teleological view of evolution became widely accepted in the United States. It played an important role in the chauvinistic notion that the United States had achieved the highest levels of social development and in the idea that cousin prohibitions were necessary to sustain the country's social progress.

With the acceptance of the Spencerian bioevolutionary view of social interaction by such nineteenth-century American thinkers as Lewis Henry Morgan, families were seen as breeding units for a society moving along an evolutionary scale of complexity (and progress). Cousin unions then became viewed as a threat to social progress, since it became widely assumed that persons closely related through common ancestry would produce offspring less healthy and less fit than those from unions of unrelated parents. In-law relationships, in contrast, no longer would be of concern since they did not threaten to produce less physically fit offspring. Under the influence of these ideas (discussed in detail in the following chapters), states joining the Union tended to pass laws forbidding the marriage of first cousins and ignore affinal proscriptions. In the older states, however, cousins continued to be permitted to wed, while in-law marriages continued to be prohibited. The absence of any federal guidelines ensured that no single uniform code governing marriage was accepted throughout the United States.

George Howard, an early twentieth-century scholar of marriage law, commented on the diversity in marital statutes among the states at the turn of the century: "The absurd conflicts touching the forbidden degrees of relationship are a positive social menace. The most serious complications may arise. For instance, a man and a woman who may be legally wed in the place where they dwell might, should they move a mile across the state line and then marry, be guilty of incestuous union and their children become bastards. Surely it ought to be possible for an enlightened people to agree upon a common rule in a matter of such vital concern" (Howard 1904, 3:194–95). Nothing much has changed since 1904, when this was written. There is still no consistent code of laws concerning marriage. More data have been collected, a fuller picture of the history of marriage rules has become available, and more sophisticated analyses of marriage have been undertaken, but the legal statutes regulating marriage between relatives in the United States have not changed accordingly. We are still left with "a field of human relations thoroughly statutized and regulated by archaic common law principles" (Chotiner 1974:32) and "characterized more by vague and somewhat inconsistent notions about legitimacy than by systematic consideration of the purposes of regulation" (Glendon 1989:57).

To understand fully the injunctions against cousin marriage in the United States, it is necessary to compare their development with that of the laws in Europe. This requires some knowledge of the details of the history of the prohibitions against cousin marriage in the Roman Catholic church. Much of this history has been discussed in Jack Goody's (1983) *Development of the Family and Marriage in Europe,* a major contribution to the exploration of the origin and development of marriage prohibitions in the West. Goody describes how the Roman Catholic church instituted a prohibition against cousin marriage in the Mediterranean world around A.D. 400 and then spread the restriction throughout Europe. Recognizing the church's prohibition against cousin marriage did not develop as a result of the genetic effects of marriage or a biblical injunction, Goody theorizes that the church attacked cousin marriage to disrupt the inheritance of the family estate and divert the wealth to itself. The establishment of prohibitions against cousin marriage unquestionably benefited the church financially. At the very least, granting dispensations generated wealth for the church because many Europeans continued to marry their cousins and paid the necessary fee (Segalen 1986). This selling of dispensations was one of the major criticisms raised during the Protestant Reformation. Whether financial gain by the church was the cause of the prohibitions or simply a result of it still remains an open question, however. That an institution might have gained financially from spreading the prohibition against cousins' marrying in Europe does not mean that this is the reason for its adoption. Increased revenues could have resulted from the prohibition without being its cause.

Goody's work is important to anyone interested in the subject of cousin marriage in Europe. While it provides important and detailed historical information, its major thesis, whether correct or not, is limited in its applicability. His materialistic explanation for the Roman Catholic church's proscriptions does not apply to the development of the prohibitions against cousin marriage in the United States. They appeared without an equivalent institution. Nor does it explain the prohibition against cousin marriage found in other parts of the world. A central and powerful religious institution that might gain economically from a prohibition against the marriage of relatives is rare.

Relatives prohibited from marrying vary from society to society, without any conformity to biological distance. In Korea, for example, traditional matrimonial rules forbid marriage between a man and a type of second cousin (the daughter of his grandfather's brother's son's daughter) but allow a man to wed a kind of first cousin (the daughter of his mother's brother). This points strongly to the influence of culture in marriage regulations. The preference for certain types of cousin marriage in specific religious groups further attests to the central role of culture. For instance, Islamic communities prefer one type of first cousin marriage—between the children of brothers. Such preferences cut across physical, geographical, and environmental lines.

Forty-three percent of the world's societies permit marriage between some type of first cousins (Pasternak 1976). *Cousins* are any two individuals descended from a pair of siblings. The term *cousin* is used in this work to designate this genealogical relationship, and thus a person's cousin is any individual descended from that person's direct ancestor's sibling. *First cousins* are the children of siblings. Your first cousin, in other words, is your parent's sibling's child. The child of a first cousin, in the terminology of the courts in the United States, is a first cousin once removed. The first cousin of a parent is also a first cousin once removed. The term is self-reciprocal. Anyone I call a first cousin once removed calls me the same. The child of my first cousin once removed is my first cousin twice removed, and the child of my first cousin twice removed is my first cousin thrice removed, and so on. (A different terminological system in the United States labels the child of a first cousin a second cousin. To avoid confusion, only one type, the courts' system, will be used in the following pages. See figure 1.)

The offspring of first cousins, in the terminological system used in the courtrooms of the United States, are second cousins. Second cousins are thus grandchildren of the original pair of siblings. They are two ancestral links removed from the sibling pair that defines their relationship. Third cousins are great-grandchildren of a pair of siblings. They are three links removed from the ancestral set of siblings that defined them as cousins. And so on down the line. In the United States no state ever forbade third or more distant cousins from marrying. Oklahoma was the only state to prohibit second cousins from marrying (Farrow and Juberg 1969:537), but it no longer does so today. Marriage between second or more distant cousins is permitted everywhere in the United States. Only first cousins, including first cousins once removed, are currently prohibited from marrying in any state.

Some exceptions are permitted among the thirty-one states that currently prohibit first cousin marriage. North Carolina, as mentioned earlier, prohibits only double first cousins from marrying. Cousins wishing to marry may do so if they descend from a common grandparent through only one set of parents—even though they are first cousins. In Illinois, Indiana, and Arizona first cousins may marry if the couple cannot bear children. In Maine first cousins may marry if they have had genetic counseling. These exceptions emphasize the concern with biogenetics in U.S. marital law.

The distinction between first and second cousins is familiar to most English speakers, but throughout the world distinctions are made between different types of first cousins that are unfamiliar to English speakers. Some societies distinguish between those cousins related to a person through males and those related to an individual through females. This is a feature of many societies with unilineal descent and is an important part of social life—especially in determining a potential spouse. In traditional China and in Korea today, for example, descent through males is important for determining social relationships. Members of the same descent group can not marry. Second or more distant cousins related through males are thus prohibited from marrying—since they belong to the same patrilineal descent group—while first cousins related only through females do not belong to the same descent group and thus can marry. There is currently an open conflict in Korea between those who wish to maintain this distinction and

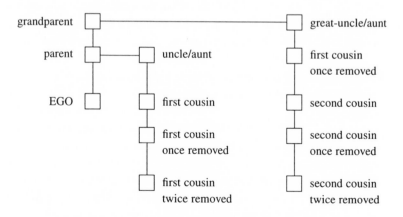

Figure 1. Cousin Terminology Used in the U.S. Court System

those who wish to ignore or change it. In determining the availability of spouses, some argue for the Western model, in which the difference between cousins on the mother's side and cousins on the father's side is ignored. Others want to maintain the traditional concern with patrilineal descent, permitting marriage between a person and any cousin related through the mother and forbidding the person from marrying any cousin related through males on the father's side of the family.

The distinction between parallel-cousins and cross-cousins is also unfamiliar to English speakers. All cousins are the descendants of siblings. When the siblings are of the same sex, their descendants are parallel-cousins. When the siblings are of the opposite sex, their descendants are cross-cousins. This distinction between these types of cousins—based on the relative sex of the ancestral sibling pair defining the cousin relationship—may seem trivial or nonsensical to someone not familiar with its role in many of the world's societies. But this distinction is as important in some societies as the distinction between siblings and cousins is in an English-speaking society. Societies with cousin marriage often permit cross-cousins to marry but forbid parallel-cousins from marrying. Like the prohibition against sibling marriage in the English-speaking world, this prohibition of marriage between parallel-cousins may be accompanied by a concern that offspring will have unwanted physical characteristics. Cross-cousin marriages, in contrast, are expected to be blessed with normal children.

Although the laws in the United States are not concerned with many of these distinctions, the prohibitions against cousin marriage in the United States should be analyzed within a general theory of cousin marriage. Such a theory must take into consideration the worldwide data. What is needed is a conception of cousin marriage that will provide a framework for understanding the comparative data on cousin marriage as well as the prohibitions against cousin marriage in the United States.

Cousin marriage prohibitions are part of the larger arena of the regulation of marriage. Marital regulations are integrally involved with issues of family and society. Questions about cousin marriage are thus not simply a matter of the relationship between culture and the law; they are essentially about the social regulation of family groups. This is a central issue for today's societies.

It is important to recognize that in any society laws enacted by legislators do not reflect all the factors governing marriage. This is certainly true for the United States, where unwritten marriage codes have played an important role in governing social relationships. Georgian statutes did not prohibit a man from marrying his daughter, yet there are no known cases in the state. The unwritten cultural distaste for such a relationship would have kept it from occurring. Similarly, an 1872 California bill forbade marriage between people of European descent and those of African descent but contained no injunction against marriage between people of European descent and those of Asian descent. Yet county clerks were instructed not to provide marriage licenses to the latter as well as the former (Wright 1889:36, note *d*). In later years the law was adjusted "to conform to popular views in the State about the undesirability of Orientals" (Sickels 1972:98).

Statutes against interracial marriage were repealed by states as early as the 1870s, and no such laws survive today in any state. (Mississippi removed the last of the miscegenation laws in November of 1987.) Nevertheless, nonstatutory means of controlling interracial marriages still exist in the United States. Even if legal statutes do not represent all the factors governing marriage, they still play an important role in social life. Most important, for the purposes of this work, they serve as key indicators of critical cultural developments.

For centuries various theories have been offered to explain cousin marriage regulations. Based on assumptions as varied as the codes themselves, they often reveal more about the cultures of the people proposing them than about the reasons for the regulations. One reason for the failure to explain the prohibitions is the absence of a comprehensive theory of cousin marriage. Without adequate knowledge of the significance of cousin marriage, it has not been possible to explain the effect of a prohibition. Explaining prohibitions against cousin marriage in the United States requires understanding what cousin marriage does.

The two most prominent explanations of cousin marriage have been breeding and alliance theories. The former treats cousin marriage as a biological mechanism, while the latter treats it as a sociocultural mechanism. Both theories fail to account for the data about cousin marriage, however.

Breeding theory assumes that marriage is primarily a mechanism of sexual reproduction and that cousin unions produce offspring that are less healthy and less fit than the offspring of parents who are not related. Chapter 5 specifically examines the American anthropologist Lewis Henry Morgan's contention that cousin marriage threatens the civilized status of a society because of its consequences to offspring. Chapter 6 continues to scrutinize breeding theory in terms of modern genetic theory and the results of recent research in population genetics, which have amply examined the potential genetic hazards to offspring of cousins. Chapter 7 examines alliance theory, based on the work of Edward Tylor. This theory, treating marriage as a primarily social phenomenon, views cousin marriage in terms of its ability to establish sociopolitical relationships. From this point of view, cross-cousin marriage is a form of exogamy in societies with unilineal descent. Marriage with a cross-cousin, according to alliance theory, is a mechanism uniting different descent groups through marriage bonds. Proponents of the theory have proposed an explanation for the preponderance of a particular form of cross-cousin marriage. Comparative analysis of the world's data reveals societies with cross-cousin marriage tend to prefer marriage between a man and his cross-cousin on his mother's side (or a woman and her cross-cousin on her father's side). Specifically, when societies express a preference for marriage between cross-cousins, three times as many prefer marriage between a man and his mother's brother's daughter than marriage between a man and his father's sister's daughter (Pasternak 1976:68–69). Claude Lévi-Strauss (1969) explained this statistical preponderance of matrilateral cross-cousin marriage systems by referring to it as an expedient means of exchanging women between different unilineal descent groups. He saw the exchange as an effective mechanism for uniting the society.

I present an alternative theory of cousin marriage in the final chapter. This theory posits cousin marriage is a mechanism for cultural continuity. Marriage regulations are then reviewed in terms of the way they assist or interfere with continuity. Marriage codes contain at least two types of rules: (1) those placing outer limits on the group of individuals a spouse can come from and (2) those placing restrictions on the relationships in the group allowed by the first type of rule. The first category covers rules of endogamy, which restrict potential marriage relationships to those within the same social unit—race, religion, community, tribe, clan, class, or caste. The second category rules operate within the social units defined by the rules of endogamy. These rules specify which members of the group cannot marry. Included in this category are marital prohibitions between people of the same descent group, family group, gender, or generation as well as interdictions against wedding spiritual kin, a person already married, or anyone with a specific disability or disease.

These two types of rules effectively establish the possible spouses available to a member of a society. Defining and restricting the possible candidates for marriage is an indispensable part of the cultural process. Endogamy tends to ensure that the spouses of the family unit share the same culture. Since the transmission of culture from generation to generation takes place primarily in the family, this kind of marriage guarantees that the children of the union will be enculturated within a common culture. When individuals of different cultures marry, the continuity of each culture is threatened. One culture may be discarded or both lost because the children are not sufficiently taught either tradition. Marriage systems based on endogamy thus can be seen as a means of ensuring the continuity of a culture through the generations.

Threats to cultural continuity, especially breeches in marriage proscriptions or challenges to the marriage rules, are often met with strong emotional disapproval, political action, and, sometimes, violence. One example of the strong reactions marriage rules can evoke is the nineteenth-century British debate over the propriety of a man's marrying his deceased wife's sister. Many viewed this as an incestuous threat to the moral order. Their strong reaction to the growing number of people engaging in this form of marriage prompted Parliament to pass, in 1835, Lord Lyndhurst's Act, which voided any such union (see chapter 4). This law remained in force until 1907. Another example is the Alabama judge who lashed out in 1938 against a man's marriage to his uncle's widow as an incestuous union that "violates the voice of nature, degrades the family, [and] offends decency and morals . . ." (quoted in Bratt 1984:258). More recently, I watched an angry American woman being interviewed by a television news reporter. She vehemently objected on camera to the integration of her neighborhood and asked, "Do you want your daughter to marry one of them?" This rhetorical question clearly expressed the importance of endogamy among some groups in the United States. The emotion the woman expressed in her question gave clear testimony to the significance of marriage codes in contemporary society.

The range of people with strong attachments to their culture knows no limits within a society. Potentially anyone in a community, from the poorest to the richest, from the least educated to university professors, will react vigorously when their marriage rules are questioned. In discussing the laws against the marriage of relatives in Europe with an eminent scholar from the Netherlands, for instance, I was told in no uncertain terms that my information was incorrect. "It was not possible that civil law in that country permitted first cousins to marry," he said. The scholar was even willing to wager a considerable sum of money that they were forbidden to marry. A member of the Dutch Reformed church, he assumed that the church's strictures against the marriage of first cousins were in agreement with the civil laws of the country. His certainty turned to incredulity when further investigation confirmed that the civil laws in the country, like those in every country in Europe, contain no statute forbidding the marriage of first cousins.

One might expect in the United States, where there is so much emphasis on individual freedom, that laws forbidding relatives from marrying would be seen as interference with an individual's right to choose. Furthermore, the constitutional separation of church and state in this country suggests that if there are to be civil laws restricting marital relationships, they should be based on a rational foundation and not simply reflect the traditional lore of one religious group. The need for a rational, nontraditional basis for marital law is especially acute in a multiethnic society, where traditional rationales for regulating marriage are diverse and the legal acceptance of one religious set of beliefs and rites prejudices the others.

To achieve legislation with a rational basis, legislators must be guided by an adequate theory of marriage, tested against historical and cross-cultural data. If no such theory exists, marital regulations will appear to be no more than senseless government interventions into personal liberties and will have no social force. The maintenance of these social regulations will be left to the devotees of diverse sects or the followers of traditional myths.

Marriage rules are expressed and defended with great emotion all over the world because marriage rules play an essential role in culture. They are fundamental expressions of a society, rationalized in myth, and rarely questioned. An adequate analysis of these rules must refer to the culture(s) of the society in which they exist. Uncovering the cultural basis for legislation against the marriage of first cousins in a society, however, does not imply that this legislation should remain intact. Changed views about the nature of families and the development of new reproductive technologies call for an adjustment of the statutes regulating the marriage of relatives. We must reexamine these laws in light of new information and in terms of current ideas and technological developments.

The subject matter of this book is sure to raise some controversy because the American myth of cousin marriage is deeply ingrained in the United States. In the nineteenth century a physician interested in the potential dangers to offspring of consanguineal unions warned researchers about the dangers of investigating the subject:

> Perhaps no opinion, upon subjects of a medical character, is more widely diffused among the public, or more tenaciously held, than that the results of the marriage of blood relations are almost uniformly un-

fortunate. This opinion has been so long held and so often reiterated, that by sheer force of these circumstances alone it has come to be regarded as an unquestioned and unquestionable fact. Almost every one, from the forward school-boy and wise old woman, to the dignified and erudite divine, will repeat that the common experience of all time and every country has proved it so conclusively, that to doubt or question its accuracy is tantamount to an exhibition of either the grossest ignorance, or the most willful and culpable obstinacy, or a weak desire of appearing wiser than one's generation by the enunciation of an astounding paradox. (Bell 1859:473–74)

This statement is still valid today. Anyone who questions the myth risks public ire and ridicule. This book takes that chance. It examines the rationale for the laws against the marriage of first cousins in the United States, challenges the myth that they act to prevent potential physical dangers to offspring, and suggests a new framework for evaluating the marriage of close relatives.

The following pages begin with a description of the laws against cousin marriage in the United States. Subsequent chapters examine their history, compare them with European laws, analyze the two major traditional theories concerning cousin marriage, and describe pertinent modern genetic research. The concluding chapter presents a modern cultural theory for the evaluation of laws prohibiting the marriage of cousins. This work thus offers more than simply an answer to why there are first cousin prohibitions in the United States. It also provides a coherent theory of cousin marriage, explores the development of an American myth, and provides a basis for legislative action to revise marital law.

1

U.S. Laws Prohibiting the Marriage of Relatives

The absurd conflicts touching the forbidden degrees
of relationship are a positive social menace.
—George Howard, *A History of*
Matrimonial Institutions

The Congress of the United States outlawed polygamy in the nineteenth century and the Supreme Court declared miscegenation laws unconstitutional in the twentieth century. Otherwise, the regulation of marriage has primarily been left to individual states. Every state regulates the marriage of relatives. Full-sibling, mother-son, father-daughter, uncle-niece, and aunt-nephew marital unions are forbidden in all states. (There is an exception to the prohibition against uncle-niece marriage. In Rhode Island, the law exempts Jews from the prohibition. Georgia at one time also had no prohibition against uncle-niece or father-daughter marriages [Farrow and Juberg 1969:537].) Beyond these five forbidden close consanguineal relationships, however, there is little agreement among the states governing the marriage of relatives. The prohibitions involving affinal relatives vary greatly, and there is no agreement about whether first cousins should be prohibited from marrying. The exact nature of the differences and the reasons for them can be best understood by examining their historical development.

Before the creation of the United States, colonists in New England, outside of Rhode Island, expressed their strong feelings against incestuous unions by making persons who violated the prohibition wear a scarlet letter *I*. Like the more famous scarlet letter *A* for adulterers, the *I* was designed to embarrass those who had breached the marriage taboos and to remind others of the proper marital relationships. Five cases of offenders wearing the scarlet *I* were recorded in Massachusetts between 1729 and 1759. These are of particular interest since they point out that incest had a different meaning at that time than it does today. In 1729 and again in 1743 the violated relationships were between a father and daughter. In 1754 the marriage between a man and his deceased wife's sister was viewed as incestuous. The incestuous relationships in 1752 and in 1759 were each between a man and his wife's daughter (Howard 1904, 2:178). Three of these cases are between affinal relations. Only the 1729 and 1743 cases were between consanguineal kin. Incest was not simply a matter of "blood relationships" in colonial New England. Affinal kin and consanguineal kin were not treated differently in the law on incest. Colonists were just as concerned about illicit affinal unions as they were about relationships between a man and his daughter, if not more so.

The forbidden relationships were formally defined in the Massachusetts colony by an act of 1695. Forbidden degrees of marriage were declared to be those Archbishop Parker of the Anglican church enumerated in a table of kindred and affinity relationships constructed in the previous century (see table 1; see chapter 2 for details). The table contained thirty relatives, two-thirds of which were affinal kin. Not everyone in the colony accepted this list as the guide to marital regulation. The law accepting the table passed only by a slight margin, reflecting a diversity of opinions in the colony, especially concerning the marriage prohibitions. Some of the colonists thought the table included relationships that should not be prohibited and omitted others that should be. For example, some were opposed to including the affinal relationship between a man and his dead wife's sister, while others were concerned that the table omitted a ban against the marriage of first cousins.

Considerable opposition to the inclusion of the wife's sister in the Church of England's list of forbidden marriages had arisen on both sides

Table 1. The List of Relatives in Archibishop Parker's Table

A. Relatives Men Were Forbidden to Marry

Consanguineal Relations	*Affinal Relations*
1. Grandmother	1. Grandfather's wife
2. Father's sister*	2. Wife's grandmother
3. Mother's sister*	3. Father's brother's wife*
4. Mother*	4. Mother's brother's wife
5. Daughter	5. Wife's father's sister

Table 1, continued

6. Sister*	6. Wife's mother's sister
7. Son's daughter*	7. Father's wife*
8. Daughter's daughter*	8. Wife's mother*
9. Brother's daughter	9. Wife's daughter*
10. Sister's daughter	10. Son's wife*
	11. Wife's sister*
	12. Brother's wife*
	13. Son's son's wife
	14. Daughter's son's wife
	15. Wife's son's daughter*
	16. Wife's daughter's daughter*
	17. Brother's son's wife
	18. Sister's son's wife
	19. Wife's brother's daughter
	20. Wife's sister's daughter

B. Relatives Women Were Forbidden to Marry

Consanguineal Relations	*Affinal Relations*
1. Grandfather	1. Grandmother's husband
2. Father's brother	2. Husband's grandfather
3. Mother's brother	3. Father's sister's husband
4. Father	4. Mother's sister's husband
5. Son	5. Husband's father's brother
6. Brother	6. Husband's mother's brother
7. Son's son	7. Mother's husband
8. Daughter's son	8. Husband's father
9. Brother's son	9. Husband's son
10. Sister's son	10. Daughter's husband
	11. Husband's brother
	12. Sister's husband
	13. Son's daughter's husband
	14. Daughter's daughter's husband
	15. Husband's son's son
	16. Husband's daughter's son
	17. Brother's daughter's husband
	18. Sister's daughter's husband
	19. Husband's brother's son
	20. Husband's sister's son

Note: Starred (*) relations are those mentioned in Leviticus.

Source: Hammick 1887:35–37.

of the Atlantic. Although only one of the twenty different affinal relationships the Anglican church forbade, it was for many years the most controversial relationship in England. The prohibition against marriage with the
widower's sister-in-law became the focus of a long and bitter series of
debates in the British Parliament, which finally ended in the twentieth century when the prohibition was removed from civil law (see chapter 2). The
colonists opposed to the prohibition argued that the marriage made social
sense since the death of one's wife made her unmarried sister, who often
had resided in the household with her sister, the best person to raise the
young children left with the widower. Furthermore, several men in the
colony had already married their wives' sisters, and the enforcement of the
act would mean having to separate these already existing families. The
deputies considered this difficulty but passed the act anyway, forcing the
separation of these couples. The deputies thought that passage of the act,
even if it meant breaking apart some marriages, would enforce morality
and make sure everyone understood that the marriage between a man and
his sister-in-law was an incestuous union against the law of God (Howard
1904, 2:213–14).

A debate over the list of collateral consanguineal relatives forbidden
in the Massachusetts act occurred as well. There was a disagreement about
whether the prohibitions should be extended to collateral consanguineal
relatives beyond siblings and, if so, how far. The Anglican table listed siblings and a man's aunt and niece (father's sister, mother's sister, brother's
daughter, and sister's daughter) as prohibited marital partners. This does
not precisely coincide with the list of relatives mentioned in the Old Testament. The niece, for one, is absent from the list of relatives mentioned
in Leviticus. The Levitical list of relatives includes mother, father's wife,
sister, half sister, granddaughter, father's sister, mother's sister, father's
brother's wife, son's wife, brother's wife, wife's mother, wife's daughter,
stepson's daughter, stepdaughter's daughter, and wife's sister while the wife
is alive. Since the Old Testament was considered the primary source for
the prohibitions, the inclusion of the niece in the table gave rise to numerous disagreements.

Other arguments arose over whether cousins should be prohibited from
marrying. A common justification in the late seventeenth century for extending the prohibitions to relationships not found in the Old Testament
was that they were logically implied and should be added to the list even
if not specifically mentioned. For example, it was argued that since the aunt
was listed, it was only rational to include the niece as well. The argument

contended that they were both of the same degree and that prohibiting the aunt implied the symmetrical prohibition of the niece. The argument that relations within the same degree should be included in a list of prohibited marriages was applied to first cousins as well. Cousins are not mentioned in either the Anglican table or the Old Testament, but some argued they should be included in any proper list of prohibited relatives. One's first cousins are as close in genealogical distance as, for example, one's uncle's wife.

After the passage of the 1695 act in Massachusetts, Samuel Sewall, a famous justice on the Massachusetts superior court, specifically decried the absence of first cousins from the list. He pointed out that "the Indians seldom marry so near as cousins-german and surely we ought not to have to go to school to them" (quoted in Calhoun 1960, 1:100). His argument resembles the one later used in the Supreme Court of the United States to justify the imposition of monogamy in the country. Both imply an evolutionary view that ties certain aspects of marriage to stages of social development. Whereas the federal government was successful in outlawing polygamy, however, Sewall's argument did not achieve his desired result. Cousins have never been added to the list of prohibited marriage partners in Massachusetts.

The prohibitions listed in the Massachusetts act of 1695 remained in force until after the American Revolution. Then in 1785 Massachusetts adopted a statute that dropped the prohibitions against marriage between a man and his wife's sister or his niece (Howard 1904, 2:214). By the time the first extensive survey of marriage statutes in the United States in the late nineteenth century was undertaken, Massachusetts had reestablished the niece in its list of prohibited marriages but not the wife's sister (Wright 1889). It also omitted other affinal relatives. The list of forbidden affinal relations at the end of the nineteenth century included only a man's stepmother, grandfather's wife, son's wife, grandson's wife, wife's grandmother, wife's mother, wife's daughter, and wife's granddaughter (Wright 1889). The affinal relations had been reduced by approximately one-third of those in the table. Prohibited, in effect, were only those affines related through lineal ascendants or descendants of a man or the close lineal relations of his spouse.

Since 1889 several changes have been made in Massachusetts's list of affinal relations. Today a man is still prohibited from marrying his stepmother, grandfather's wife, grandson's wife, and wife's mother but not the son's wife, wife's grandmother, wife's daughter, and wife's granddaughter. A woman is prohibited from marrying her stepson, husband's grandson, husband's grandfather, and daughter's husband.

The forbidden consanguineal relatives for a man in Massachusetts at the end of the nineteenth century were his grandmother, mother, mother's sister, father's sister, sister, daughter, sister's daughter, brother's daughter, and granddaughter. There was a corresponding list of relatives for a woman. The list of consanguineal relatives of the late nineteenth century remains unchanged under current Massachusetts law.

Connecticut adopted the Massachusetts act of 1695 in 1702. Over the years it has also changed its list of prohibited relationships, but the course taken by the state was different from that followed in Massachusetts. Marriage with the daughter of a former wife's sibling was no longer prohibited by law in 1750. The prohibition against marriage with a deceased wife's sister was dropped in 1793, and in 1816 marriage with the deceased brother's wife was no longer considered incestuous (Howard 1904, 2:397). By 1889 Connecticut had dropped all affinal relationships from its list of forbidden marriages except for stepmother and stepdaughter (Wright 1889). Today no affinal relatives are prohibited from marrying. Prohibited consanguineal relationships remain limited to those closer than first cousins.

New Hampshire adopted the 1695 Massachusetts act in 1714. Like the other two New England states, New Hampshire modified the list of relations in the Anglican table. Unlike the others, however, it added first cousins to the list of forbidden consanguineal relations. In 1869 the state added the father's brother's daughter, mother's brother's daughter, father's sister's daughter, and mother's sister's daughter to the list of relatives men were forbidden to marry. Corresponding prohibitions were passed for a woman. Before the beginning of the twentieth century, New Hampshire prohibited a man from marrying his mother, daughter, aunt, niece, granddaughter, grandmother, stepmother, wife's mother, wife's daughter, son's wife, grandson's wife, and first cousin. A woman was prohibited from marrying her corresponding relatives (Wright 1889). This list of prohibitions was maintained through the 1920s (Morland 1946). Since then the list has been reduced, and today the prohibited marriages are between a man and his daughter, granddaughter, stepdaughter, sister, aunt, niece, first cousin, mother-in-law, or the widow of his father, son, or grandson. There are corresponding prohibitions for a woman.

The other New England states, Maine, Rhode Island, and Vermont, maintained the same set of forbidden consanguineal relatives as those in

Massachusetts throughout the nineteenth century. These three states did not allow marriage between a man and his mother, daughter, sister, aunt, niece, granddaughter, or grandmother. The prohibited affinal relatives were the stepmother, grandfather's wife, son's wife, grandson's wife, wife's mother, wife's grandmother, wife's daughter, and wife's granddaughter. A woman was proscribed from marrying her corresponding relatives. Rhode Island has maintained this list of prohibited relatives. Both Vermont and Maine have dropped the affinal relationships. Maine dropped its affinal prohibitions in 1981 and amended its marital regulations in 1985 to add first cousins to its list of consanguineal relatives. The 1985 statute prohibited a man from marrying "the daughter of his father's brother or sister or the daughter of his mother's brother or sister" (19 Maine Revised Statutes Annotated 1985 §31). Likewise, a woman was prohibited from marrying the son of her father's brother or sister or the son of her mother's siblings. Legislators who sponsored the bill introduced it under the supposition that it would prevent offspring with defects (Maine Representative Leland Davis, personal communication). No survey was ever undertaken in the state to find out whether this was, indeed, a problem.

In 1987 legislative action amended the 1985 Maine statute to permit first cousins to marry under certain conditions. As a result of the amendment, these cousins can marry today in Maine if they provide the town clerk with a physician's certificate of genetic counseling at the time their marriage intentions are recorded.

In the Middle Atlantic colonies Pennsylvania had marriage laws that were originally based on Quaker regulations. The Quakers were prominent in the colony from its inception and constituted a majority of the assembly that adopted marriage laws in the early eighteenth century (Gough 1989:128). The earliest Pennsylvania statutes outlawing incest in 1682 and 1700 did not clearly define what relationships were incestuous and were disallowed for vagueness. Legislation based on earlier English law was enacted in 1705 to clarify the issue (Frost 1973:160). This legislation established the main principles of marriage law in Pennsylvania (Howard 1904, 2:318). The 1705 act, like the one passed in England over a century earlier under King Henry VIII, prohibited only those relationships mentioned in the Bible: mother, stepmother, sister, half sister, granddaughter, father's sister, mother's sister, father's brother's wife, son's wife, brother's wife, wife's mother, wife's daughter, stepson's daughter, stepdaughter's daughter, and wife's sister while the wife is alive. (Daughter is not mentioned, but it is usually included in any list of prohibited relatives. The niece is also absent, although most states have included the niece in their list of forbidden consanguineal relatives.)

By the first half of the eighteenth century the Quakers had added to the list of prohibited relatives. They lengthened their list of incestuous relations by adding first cousins and the wife's cousin for a man (Howard 1904, 2:322–23). Many Quakers had been opposed to cousin marriage. Frost (1973) points out that "meetings forbade first cousins to wed and discouraged marriage between second cousins. New England's discipline asked that even third cousins not marry, and advised meetings to discourage although not forbid wedlock between second cousins. Rhode Island Monthly Meeting did permit children of first cousins to marry in 1728" (161). In Philadelphia, before the Revolution, first cousins who married were automatically expelled from Quaker meetings, although some exceptions were made (Frost 1973:161). In spite of Quaker influence in early Pennsylvania history, however, the state did not add first cousin marriage to its list of forbidden relations until 1902 (Farber 1968:27).

Pennsylvania does not forbid marriage between any affinal relatives today, but marriage between a man and his father's wife, son's wife, wife's daughter, and wife's child's daughter were still prohibited in Pennsylvania before the close of the nineteenth century (Wright 1889). Some relationships forbidden by an act of the legislature in 1860 were legalized in 1868 (Howard 1904, 2:474, note 1), but marriage between a stepparent and a stepchild, along with any marriage between a person and the spouses of their ascendants or descendants, was still forbidden in the 1940s (Morland 1946). Marriages between a man and his father's wife, wife's daughter, wife's granddaughter, or son's wife and between a woman and her mother's husband, husband's son, husband's grandson, or daughter's husband were still prohibited in the 1960s (Farrow and Juberg 1969:537).

The state of New York outlined its list of forbidden marriages in 1830. It legislated that only marriages between relatives in the ascending and descending lines and between full and half siblings were incestuous and void (Kent 1848:83). In contrast to the states mentioned earlier, New York has never prohibited first cousin marriage or affinal unions. It is also the only state to have joined the Union before the nineteenth century that has not prohibited steprelatives or in-laws from marrying. Today New York's statutes void marriage between uncle and niece or aunt and nephew as well as those between siblings and ascendants/descendants.

North Carolina established the table of the Church of England as a guide for magistrates and ministers in 1715, reaffirming an earlier marriage act passed in 1669 (Semonche 1965:331). In 1741 marriage statutes were enacted that provided for the filing of a bond of fifty pounds (changed to five hundred pounds in 1778 and a thousand dollars in 1836 and abolished in 1868) by marriage applicants. The bond became "payable to the King of England, and after independence to the governor, if any disability was found to obstruct the marriage" (Semonche 1965:334). There is no evidence that a marriage bond was ever forfeited. Since the Revolutionary War North Carolina has not forbidden affinal relatives from marrying, and throughout the nineteenth century the state forbade marriage only between those persons consanguineally related who were closer than first cousins. During the first half of the nineteenth century cousin marriage was an accepted institution among planters in the state, and nearly 10 percent of these marriages were between first or second cousins (Censer 1984:84–87). North Carolina passed a prohibition against double first cousins in this century (Morland 1946). When two brothers from one family marry two sisters from another or when a brother and sister from one family marry a brother and sister from another family, the children of the two marriages are double first cousins. Otherwise, North Carolina permits marriage between first cousins.

The southern colonies used the list of forbidden marriages of the Anglican church in England, either incorporating them directly into law or using them as a model for regulating marriage. Virginia passed a statute in the early eighteenth century prohibiting marriages forbidden by "the laws of England" (quoted in Howard 1904, 2:234). In 1788 it adopted a statute that expressly forbade marriage with a brother's widow or with a deceased wife's sister. The latter prohibition was removed in 1849, and the prohibition against marrying a brother's widow was removed in 1860. By the end of the nineteenth century Virginia forbade marriage between a man and his mother, grandmother, stepmother, sister, daughter, granddaughter, half sister, aunt, son's widow, wife's daughter, wife's granddaughter, wife's stepdaughter, brother's daughter, and sister's daughter. A woman could not marry her corresponding relatives, plus the husband of her brother's or sister's daughter (Wright 1889). The Virginia Code of 1942 prohibited ascendants and descendants, brothers and sisters, uncles and nieces, and aunts and nephews from marrying. It also forbade marriage with surviving spouses of ascendants or descendants and with a spouse's ascendants or descendants (Morland 1946). Currently, adopted siblings have been added to the list, but affinal relatives are no longer prohibited from marrying. Cousins have never been prohibited.

In Maryland an Episcopal minority wrested control of religious matters from a Catholic and Quaker majority in the late seventeenth century and passed a statute in 1702 forbidding marriage contrary to the Anglican Table of Kindred and Affinity (Howard 1904, 2:242). The 1702 law continued in force through the Revolutionary War. It was reaffirmed in the statutes of 1777 (Domesticus 1827:39), but soon afterward the prohibition against marriage with the sibling of a deceased spouse was repealed. All collateral relatives by affinity have since been removed, and today only marriages between ascendants and descendants, ascendants or descendants by affinity, brothers and sisters, uncles and nieces, or aunts and nephews are forbidden.

South Carolina's list of forbidden marriages is the same as Maryland's. The Church of England was established by law in 1704 in the colony, making the archbishop's table the official mechanism for determining the forbidden degrees in marriage. Since then the collateral affinal relationships—uncle's wife, wife's aunt, sister-in-law, nephew's wife, and wife's niece—have been dropped from the list of prohibited degrees.

Georgia, originally part of South Carolina, did not rigidly enforce the Anglican table after James Ogelthorpe was given a charter in 1732. He attracted a number of Puritans, who did not concur with the list of prohibitions in the Anglican table (Howard 1904, 2:262). The Puritans were particularly opposed to cousin marriage (Howard 1904, 2:212–13). Their presence in Georgia may explain why first cousin marriage was prohibited there from 1863 to 1865 (Howard 1904, 2:433). The Georgia House of Representatives, by a small majority (56 to 52), had passed a bill in the 1850s prohibiting first cousin marriage "under a severe penalty and cutting off the inheritance of issue. The preamble to the bill asserts that many deformations of mind and body are of congenital origin, from the practice of near kindred intermarrying with each other" (*Kansas Herald of Freedom* [Lawrence, Kansas], December 18, 1858, quoting the *Alton Courier*). Cousin marriage has not, however, been condemned by the state since 1865, although a range of in-laws has been. The current laws of Georgia forbid marriage between a father and daughter or stepdaughter; mother and son or stepson; brother and sister of whole or half blood; grandparent and grandchild; aunt and nephew; and uncle and niece (Georgia Code 1991, §19-3-3).

Louisiana civil statutes of 1808, 1825, and 1870 dropped the prohibitions against marriage between affinal relatives that had been in force under the old Spanish code and had been incorporated into the Civil Code Project of 1804 (Dominguez 1986:59). Marriage was prohibited "between all ascendants and descendants, legitimate or natural, and between those connected by marriage in the same line" in 1804 (Louisiana Civil Code 1804, art. 94). The later nineteenth-century statutes added half siblings to the list of forbidden relatives but did not include first cousins. These were added at the beginning of this century: "In 1900, in a move that was apparently unpopular, the state legislature amended article 95 of the revised Civil Code of 1870 to include first cousins . . ." (Dominguez 1986:60). People in the state evaded the law, however, and continued to marry their first cousins by going to neighboring states where such a marriage was valid. The two Louisiana legislative houses failed to concur in an amendment to the bill determining the effective date of the legislation, and consequently the act was found defective and held unconstitutional in 1901. The legislature then passed another bill against cousin marriage in 1902, which remains today. Louisiana has occasionally granted dispensations for first cousin marriage, and in 1987 an act of the legislature legalized marriages between collateral relations contracted prior to September 11, 1981. This act was put into effect January 1, 1988.

California, Florida, and Texas, like Louisiana, have a history of Spanish influence. Because of the prohibition against cousin marriage in the Roman Catholic church and the role of the church in Hispanic culture, one might suspect these states would also have such a prohibition, but they have never added one. California and Florida today prohibit marriage between a man and his aunt, niece, sister, mother, daughter, and granddaughter. Texas forbids marriage between any lineal relatives, between siblings, and between individuals and their parents' siblings or their siblings' children, whether the relationship is by consanguinity or adoption. Texas is the only one of these three states that has had prohibitions against affinal relationships. Marriages between a man and his father's widow, son's widow, wife's daughter, and wife's granddaughter were prohibited in Texas during the nineteenth century (Wright 1889). Today marriage to a stepparent or stepchild is all that remains of the list of affinal prohibitions.

Ohio, which joined the Union in 1803, enacted legislation in that year allowing marriage between persons "not nearer of kin than first cousins" (Acts of the State of Ohio 1803, vol. 3). The legality of marriage between first cousins was reaffirmed in 1810 and again in 1824. In 1870, however, Ohio amended its laws and added first cousins to its list of forbidden relatives, as New Hampshire had done a year earlier. The Ohio legislature passed a bill establishing second cousins as the closest kin that could legally marry, which remains in force today. As it is written, the law precludes first cousins once removed as well as first cousins from marrying since both are closer than second cousins.

No affines are prohibited from marrying today in Ohio. Furthermore, Ohio courts have determined that "sexual relations between cousins are not incestuous" (Mazzolini v. Mazzolini, 155 N.E. 2d 208). They have also established that first cousins who marry in a state where it is legal would have their marriage legally recognized if they moved to Ohio (Mazzolini v. Mazzolini, 155 N.E. 2d 206).

Before the end of the nineteenth century Arkansas and Illinois followed Ohio in enacting first cousin marriage prohibitions. Arkansas enacted legislation against cousin marriage in 1875, which remains in effect today. Illinois statutes in 1819 used the sixteenth-century language of English law and allowed marriage between any persons "not prohibited by the laws of God" (Gilman 1869:622). Marriages between first cousins were considered incestuous and rendered void in 1887, when the revised statutes of 1874 were amended. This legislation has since been amended, and first cousins who are fifty years or older are now permitted to marry. First cousins can also marry if either perspective spouse presents to the county clerk a certificate signed by a licensed physician stating that the person is permanently and irreversibly sterile.

Indiana allowed marriages "not prohibited by the laws of God" in an act of 1818 (State v. Tucker, 174 Ind. 715). The revised statutes of 1852 allowed couples "not within the prohibited degrees of consanguinity" to marry, but they did not specify what the degrees were. In 1873 Indiana legislated that marriages prohibited by law on account of consanguinity were to be absolutely void, but this statute also neglected to state precisely what the prohibited degrees were (Indiana Acts 1873, chap. 43, sec. 1). Newman (1869) reported that "the union of cousins is forbidden" in Indiana (117). Wright (1889) also mentioned that only those "not nearer of kin than second cousins" could marry in the state (32). But not until 1907 did it become certain under Indiana law that first cousins were proscribed from marrying. Legislation enacted in that year clearly spelled out that first cousins were not permitted to marry. The law declared that all marriages between persons nearer of kin than second cousins were void (making the marriage between first cousins once removed prohibited as well). The act also legalized and declared valid all marriages between first cousins undertaken before the law went into effect, clearing up any uncertainty over their legal status (Indiana Acts 1907, chap. 68, sec. 1). This law has since been amended. In 1977 legislation approved exceptions to the prohibition.

It allowed that "marriages entered into after September 1, 1977, between first cousins sixty-five (65) years of age and older shall not be void" (Indiana Code 1982, Vol. 6, Title 31).

Of the states that joined the Union after the middle of the nineteenth century, Kansas was the first to prohibit first cousins and not affines from marrying. Before achieving statehood, the Territory of Kansas passed a law in 1855 prohibiting marriages between lineal consanguines, half and full siblings, uncles and nieces, and aunts and nephews. The territory also forbade a "step-father to marry the daughter of his deceased wife and for a step-mother to marry the son of her deceased husband" (Statutes of Kansas Territory 1855, chap. 108, sec. 2). In 1858 the steprelatives were removed, and the list of consanguineal kin was expanded to include "cousins." This meant, technically, that all people descended from a pair of siblings were forbidden to marry. This, evidently, was not what the legislators had intended, and in the following year they amended the law specifying that "first cousins" were prohibited from marrying. When Kansas was admitted to the Union shortly afterward, in 1861, it became the first state to prohibit first cousins from marrying. Its list of forbidden relatives included only consanguineal kin, not affinal kin.

Kansas marital law of 1861 marked the beginning of a distinct change in the pattern of marriage laws in the United States. A large majority of the sixteen states entering the Union after Kansas prohibited first cousin marriage. Few had any affinal prohibitions. Today twelve of the sixteen (75 percent) forbid first cousin marriage. Only Hawaii, Alaska, Colorado, and New Mexico permit cousin marriage. This contrasts sharply with the earlier states in the Union, which, for the most part, did not prohibit first cousins from marrying but did prohibit a range of affinal kin (see table 2).

New Mexico, while a territory, briefly prohibited first cousin marriage from 1876 to 1880. This form of marriage was fairly common among the families of Spanish descent in the territory (Chavez 1982). Probably because of this tradition, the following proviso was added to the 1876 statute prohibiting first cousin marriage: "the marriage of all persons within three months from the passage of this act, who may be related to each other in the grade of first cousins, shall be held legal and not effected by this or any other act" (New Mexico Acts of the Legislative Assembly 1876–78, chap. 12, sec. 2). Pressure from the Spanish community probably underlay the repeal of the cousin marriage prohibition four years later (New Mexico Statutes 1986 Replacement, 7:6, compiler's notes). After becoming a state in 1912, New Mexico continued to permit first cousin marriage.

Table 2. First Cousin and Affinal Prohibitions

		Nineteenth Century		Today	
State	Entered Union	Affines	First Cousins	Affines	First Cousins
New Jersey	1787	X			
Pennsylvania	1787	X			X
Delaware	1787	X			X
Georgia	1788	X		X	
Maryland	1788	X		X	
Massachusetts	1788	X		X	
New Hampshire	1788	X	X(1869)	X	X
New York	1788				
South Carolina	1788	X		X	
Connecticut	1788	X			
Virginia	1788	X			
North Carolina	1789				X
Rhode Island	1790	X		X	
Vermont	1791	X			
Kentucky	1792	X			X
Tennessee	1796	X		X	
Ohio	1803		X(1870)		X
Louisiana	1812				X
Indiana	1816				X
Mississippi	1817	X		X	X
Missouri	1817				X
Illinois	1818		X(1887)		X
Alabama	1819	X		X	
Maine	1820	X			X
Arkansas	1836		X(1875)		X
Michigan	1837	X			X
Texas	1845	X		X	
Florida	1845				
Iowa	1846	X			X
Wisconsin	1848				X
California	1850				
Minnesota	1858				X
Oregon	1859				X
Kansas	1861		X		X
West Virginia	1863	X			X
Nevada	1864		X		X

Table 2, continued

State	Year				
Nebraska	1867				X
Colorado	1876		X		
South Dakota	1889	X	X	X	X
Washington	1889	X	X		X
North Dakota	1889	X	X		X
Montana	1889		X		X
Idaho	1890				X
Wyoming	1890		X		X
Utah	1896				X
Oklahoma	1907			X	X
New Mexico	1912				
Arizona	1912				X
Hawaii	1959				
Alaska	1959				

Note: The date of cousin prohibition is given in parentheses for those states entering the Union prior to 1861.

According to Arner (1908:14), the territory of Alaska at one time forbade first cousin unions, but by 1933 the territory's statutes only prohibited marriage between individuals "related to each other within and not including the fourth degree of consanguinity, whether of the whole or half blood computed according to the rules of the civil law" (quoted in Morland 1946:1067–68). This does not prohibit first cousins from marrying since they are relatives of the fourth degree, according to the civil method of reckoning distance. The number of degrees between two relatives is calculated in the civil method by summing the number of ties between each relative and the common ancestor. For example, a brother and sister are in the second degree of relationship. It is one degree from each one of them to their common ancestor, their parent. Nephew-aunt and niece-uncle are both in the third degree of relationship. First cousins are in the fourth degree of relationship. Each individual has two degrees of relationship to a common ancestor, their grandparent. Mackay (1957:25) stated that Alaska's laws of 1949 prohibited relatives as distant as second cousins from marrying, but this is probably due to a miscalculation on his part or a confusion between the civil and canonical methods of calculating distance (see chapter 2 for a detailed discussion of the difference between the two methods of calculation). Since Alaska became a state in 1959, its statutes on consanguinity in marriage have been identical to the 1933 ones. Only relatives closer than first cousins are prohibited from marrying (Martindale-Hubbell 1995).

Colorado prohibited cousin marriage at one time. The state forbade it in 1864, but exempted those people living in that portion of the state acquired from Mexico. They were permitted to marry cousins according to Mexican law (Wright 1889:37, note a). The prohibition against first cousins' marrying remained through 1877 but was absent from the Session Laws of 1883, although "Mills, Ann. Stat. (1891), sec. 1320, p. 931, declares the marriage of first cousins incestuous and void" (Howard 1904, 2:474, note 4). Mackay (1957:21) thought Colorado's Annotated Statutes of 1935 prohibited first cousins from marrying, but Morland (1946) and Indovina and Dalton (1945) state that Colorado permitted first cousins to marry at that time. Cousin marriage is not prohibited today. The state's current statutes spell out that only marriages between ancestors and descendants, between brother and sister of half or whole blood, between uncle and niece, and between aunt and nephew are incestuous and absolutely void.

West Virginia was formally admitted to the Union in 1863, after having been formed as an independent entity separate from Virginia. When it joined, cousins were permitted to marry, and a number of affinal relationships were prohibited, in keeping with the laws of Virginia (a man could not marry his stepmother, wife's daughter, son's wife, and wife's granddaughter) and most of the states already in the Union. West Virginia's list of forbidden in-laws, however, also included a man's nephew's widow, which was the only case in which a state has forbidden this relationship. In 1906 the list of forbidden relatives in West Virginia for a man included his mother, grandmother, stepmother, sister, daughter, granddaughter, half sister, aunt, uncle's wife, son's wife, wife's daughter, wife's granddaughter, wife's stepdaughter, brother's daughter, sister's daughter, brother's son's wife, and sister's son's wife. Marriage between a man and his deceased brother's wife was legal. In 1955 first cousins and double cousins were added to the list, and the uncle's wife was removed. The corresponding prohibitions for a woman were also spelled out. It was also declared that if a man had previously married his brother's widow, uncle's widow, first cousin, or double cousin, the marriage was legal. West Virginia dropped all of the affinal relationships in 1986 and specified that the prohibition against first and double cousins should not include those related by adoption.

Nebraska, Idaho, and Utah, like West Virginia, did not prohibit cousin marriages when they first became states in the late nineteenth century but do so today. Oklahoma, when it became a state in 1907, forbade first and second cousins from marrying. It has the distinction of being the only state that forbade marriage between second cousins. This consanguineal union was prohibited until 1969. Legislation passed in 1965 recognized the legitimacy of second cousin marriage performed in other states, and in 1969 second cousin marriage was removed from the list of prohibited marriages. First cousin marriages are still prohibited today. Nevada, South Dakota, Wyoming, North Dakota, Washington, Montana, and Arizona, the remainder of the states that entered the Union after Kansas, all prohibit first cousin marriage.

No state in the Union before the 1860s had civil regulations preventing the marriage of first cousins. Of these states, only Arkansas, Illinois, New Hampshire, and Ohio prohibited first cousin marriage before the end of the nineteenth century. Delaware, Indiana, Iowa, Kentucky, Louisiana, Maine, Michigan, Minnesota, Missouri, Mississippi, North Carolina, Oregon, Pennsylvania, and Wisconsin passed legislation prohibiting first cousins from marrying in the twentieth century. The remaining states that joined the Union prior to the 1860s (Alabama, California, Connecticut, Florida, Georgia, Massachusetts, Maryland, New Jersey, New York, California, Rhode Island, South Carolina, Tennessee, Texas, Vermont, and Virginia) have no prohibitions against cousin marriage.

Twenty-one of the thirty-three states (63.6 percent) in the Union before 1861 prohibited affinal relatives from marrying. Only twelve (Arkansas, California, Florida, Illinois, Indiana, Minnesota, Missouri, New York, North Carolina, Ohio, Oregon, and Wisconsin) had no affinal proscriptions. Louisiana dropped affinal prohibitions in the second half of the nineteenth century, and Connecticut, Delaware, Iowa, Kentucky, Maine, Michigan, New Jersey, Pennsylvania, Vermont, and Virginia dropped them in the twentieth century. Iowa, for example, prohibited marriage between a man and his father's widow, wife's mother, wife's daughter, son's widow, son's son's widow, and daughter's son's widow until 1985, when it dropped all affinal relationships from its list of void marriages. Alabama, Georgia, Maryland, Massachusetts, Mississippi, New Hampshire, Rhode Island, South Carolina, Tennessee, and Texas, the remaining states with affinal prohibitions prior to 1861, still maintain them today.

Marriages between the stepmother and stepson and the stepfather and stepdaughter are prohibited in these states. Mississippi also declares incestuous and void relationships between a man and his legally adopted daughter, stepsister, son's widow, wife's daughter, and wife's granddaughter. In Alabama relationships between a man and his son's widow, wife's granddaughter, and uncle's widow were also considered incestuous until 1947, when the uncle's widow was deleted (Indovina and Dalton Supplement 1956). Georgia, since the nineteenth century, has also considered these affinal relations incestuous but added the wife's mother. South Carolina includes the grandfather's wife, the wife's grandmother, and the grandson's wife in its list of forbidden relatives. Tennessee has not dropped any of the prohibited in-laws or steprelatives from its nineteenth century list of prohibitions and continues to forbid marriage to the spouse of a parent, the spouse of a lineal descendant, and the lineal descendant of a spouse.

Of the seventeen states that joined the Union after 1860, only four (23.5 percent) have enacted proscriptions against marriage between nonconsanguineal relatives. North Dakota, Washington, South Dakota, and Oklahoma have forbidden certain in-laws or steprelatives from marrying. North Dakota at one time forbade marriage between a man and his stepmother or stepdaughter but no longer does. Washington at one time banned marriage between a man and his father's widow, wife's mother, wife's daughter, son's widow, and grandson's widow. There were the corresponding prohibitions for a woman. Today the state does not prohibit any affines from marrying. Only South Dakota and Oklahoma continue to ban nonconsanguineal unions. Each prohibits a man from marrying his stepmother or stepdaughter.

If 1861, the year Kansas entered the Union, is taken as a dividing point, it is evident that the laws prohibiting marriage between in-laws and steprelatives have significantly decreased. Twenty of the thirty states (67 percent) in the Union during the first half of the nineteenth century had affinal prohibitions. After the 1860s states that joined the Union generally did not adopt any affinal prohibitions. Furthermore, most states since then either dropped their prohibitions against affinal marriage or have reduced the number of relationships prohibited.

No state bans all the affinal relatives listed in Archbishop Parker's Table of Kindred and Affinity, and only twelve (Alabama, Georgia, Maryland, Massachusetts, Mississippi, New Hampshire, Oklahoma, Rhode Island, South Carolina, Tennessee, South Dakota, and Texas) of the fifty states (24 percent), plus the District of Columbia, maintain affinal prohibitions today. Oklahoma and Texas prohibit marriage between a man and his stepmother or his stepdaughter. Maryland, Michigan, Rhode Island, South Carolina, and Tennessee prohibit marriage between a man and his grandfather's wife, wife's grandmother, stepmother, mother-in-law, stepdaughter, daughter-in-law, grandson's wife, and his wife's granddaughter. Massachusetts at one time prohibited the same relatives from marrying, but since 1983 a man has been permitted to marry his daughter-in-law. There are corresponding prohibitions for a woman. Thus, in Massachusetts a man is forbidden to marry his wife's mother but can marry his son's wife. Likewise, a woman in Massachusetts is prohibited from marrying the husband of her daughter but can marry the father of her husband.

Thirty-eight states (Alaska, Arizona, Arkansas, California, Colorado, Connecticut, Delaware, Florida, Hawaii, Idaho, Illinois, Indiana, Iowa, Kansas, Kentucky, Louisiana, Maine, Michigan, Minnesota, Missouri, Montana, Nebraska, Nevada, New Jersey, New Mexico, New York, North Carolina, North Dakota, Ohio, Oregon, Pennsylvania, Utah, Vermont, Virginia, Washington, West Virginia, Wisconsin, and Wyoming) do not forbid marriages between any in-laws or steprelatives. In general, states have either reduced or eliminated affinal prohibitions.

In contrast to the decrease in affinal prohibitions since the middle of the nineteenth century, there has been an increase in legislation forbidding first cousins from marrying. Before 1861 no state prohibited cousin marriage. An overwhelming majority of the states that joined the Union since that time prohibit first cousins from marrying, and most of the other states have added first cousins to their list of prohibited marriages. When the Bureau of Labor undertook the country's first comprehensive survey of marriage in the 1880s, thirteen states and territories had passed legislation forbidding cousins from marrying (Wright 1889). By 1908 there were sixteen states with first cousin prohibitions (Arner 1908:14). Since then the number of states with first cousin prohibitions has nearly doubled. Most recently, Maine revised its marriage laws in 1985 and prohibited first cousin marriage. This made a total of thirty-one states with proscriptions against cousin marriage. States that do not allow first cousin marriage are Arizona, Arkansas, Delaware, Idaho, Illinois, Indiana, Iowa, Kansas, Kentucky, Louisiana, Maine, Michigan, Minnesota, Mississippi, Missouri, Montana, Nebraska, Nevada, New Hampshire, North Carolina (which forbids only double first cousins from marrying), North Dakota, Ohio, Oklahoma, Oregon, Pennsylvania, South Dakota, Utah, Washington, West Virginia, Wisconsin, and Wyoming (see table 3).

Because of the way marital law is currently written in Indiana, Kentucky, Nevada, Ohio, Washington, and Wisconsin, first cousins once removed as well as first cousins are forbidden to marry. The law in these states prohibits marriage between people more closely related than second cous-

Table 3. First Cousins Plus the Relatives in Archbishop Parker's Table a Man Is Forbidden to Marry Today, by States

	Consanguineal											Affinal																			
	GM	FZ	MZ	M	D	Z	SD	DD	BD	ZD	C	GFW	WGM	FBW	MBW	WFZ	WMZ	FW	WM	WD	SW	WZ	BS	SSW	DSW	WSD	WDD	BSW	ZSW	WBD	WZD
Alabama	X	X	X	X	X	X	X	X	X	X	X							X		X	X					X	X				
Alaska	X	X	X	X	X	X	X	X	X	X	X																				
Arizona	X	X	X	X	X	X	X	X	X	X	X[a]																				
Arkansas	X	X	X	X	X	X	X	X	X	X	X																				
California	X	X	X	X	X	X	X	X	X	X	X																				
Colorado	X	X	X	X	X	X	X	X	X	X	X																				
Connecticut	X	X	X	X	X	X	X	X	X	X	X																				
Delaware	X	X	X	X	X	X	X	X	X	X	X																				
Florida	X	X	X	X	X	X	X	X	X	X	X																				
Georgia	X	X	X	X	X	X	X	X	X	X	X							X		X											
Hawaii	X	X	X	X	X	X	X	X	X	X	X																				
Idaho	X	X	X	X	X	X	X	X	X	X	X																				
Illinois	X	X	X	X	X	X	X	X	X	X	X[a]																				
Indiana	X	X	X	X	X	X	X	X	X	X	X[a]																				
Iowa	X	X	X	X	X	X	X	X	X	X	X																				
Kansas	X	X	X	X	X	X	X	X	X	X	X																				
Kentucky	X	X	X	X	X	X	X	X	X	X	X																				
Louisiana	X	X	X	X	X	X	X	X	X	X	X																				
Maine	X	X	X	X	X	X	X	X	X	X	X																				
Maryland	X	X	X	X	X	X	X	X	X	X	X	X						X	X	X	X	X		X	X	X	X				
Massachusetts	X	X	X	X	X	X	X	X	X	X	X	X						X	X	X			X	X	X	X	X				
Michigan	X	X	X	X	X	X	X	X	X	X	X	X						X	X	X	X	X	X	X	X	X	X				
Minnesota	X	X	X	X	X	X	X	X	X	X	X																				
Mississippi	X	X	X	X	X	X	X	X	X	X	X							X		X						X	X				

State																	
Missouri	X	X	X	X	X	X	X	X	X	X	X							
Montana	X	X	X	X	X	X	X	X	X	X	X							
Nebraska	X	X	X	X	X	X	X	X	X	X	X							
Nevada	X	X	X	X	X	X	X	X	X	X	X							
New Hampshire	X	X	X	X	X	X	X	X	X	X	X	X	X	X	X		X	X
New Jersey	X	X	X	X	X	X	X	X	X	X								
New Mexico	X	X	X	X	X	X	X	X	X	X								
New York	X	X	X	X	X	X	X	X	X	X								
North Carolina	X	X	X	X	X	X	X	X	X	X^b								
North Dakota	X	X	X	X	X	X	X	X	X	X	X							
Ohio	X	X	X	X	X	X	X	X	X	X	X							
Oklahoma	X	X	X	X	X	X	X	X	X	X	X		X					
Oregon	X	X	X	X	X	X	X	X	X	X	X							
Pennsylvania	X	X	X	X	X	X	X	X	X									
Rhode Island	X	X	X	X	X	X	X	X	X	X	X	X	X	X	X	X	X	X
South Carolina	X	X	X	X	X	X	X	X	X	X	X	X	X	X	X	X	X	X
South Dakota	X	X	X	X	X	X	X	X	X	X	X							
Tennessee	X	X	X	X	X	X	X	X	X	X	X	X	X	X		X	X	X
Texas	X	X	X	X	X	X	X	X	X	X	X	X						
Utah	X	X	X	X	X	X	X	X	X	X	X							
Vermont	X	X	X	X	X	X	X	X	X	X	X							
Virginia	X	X	X	X	X	X	X	X	X	X	X							
Washington	X	X	X	X	X	X	X	X	X	X	X							
West Virginia	X	X	X	X	X	X	X	X	X	X	X							
Wisconsin	X	X	X	X	X	X	X	X	X^a	X	X	X						
Wyoming	X	X	X	X	X	X	X	X	X	X	X							

a. Permitted when the couple will not bear children.

b. Double first cousins only.

Note: G = grand; M = mother; F = father; Z = sister; D = daughter; S = son; B = brother; W = wife; C = cousin. GFW is read as grandfather's wife, etc.

ins. A Minnesota attorney general's opinion stated that first cousins once removed cannot legally marry in that state, although the law only specifies first cousins (Op. Atty. Gen., 300-G, Feb. 26, 1953).

It is possible to legally marry a first cousin in nineteen states: Alabama, Alaska, California, Colorado, Connecticut, Florida, Georgia, Hawaii, Maryland, Massachusetts, New Jersey, New Mexico, New York, Rhode Island, South Carolina, Tennessee, Texas, Vermont, and Virginia. First cousins are also permitted to marry in the District of Columbia.

Michigan courts have held that marriage between first cousins was "not void as contrary to law of nature (Miller's Estate [1927] 214 N.W. 428, 239 Mich. 455) and that the prohibition applies only to marriages solemnized in the state (Toth v. Toth [1973] 212 N.W. 2d 812, 50 Mich. App. 150). The attorney general also has given the opinion that first cousins residing in Michigan who legally marry outside of the state will have the marriage recognized on their return (Op. Atty. Gen. 1939–40, 177).

First cousins are also legally permitted to marry under special conditions in Maine, Arizona, Illinois, and Wisconsin. Maine's 1985 legislation forbidding first cousins to marry was amended in 1987 to permit a couple to marry if either partner presents documented evidence that the couple has had genetic counseling. Arizona since 1990 has permitted first cousins to marry if each of the couple is more than sixty-five years old or if one of them is unable to reproduce. Illinois permits first cousins to marry if they are fifty years old or older or if one of the partners is sterile. Wisconsin permits first cousins to marry if the female is at least fifty-five years old or the couple, when applying for a marriage license, presents to the clerk a physician's affidavit that one of them is permanently sterile.

The reasoning underlying the exceptions in Maine, Arizona, Illinois, and Wisconsin is clearly that first cousin marriage has the potential for producing offspring with physical debilities that will be costly to the state. Couples that pose such a risk are thus forbidden to marry, while those that do not are excepted from the injunction. The underlying supposition that first cousin marriage poses a significant risk is questionable, however (see chapter 6).

Adopted relatives as close as siblings are permitted to marry in some states (Wadlington 1984:151). This raises a potential problem. An adopted individual may have close consanguineal ties to the prospective spouse. These ties would void the marriage, but they may be unknown because the adoption records were sealed. West Virginia has included a procedure in its statutes that deals with this problem. When first cousins by adoption apply for a marriage license, the courts can confidentially examine adoption records, ascertain whether the couple has any close consanguineal ties, and then inform the clerk to issue or deny the marriage license. Another way to avoid the problem is not to permit close adopted relatives to marry. New Hampshire, for example, prohibits cousins by adoption from marrying. The problem with adopted relatives who may be consanguineally related but want to marry is dealt with differently in, for example, Sweden. There consanguineal relatives as close as half siblings are not forbidden to marry.

To recapitulate, every state regulates the marriage of relatives. Each forbids marriage between full siblings, between parents and children, between uncles and nieces, and between aunts and nephews. There is considerable variation with other relatives. Some forbid affinal as well as consanguineal relatives from marrying, and there is no uniformity regarding first cousins. Thirty-one states forbid first cousin marriage, and nineteen do not. While the common notion that southern states are more apt to allow first cousins to marry does not fit the data, there is a pattern to the injunctions against first cousin marriage. There is a tendency for states in the western part of the United States to have a prohibition against first cousin marriage. States that joined the Union after 1860, most of which were in the West, tended to prohibit it. Later other states amended their marital laws to forbid first cousin marriages. The increase in the number of states forbidding the marriage of first cousins over the past century and a half has been accompanied by a decrease in the number of affinal relatives prohibited from marrying. After the middle of the nineteenth century states tended not to prohibit affines from marrying, and those that previously had done so reduced or eliminated their proscriptions. Nearly two-thirds of the states had some injunction against marriage between affinal relatives before 1861. Today only twelve states have affinal prohibitions.

2

The Reasons for
U.S. Laws against
First Cousin Marriage

That there has existed, at least in all modern times, what is
called a "feeling" against the intermarriage of blood relations, is a fact that cannot be denied, but of which the scientific value cannot be rated very high.

—*Westminister Review*, 1893

When searching for an explanation of the prohibitions against cousin marriage in the United States, the sociologist Bernard Farber noticed the "tendency for states that forbid first cousin marriage to permit marriage of affines (and vice versa)" (Farber 1968:28). He also recognized that this
tendency had a general geographical distribution. A statistical association
between laws against cousin marriage and a lack of affinal prohibitions exists in the western and midwestern states. Conversely, an association between the absence of cousin marriage prohibitions and the existence of laws
prohibiting affinal relationships exists in New England and the southern
states (Farber 1968:29). Focusing on the geographical distribution of the
two types of associations, Farber sought to explain the marriage regulations
in sociological terms. The western states, where cousin marriage is prohibited and affinal relationships are permitted, were settled later than those
in the East, and he postulated that they were settled by immigrants with a
diverse ethnicity who "invited an individualistic, preferential-descent system by which the individual derived his kinship identity from his parents"
(Farber 1968:39). The prohibition against cousin marriage strengthened this
individualism. Farber noted that cousin marriage facilitated control over
nuclear families by kin and helped ensure the continuous transmission of

tradition. He concluded from this that the western states forbade cousin marriage to support the breakdown of the continuity of family culture in support of individuality. The states in the East and South, which had been settled earlier, Farber saw as having a greater ethnic homogeneity (although with a class structure) and having maintained their cultural traditions. He thought cousin marriage was not prohibited in these states because it served to maintain the ethnic traditions by creating extended family units.

Farber's attempt to explain the distribution of marriage laws is, at best, unnecessarily complex. The geographical distribution of states with a ban on cousin marriage can be explained much more easily. It is not necessary to connect cousin marriage with late settlement, ethnic diversity, cultural transmission, and individualism. Nor is it necessary to assume that states with cousin prohibitions are more ethnically heterogeneous than those without them, something that is not supported by the evidence. Iowa and Maine, for example, have prohibitions against cousin marriage today, while New York and California do not. Maine and Iowa are not more ethnically complex than New York and California. Comparing two neighboring western states, Kansas and Colorado, one discovers that in the former first cousin marriage is prohibited, while in Colorado, partly because of its Mexican heritage, there is no such prohibition. This is precisely the opposite of what Farber's hypothesis would predict.

Farber's assumption that diverse ethnicity implies individualism or, put another way, that individualism provides the impetus to ban cousins from marrying does contain an essential truth about cousin marriage. As discussed in chapter 7, cousin marriage is an important mechanism of cultural continuity and, as such, functions to maintain a group. But this can not explain the distribution of the laws against cousin marriage. For one thing, it is doubtful that individualism is more pronounced in states with a prohibition against first cousin marriage or that the passage of a prohibition in Maine in 1985 was the result of increasing individualism in the state. Furthermore, that individualism can account for a prohibition does not stand up under analysis when important comparative data are included. The British, for example, were part of the social, political, technological, and economic changes over the last two centuries that accompanied the rise of individualism throughout the Western world. They also have witnessed a decline in the importance of the notion that marriage joined two individuals into a single unit. They also have repealed the prohibitions against marriage with collateral affines. But, as will be discussed in detail in the following chapters, the British have not forbidden the marriage of cousins.

The geographical distribution of the laws regulating the marriage of relatives noted by Farber can be explained parsimoniously, without the complex ratiocination of his hypothesis, by recognizing the significance of the temporal factor. The discussion of the American laws in chapter 1 makes it clear that the regulation of marriage between relatives in the United States has not remained constant. Statutes have been repealed, replaced, or amended since their earliest inception and continue to be modified today. In general over the last century and a half the United States has tended to give less weight to affinity as grounds for prohibiting marriage. At the same time, it has increasingly stressed consanguineal relationships (Clarke 1957:100). This has led over the past century and a half to an increased percentage of the states with first cousin prohibitions and a decline in the number of states with laws prohibiting affines from marrying. With an increasing emphasis on consanguinity and a decreasing emphasis on affinity in the U.S. legal tradition, western states would have laws prohibiting cousin marriage and lack those prohibiting affinal relationships simply because their statutes were enacted at a later date than those in the eastern and southern parts of the United States. Simply put, the distribution of the statutes on marriage between relatives reflects the increased emphasis on regulating consanguinity in marriage in the United States since the middle of the last century.

What requires explanation is the change in emphasis. This change can be best understood by relating it to an important cultural shift the United States underwent during the middle of the nineteenth century. The basis of the relationships between the individual, marriage, family, and society changed from human rationality and moral persuasiveness to bioevolutionary concerns (Grossberg 1985:144–45; Rosenberg 1976:25–53).

Acrid debates over marital law in the country during the first half of the nineteenth century were dominated by concerns with the moral consequences of affinal marriages. Incestuous relationships in general were viewed in terms of the social and moral implications of marriage. Affinal kin were treated no differently from consanguineal kin in legislating prohibitions. Each side in these debates relied primarily on biblical interpretation and ecclesiastical authority for their arguments. Consequently, scriptural experts played major roles in the debate.

By the middle of the nineteenth century the debates over the regulation of marriage no longer focused on biblical exegesis and moral concerns. The emphasis had shifted to the results of empirical investigations into the health of various human groups and to the possible physical consequences of consanguinity for offspring. Bioevolutionary fitness became the major concern, and medical doctors became the chief protagonists in the debates. This trend was sharply accelerated in the United States after the middle of the nineteenth century.

This change is clearly illustrated by the increased concern with consanguineal relationships and the decreased anxiety over affinal unions in the debates over prohibited marriages. The most debated relationship in the United States during the first half of the nineteenth century was the relationship between a man and his former wife's sister. Archbishop Parker had included sister-in-law in his list of affinal relatives a man was forbidden to marry, although many thought it applied only to sororal polygyny, that is, to the marriage between a man and his sister's wife when his wife was still alive (Mielziner 1901). The prohibition against marriage between a man and his sister-in-law was the cause of stormy parliamentary debates throughout most of the nineteenth century in England, and it was not removed until the early twentieth century (see chapter 4 for details). In the United States the prohibition was successfully opposed much earlier.

Noah Webster had raised objections to the prohibition against the marriage between a man and his dead wife's sister in the late eighteenth century. In 1789 he wrote a brief argument outlining his opposition to the proscription (Webster 1790). To those who argued that the prohibition was based on the Old Testament, Webster responded by dismissing the biblical prohibitions as pertinent only to the ancient Hebrews and not binding on others. He argued that moral laws, such as proper marriages, must ultimately be based on the concept of "fitness." This meant that marriages must follow the requirements of natural laws. Webster recognized two natural laws. His first law required that "marriage, which iz a social and civil connection, should not interfere with a natural relation, so az to defeet or destroy its duties and rights" (323). This law reiterated the age-old concern that improper marriage confuses the roles of family members. It has often been feared, for example, that were a nephew to marry his aunt or a godmother her godson, the social roles required in the consanguineal or spiritual relationships would conflict with those required by the affinal relationships. This conflict, so the argument goes, would result in chaos and the destruction of the family units. Webster's second natural law to determine the fitness of marriage prohibitions was that close breeding led to deleterious physical effects in offspring: "It iz no crime for brothers and sisters to intermarry, except the fatal consequences to society; for were it generally practised, men would soon become a race of pigmies. It iz no crime for brothers and sisters children to intermarry, and this iz often practised; but such near blood connections often produce imperfect children" (324). Webster concluded that marriage with the former wife's sister should not be prohibited since it does not inhibit natural fitness. It does not threaten to confuse family roles or to produce "imperfect offspring."

Webster's laws were a combination of ancient and modern ideas. His first law was an expression of the ancient view that marriage is an institution essential for the maintenance of social order. His second law was an early expression of the contemporary American view that marriage is essentially a breeding mechanism, which, when it involves close relatives, will produce unfit offspring. Webster's disregard for the Mosaic prohibitions, his focus on naturalistic arguments, and his concern with the possible deleterious effects on the offspring in a consanguineous marriage portend the American myth of cousin marriage. At the time Webster wrote, however, no widely accepted theoretical framework for his ideas existed, and there was only impressionistic evidence for his contention that cousin marriage led to imperfect offspring. Arguments about the fitness of types of marriage remained centered on social or moral concerns. Nor was fitness a bioevolutionary doctrine. It was not until well into the nineteenth century that physicians would begin to publish the results of their investigations of the impact of consanguineal unions on offspring and a natural theory of social evolution would become widely accepted. These were the missing essential ingredients to make Webster's second law a factor in the legislation of cousin marriage. Only in the nineteenth century would marrying outside of the circle of close relatives become synonymous in the United States with proper breeding, survival, and biological fitness. Social progress would be accomplished through proper marriages, and outbreeding would become the dominant concern of marital law in the United States.

Early in the nineteenth century, after the Presbyterian church suspended Archibald McQueen, a Fayetteville, North Carolina, minister, for marrying his deceased wife's sister, a public debate arose in the church about the propriety of marriage between a widower and his sister-in-law. The arguments in this debate illustrate the fundamental changes in the underlying attitudes toward marital regulations. The debate opened when a clergyman, writing under the pseudonym Domesticus, answered the question, "Which of the Levitical bans apply to contemporary social situations?"

> The obvious reply to this is,—just so much as agrees with the physical, moral and political circumstances of modern society, and the rule

is *General Expediency,* as apprehended by the common sense of mankind. Before therefore a Mosaic statute can be acknowledged to possess a binding authority over me, or the community of which I am a member, I must ascertain its *reason,* its principle. If on a fair and candid examination, I discover that the reason *fully holds,* the statute I pronounce to be *binding.* If there be a difference of circumstances, not however destructive of the general reason, I am bound to *modify* so as to suit the peculiarity.—If the circumstances be so different, that the reason ceases altogether, it is *abrogated.* (Domesticus 1827:7)

He went on to explain that what he meant by "general expediency" was "fitness." Fitness was the promotion of happiness, which was the same as the tendency to promote the public good. Reasoning would lead to its discovery, and what was being discovered was, ultimately, the will of God.

Domesticus also summarized the reasons proposed in the past for prohibiting marriage between a man and his deceased wife's sister: (1) certain relationships are abhorrent to nature; even animals avoid them; (2) incest taboos extend friendships and family relationships; were there none, "a spirit of clanship would be perpetuated to the serious injury of society" (11); (3) crossbreeding has a good effect; (4) the taboos should only apply to marriage between ascendants and descendants because this would destroy the respect due elder relatives, particularly if a son would marry a mother; and (5) the prohibitions were only to guard against marriage between persons of unequal age, which would result in degenerate offspring or infertility.

While arguing that the prohibition against marriage between a man and his wife's sister was necessary, Domesticus did not concur with all of the reasons given in the past for outlawing sister-in-law marriage. He did not accept that there was an instinctual avoidance of incest and attempted to refute the claim with ethnographic data. Citing cases from non-Western peoples, he concluded that "the feeling of repugnance . . . is generated by custom and education" (11). His argument for maintaining the prohibition rested on a belief that there is a need for injunctions against marrying relatives to maintain society. If not for the prohibitions, "the best organized society, that the earth has ever seen upon its surface, would become in a few years, a hideous mass of corruption and rottenness" (12).

Domesticus viewed the marriage of close relatives as essentially a threat to the social order. He believed that were a man permitted to marry his sister-in-law, the result would be general licentiousness and the destruction of structured social relationships. He specifically feared that permitting the marriage between a widower and his wife's sister would destroy any inhibitions the man might have about her sister while his wife was alive. The tranquility of domestic organization thus would be disrupted by sexual desire:

> We shall hear by and by, tales that will make our ears to tingle. We shall hear from this part of the country,—and that part,—and a third part, of the dreadful misfortune that happened in such a family: We shall hear of a lovely and accomplished girl rushing as she thought to an asylum opened to her by Heaven itself;—and finding but too late, that she had fallen into the clutches of a demon. We shall hear of a wife dying with a broken heart, her children weeping about her bed, knowing not well what has taken place,—yet feeling that some desolating whirlwind has come over them! (31)

In reply to Domesticus, another Presbyterian minister, writing under the pseudonym Clericus (1827), argued that there was no explicit ban against marrying the sister of a deceased wife in the Bible and that adherents have wrongly inferred the prohibition. Furthermore, there was no natural basis for the prohibition. Clericus contended that the arguments of inference were inconsistent and absurd and that the Levitical prohibitions must be understood in sociological and historical terms. The scriptural prohibitions came about when neighboring contemporaneous people of the Hebrews combined wool and linen in their garments, sowed barley and grapes together, and plowed with both ox and ass. The prohibitions enabled the ancient Hebrews to distinguish themselves from these neighboring peoples. Likewise, the Old Testament marriage prohibitions were a device of social organization, appropriate to the peoples of the Old Testament, but not binding on people today. Clericus thought that allowing a man to marry his dead wife's sister was not a threat to social well-being. On the basis of a sociohistorical explanation for the biblical prohibitions and an assertion that their purposes were not served in the contemporary world, Clericus concluded that marriage between a widower and his sister-in-law should not be banned.

A third voice in this debate was raised by Philip Milledoler, who was in favor of maintaining the prohibition. Distinguishing between consanguineal and affinal relationships, he argued that sister-in-law marriage must be prohibited "to prevent sinful familiarity between members of the same family, allied by affinity—to promote domestic tranquillity—and generally to enlarge the sphere of human benevolence and kind offices" (Milledoler 1843:14). These traditional reasons for the prohibition were augmented by referring to the concern that was about to dominate nineteenth-century marital legislation in the United States. Milledoler argued that consanguineous marriage was against nature. Close consanguineal kin, including first cousins, should be forbidden to marry because there is an evolutionary danger: "Is there not a law of nature which proves the deterioration, and even extinction of whole families who have long practised kindred marriage?" (17). His conviction that the marriage of close relatives threatened the deterioration or extinction of families led him first to conclude that cousin marriage should be prohibited and then to extend the evolutionary argument to affinal kin. He reasoned that if the marriage of first cousins threatened the extinction of the social group, so must any marriage with kin, affinal or consanguineal, as close or closer in relationship. Thus, he concluded, marriage with the wife's sister must also be forbidden.

The debate in the Presbyterian church over marriage between a man and his wife's sister effectively ended in 1846 with the reinstatement of the Reverend Archibald McQueen, shortly after Milledoler's argument was published. The reverend was reinstated because affinal relationships were no longer the major concern in regulating marriage. Previously, the arguments about marital regulations had primarily focused on the potential destruction of society through the breakdown of civil behavior unleashed by the failure to prohibit marriage (which implied sexuality) between family members. These family members could be related either consanguineally or affinally. By 1846, in the Presbyterian church, the focus had shifted to the notion of evolutionary fitness.

The maintenance of society was now threatened not by the failure to preserve the moral order within families but by the failure to breed viable and fit offspring. With this change broadly accepted in the United States, affinal unions became conceptually and legally separated from consanguineal unions, and prominence was accorded the latter. Affinal unions would no longer be of concern for much of the United States. This was evident in civil law by 1842. All of the states but Virginia had already permitted marriage with the deceased wife's sister (Cooke 1842:3). The Vermont Supreme Court had thrown out an appeal in 1837 that claimed prejudice in a case on the basis of affinal ties. The judges not only rejected the appeal but also ruled it was permissible for a man to marry his deceased wife's sister (Clarke 1957:100). By 1852 the perceived threat to social well-being that marriage with the deceased wife's sister had held for some in the past was so diminished in the United States that the educational reformer Horace Mann could state the prohibition was "silly and superstitious" (quoted in Grossberg 1985:113). In civil law the question of whether this form of marriage threatened society had been clearly answered in the negative.

Marriage in the United States in the nineteenth century was no longer primarily a social mechanism in which individuals ensured their sinlessness and through which they were granted access to heaven. Nor were marriage prohibitions any longer primarily a means for society to ensure harmony in the domestic unit. By the middle of the nineteenth century, marriage was widely viewed in terms of social evolution and as a mechanism necessary to society's survival and progress. Marriage between "natural" relatives (i.e., cousins) became the concern now rather than marriage between "contractual" relatives (i.e., in-laws). The former now were seen to harbor potential dangers to society and had to be carefully regulated.

One of the most influential American social theorists of the nineteenth century, Lewis Henry Morgan, clearly expressed the change that occurred in the United States with regard to marriage and its regulation. Morgan was a lawyer in Rochester, New York, who married his first cousin in 1851 (Trautmann 1987:244). This marriage was a legal union since New York State, like every state in the Union at that time, did not prohibit cousin marriage. The 1830 New York statutes governing marriage treated incestuous and void only those marriages that were "between relatives in the ascending and descending lines, and between brothers and sisters of the half as well as the whole blood" (Kent 1848:83, note a). Morgan's marriage did not meet with everyone's approval, however. One person in particular who opposed the idea of cousin marriage was Joshua McIlvaine, the pastor of Rochester's First Presbyterian church. Morgan was not religious, but his wife was a devout member of the First Presbyterian church, and Morgan became a good friend of the church's pastor. The pastor was an outspoken opponent of consanguineal marriage. He was also one of the cofounders, with Morgan, of a literary club that their wives referred to as "The Pundit Club." In the club, McIlvaine spoke to the Pundits about the degradation and inferiority of American Indians because they practiced cousin marriage (Trautmann 1987:244).

Less than a quarter of a century after his marriage to his mother's brother's daughter, Morgan wrote of a discovery by ancient peoples of "the advantages of marriages between unrelated persons" ([1877] 1958:467), the consequent rise of superior groups of humans through crossbreeding ([1877] 1958:39), and the necessity of avoiding "the evils of consanguine marriages" ([1877] 1958:68). The sharp contrast between Morgan's marriage to his first cousin in 1851 and his condemnation of consanguineal marriage by 1877 accentuates the cultural change that took place in the United States. His life and work encapsulate the change in the perception of marriage that occurred for many people in the United States around the middle of the nineteenth century (Ottenheimer 1990). During the second half of the century, as Morgan expressed in his publication, marriage was treated as an evolutionary mechanism. Marriage was a means for social progress, and its regulation was necessary to ensure that physically fit offspring would accomplish this. During this period in American history physicians also began systematically to investigate inheritance as a factor in disease, eugenics became popular, and miscegenation laws became widespread.

The transition in the United States from a concern with marriage regulations as a social means for maintaining morality and the social order to the concern with physical conditions and the evolutionary fitness of offspring was also reflected in Joel Bishop's *Commentaries on the Law of Marriage and Divorce,* an influential nineteenth-century legal work. In the 1852 edition the dangers of immorality, the advantages of alliances, and the potential disruption of family order are the reasons given for the legal marriage prohibitions. In the 1872 edition the traditional social arguments for the prohibitions were replaced by references to the dangers of inbreeding. The reasons for the injunctions against the marriage of close relatives in this edition are that "marriages between persons closely allied in blood are apt to produce an offspring feeble in body, and tending to insanity in mind" (quoted in Grossberg 1985:145).

Nineteenth-century scholars searched for a natural foundation of human society that could serve as a basis for the regulation of marriage. They soon turned to the hereditary transmission of disease as reflected in the illness of family members as the source for marital law. Physicians became particularly concerned with maintaining the health of individuals in the United States by controlling marriage. One nineteenth-century physician expressed his feelings by comparing two distinct groups:

> The Turkish monarchs from the time of Mahomet the Great brought their wives from the mountains of Circassia, inhabited by the boldest, most independent, *beautifully formed* and intelligent race in Asia, and the consequence was that the great deeds of the father were eclipsed by the superior achievements of the son.
> The Spanish monarchs, on the contrary, from the time of Charles 5th, selected wives, often nearer relatives, from considerations of mere personal aggrandizement, being of royal, Spanish blood, indubitably,

(if we rely on Spanish authority,) the most pure, and most honorable
in the world! And the consequence has been that the race is, as it ought
to be, nearly extinct, exhibiting to the world a *beautiful specimen* of a
queen in the person of the present lecherous fugitive! Is it not passing
strange that men of high intellectual attainments should be so infatu-
ated, so reckless of future happiness as to form a matrimonial alliance
in a family for mere pecuniary considerations, in which some hereditary taint, physical or moral or personal deformity, has afflicted generations, and thus wickedly taint, and corrupt, and poison his own offspring? (Steger 1855:191)

Webster's fears, Milledoler's concerns, and McIlvaine's views of social inequality had now come to the foreground. The natural theory of society with a focus on consanguinity that had been in the background of the
debate over marriage with the dead wife's sister now dominated legislation. The moral or social influences of marriage laws were no longer the
major concern. As Allen (1869) pointed out, "But what of late years has
interested the public most, particularly the scientific portion, is the physiological bearing of those laws" (261). The general opinion was that "im-
becility and disease" was caused by consanguinity in marriage (Pendleton
1863:25). The resulting disapproval of consanguineal marriage was entwined with the evolutionist's idea that those groups practicing close marriage were less civilized and less fit than those who opposed it. Cousin
marriage was thought of as an early form of human social behavior, discarded by people who recognized its physical evils in their struggle for
survival and who were thus able to achieve civilization. Prohibitions against
consanguineal marriage were a means to ensure "survival of the fittest" in
a struggle among the different human races.

The development of a bioevolutionary framework for marriage regulations and the suggestion that various afflictions were inherited were accompanied by inquiries into the possible physical disorders caused by consanguineal marriage. Results of empirical investigations into inherited
disorders began to appear in France as early as 1846 with Francis Devay's
Hygiene des familles (see Bell 1859:475). Soon afterward, in 1848, the
governor of Massachusetts appointed a commission headed by the physician S. G. Howe to study "idiots" in the state. Its conclusions supported
the notion that consanguinity was responsible for idiocy. The commission's
report became well known (Rosenberg 1976:34). Within a few short years
a great deal of literature on the subject of the consanguineal effects on
health and physical condition appeared. (Among them are Bemiss 1857 and

1858; Brooks 1856; Child 1862; Crossman 1861; Gardner 1861; Mitchell 1886; and Morel 1857. See Huth 1875 for an extensive bibliography). These works were often authored by physicians who were concerned with consanguinity in marriage and investigated the possible hereditary causes of physical ailments.

Members of the American Association for the Advancement of Science at their ninth annual meeting in Providence were concerned about how consanguinity in marriage affected the "improvement and prosperity of thousands of families" and "the safety and elevation of society" (Brooks 1856, quoted in Bittles 1993:3). Furthering the concern with consanguinity was the mid-century report of the state of Kentucky's Deaf and Dumb Asylum. It noted that 10 to 12 percent of the deaf mutes in the institution were offspring of cousins. The report asserted that such marriages violated the laws of nature and resulted in deafness, blindness, and idiocy. It also concluded that Kentucky had a right to protect itself by preventing such unions (Report of the Kentucky Deaf and Dumb Asylum, quoted in Allen 1869: 258). Shortly thereafter, in 1855, Ohio legislators passed a law requiring assessors in the townships of each county to inquire into the degree of relatedness between parents of the deaf and dumb, blind, insane, and idiotic. The assessors were to report the results of their inquiries to the county and eventually to the secretary of state of Ohio by July 1, 1856 (Allen 1869:258; Bemiss 1857). S. M. Bemiss, a physician from Louisville, Kentucky, began his investigations into "the evil results of marriages of consanguinity" in the following year with a collection of information from thirty-four marriages between cousins (Bemiss 1857:368). He thought the dire consequences of cousin marriage would be better prevented by demonstration of its evils and appropriate action by reasoned individuals rather than by civil legislation. Besides, he figured it would be "difficult to convince either legislators or communities that there could be a necessity for going beyond the requirements of Levitical law" (Bemiss 1857:377). It turned out, however, not to be too difficult at all.

The inquiries into the relationship between consanguinity and physical disorders in Kentucky and Ohio led their governors in their annual messages of 1860 to urge their respective legislatures to enact "a penal statute against the marriages of blood relations, on the ground that those States were already heavily burdened with the deaf and dumb, blind, imbecile, and idiotic offspring of such marriages" (Pendleton 1863:14). Ten years later Ohio passed an injunction against marriage between kin related more closely than second cousins.

Kansas had joined the Union in 1861 with a statute against the marriage of first cousins. Prior to its becoming a state, the Territory of Kansas had passed a law in 1858 forbidding the marriage of cousins, which was amended the following year to restrict the prohibition to first cousins. A Lawrence, Kansas, newspaper reported the passage of the bill and gave a rationale for it:

> It has been ascertained by careful investigation into the marriages of consanguinity, that over ten per cent. of the blind, and nearly fifteen per cent. of the idiotics, in the various State institutions, are the offspring of kindred parents. Making an estimate based upon the best ascertained data there would be found in the twenty millions of white inhabitants in the United States, six thousand three hundred and twenty-one marriages of cousins, giving birth to three thousand nine hundred and nine deaf and dumb, blind, idiotic and insane. (*Kansas Herald of Freedom,* June 25, 1859)

The recording of the family histories of asylum inmates and the medical histories of selected populations and widespread investigations of the offspring of consanguineal marriages were systematically undertaken throughout the United States. Many investigations were sponsored by the American Medical Association, and their results were widely published. One of the most influential of the mid-century publications on the harmful effects of consanguineal marriage was the Bemiss report of 1858. The American Medical Association had appointed Dr. S. M. Bemiss to head a committee to investigate "the popular idea of deterioration of offspring from such marriages" (Bemiss 1858:321). The committee solicited data from doctors by asking them to comment on the state of health of the families with consanguineal marriage in their area. It collected 873 cases from twenty-five states. Of these consanguineal unions, 630 were between first cousins, 120 between second cousins, 13 between third cousins, 27 between double first cousins, and 61 between relatives who were themselves the descendants of related people. There were also 12 cases of "marriage or incestuous intercourse" between uncle and niece or aunt and nephew, plus 10 cases of brother and sister or parent and child relationships. Bemiss had hoped to collect a large number of cases in which spouses were not related by consanguinity to serve as a basis for comparison, but he obtained only 125 and considered this insufficient to represent this class of marriage. He nevertheless published the remaining data without this set for comparison.

Bemiss's data on consanguineous marriages were published as a lengthy table with columns for marking the number of the case, descriptions of the temperament of the spouses, their occupations, date of marriage, and their age at marriage. Columns for the number of children of the consanguineous marriage, their sex, and their condition were also included. The condition of the children was displayed in thirteen columns. Seven were for indicating the number of defective, deaf and dumb, blind, idiotic, insane, epileptic, and scrofulous children. Two were used to indicate their sex, and three columns indicated how many offspring died young, their age at death, and the cause of death. The final column contained the reporting doctors' remarks on the condition of the children.

To indicate the nature of the evidence in the Bemiss report to the American Medical Association, I cite the first four cases in the table that have remarks about the children's condition. The first case is a farmer married to his half sister. The reporter noted that their temperament was "sanguine" and called all of their seven children defective. One was reported as idiotic, and the other six were called defective because they "cannot speak so as to be understood, except by their immediate family" (Bemiss 1858:335). The next case is married half siblings whose temperament was listed as unknown and who had one child, sex not stated, described as defective. The only comment about this child categorized as idiotic was that the child was "marked with the singular peculiarity of having one blue and one black eye" (Bemiss 1858:335). It is not clear whether this peculiarity was the reason the child was listed as idiotic. The next case is also married half siblings. They had five children, all rated defective. Each was listed as idiotic. The reporter's remark was that "three are complete idiots, the other two imbeciles" (Bemiss 1858:335). The fourth case is unmarried siblings with one child. The father's temperament was described as "nervo-lymphatic" and the mother's as "sanguine." Their only child was a daughter of twenty, who was described as "healthy, bright, and active" (Bemiss 1858:335).

The report's poor quality is obvious, due in part to hindsight based on more than a century of improvements in social scientific research methodology. The information is primarily derived from the subjective judgments of questionable sources. The statistics are a compilation of data derived from poor samples containing unreliable information.

The Bemiss report was sharply criticized soon after its publication. Bell (1859) pointed to the "multitude of influences that concur to render the statistics obtained in this manner unworthy of reliance" and discussed "how a preconceived prejudice blinds the minds of those possessed by it" (477). Subsequent investigators also pointed to the inadequacies in the Bemiss report. Withington (1885) noted that the "percentage of the 'defective' in the children of third cousins is actually greater than in the offspring of second or even of first cousins" (8). This result would not be expected if, in fact, the defects were due simply to the degree of consanguinity. Ironically, Bemiss had made this point earlier in his original study of cousin marriage (1857:373–74).

Careful investigations undertaken after Bemiss's report contradicted his findings, and researchers began to suspect that inherited defects were because of transmitted genetic material rather than simply the degree of the parents' consanguinity. Cousin marriage in itself, they believed, could not account for the illnesses of the offspring of related parents. The Report of the Committee on the Result of Consanguineous Marriages, presented by Robert Newman to the New York Medical Society in 1869, for example, stated that the appearance of unwanted characteristics in the offspring was because of the transmission of those characteristics, not close marriage. It found no reason to ban cousin marriage. The report also pointed out that "material already before the public, proved little more than a chaotic mass of fact and opinion, most frequently given to sustain some preconceived theory, or to favor popular prejudices, based on incomplete physiological hypotheses" (Newman 1869:109). New York State, in agreement with this report and in spite of the growing belief that unhealthy offspring were produced by consanguineal relations, did not ban cousin marriage. It still does not prohibit it today.

Several investigators in the 1860s advanced "the theory that any ill effects of consanguineous marriage should be attributed to the intensification of inherited characteristics" (Arner 1908:13). There was also the notion that the transmission of a "quantum and kind of vital element" (Newman 1869:112) was the factor in the appearance of unwanted characteristics in progeny. This precursor to the modern concept of the gene found in investigations of the time grew out of an awareness that the marriage of consanguineal relatives did not necessarily lead to genetic defects in offspring. In an address to the Ohio State Medical Society a physician stated that the belief in the evil effects of consanguineous marriages on offspring had no basis. This statement was based on several points:

> Among the eighteen conclusions drawn as the result of the author's studies are the following: 1. Like breeds like, good or bad, entirely independent of consanguinity. 2. Intemperance, luxury, dissipation, sloth and shiftlessness, as well as hygienic surroundings and innumerable other causes, should bear much of the responsibility laid at the door of

consanguinity. 3. Data are of doubtful reliability, full of flaws and false reasoning. 4. Statistics show about the same proportion of deaf-mutes, idiots, and insane persons, descendant from consanguineous marriages, to the whole number of those unfortunates, as the number of consanguineous marriages is to the whole number of marriages. 5. Consanguineous marriages which bring together persons having a disease or morbid tendency in common are dangerous to the offspring; not, however one whit more so than the marriage of any other two persons not related, yet having an equal amount of tendency to disease in common. 6. The half a hundred abnormalities ascribed to consanguinity, including almost all the ills that flesh is heir to,—among others, whooping-cough,—approaches the ludicrous. 7. Consanguineous marriages, no other objection being present, should not be opposed on physiological grounds. ("Literature, Art and Science" 1886:132)

Some writers even argued that cousin marriage had a positive benefit. Some thought that marrying cousins could help ensure the health and vigor of a family: "If then both parents, although cousins, are perfect in constitution and health, and have nothing to transmit but power, then their children have a double security against constitutional imperfection, and a double warranty of inherited capacity and strength" (Newman 1869:113). Only if the ancestors of the spouses had some deleterious element would cousin marriage raise the possibility that the children would suffer from the union.

The many criticisms of the Bemiss report pointed out that it had information of dubious quality, lacked any basis for comparison to make it scientifically meaningful, and was misguided in blaming consanguinity for health problems resulting from other factors. Nevertheless, the results of the report gained wide acceptance. The report's true significance thus lies not in its contribution to the scientific study of the relationship between consanguinity and the health of offspring but in its symbolic value. The conclusion "that multiplication of the same blood by in-and-in marrying does incontestably lead in the aggregate to the physical and mental depravation [sic] of the offspring" (Bemiss 1858:332) reflected the conviction that cousin marriage was dangerous and was widely quoted as proof of this conviction. The report thus legitimized in a modern idiom the concern with forbidden relatives. It gave clear expression to the fear in the United States of consanguinity in marriage and justified this fear with empirical research and statistics, however flawed, indicating the dangers of inheriting physical characteristics.

Those empirical investigations contradicting the proposition that cousin marriage was dangerous, the arguments that legislation to enjoin cousin marriage was unnecessary, and the suggestions that cousin marriage was potentially advantageous were drowned out in the United States by a rising tide of fear in the dangers in consanguineal unions. In the first decade of the twentieth century, when the arguments and data about cousin marriage were reviewed by Arner (1908), not only had it become widely accepted that cousin marriage was dangerous, but also numerous states had passed laws prohibiting such unions. Arner recognized that the supposed physical threats to the offspring in consanguineous marriages were enormously exaggerated and nowhere as great as popularly thought. "Nevertheless," he wrote, "since it is undoubtedly true that on the average such marriages do not produce quite as healthy offspring as do non-consanguineous unions, and since public sentiment is already opposed to the marriage of cousins, it is perhaps just as well that existing laws on the subject should remain in force" (93).

Arner mistakenly believed that the natural development of American society would eventually remove the legal barriers to cousin marriage. He thought that cousin marriage implied the endogamy of a caste system and that this manifested itself in the ethnic differentiation prominent in the United States during the nineteenth century. He anticipated that this ethnic diversity would break down and that a diminished percentage of cousin marriages would result. Furthermore, Arner believed lawmakers would eventually recognize the genetic causes of inherited diseases and disabilities. At that time, any possible genetic dangers of inbreeding would be dealt with by laws based on eugenics rather than on forbidden degrees of kinship. "And," he added, "when rational laws prohibit the marriage of the diseased and the degenerate, the problem of consanguineous marriage will cease to be of vital importance" (95).

The number of first cousin marriages in the United States has decreased significantly since the middle of the nineteenth century. Arner estimated that the frequency of cousin marriages in the early twentieth century was half "as in the days of the stage coach" (28). Reid (1988) found that before the middle of the nineteenth century 20 percent of the 142 marriages in a group of Scotch-Irish American families were with first cousins (401). After 1850 only 1 marriage out of the 36 recorded in the group was between first cousins (401). A decrease in the number of first cousin marriages was also found in a study of the descendants of a Swiss couple who immigrated to the United States in 1853 (Hammond and Jackson 1958). In their investigation of the frequency of consanguineous marriage among Mormons and their relatives in the United States, Woolf et al. (1956) discovered a significant drop in the number of first cousin marriages. The percentage of first cousin marriages among the Mormons and their relatives was never very high in the United States, despite the fact that the church never prohibited them, but there was a notable difference in frequency over time. The percentage of first cousin marriages dropped from a high of 1.17 percent from 1720 to 1739 to 0.08 percent from 1940 to the mid-1950s. The frequency of first cousin marriages from the period 1847–69 to 1930–50 just in the state of Utah dropped from 0.16 percent to 0.0 percent (238–43). Lebel (1983) found in his study of Roman Catholic marriages in a Wisconsin diocese that there was only a small average rate (0.10 percent) of first cousin marriages in the period from 1842 to 1981. The highest percentages occurred before World War I, reaching a high of 0.33 percent in the decade from 1902 to 1911. In the next decade (1912–21), the percentage of cousin marriages fell to 0.19 percent, and in the last decade of the study (1972–81), the percentage reached a low of 0.10 percent (Lebel 1983:550).

One study (Freire-Maia 1957) estimated the percentage of cousin marriages in the United States during the 1950s was less than 0.01 percent (136). A survey of consanguineous marriages among Italian Catholics in Chicago from 1936 to 1956 found 107 married couples who were first cousins (Slatis, Reis, and Hoene 1958:447). There were this many in spite of the fact that first cousin marriage was prohibited under Illinois law. Cousin marriage still had not disappeared by the 1980s: "Despite many contrary influences, it continues at a very low frequency, on the order of about 1/1,300 marriages" (Lebel 1983:554).

Contrary to Arner's prediction that the laws against cousin marriage would disappear, however, first cousins are still forbidden to marry in a majority of states. In spite of an amalgamation of different ethnic groups in the country (although probably not to the degree Arner expected), a decrease in the number of cousin marriages, and legislation enacted in some states for the medical examination of potential marriage partners to prevent "the diseased and the degenerate" individuals from marrying, the number of laws forbidding consanguineous marriage has not decreased. Furthermore, the genetic transmission of human traits has become much better understood since the nineteenth century, and modern research indicates there is no justification for the prohibitions against cousin marriage (see chapter 6). Nonetheless, the twentieth century saw no state drop cousins from its list of forbidden marriage partners.

Although people in the United States continue to marry their first cousins, this form of marriage is rarely discussed because of the widespread opprobrium attached to it. I personally am aware of several such unions. In addition, Arizona, Illinois, Indiana, Maine, and Wisconsin, where the laws have been amended to allow first cousins to marry under special conditions, must have a number of couples who have taken advantage of these amendments. Outside of occasional anecdotal reports in the news media, however, little information about these couples exists. Recent migrants to this country have traditions of cousin marriage, and they will likely continue their traditional practices here. This will undoubtedly have some impact on the incidence of cousin marriages in the United States over the next decade or longer.

The probability that there will be an increase in the number of people in the United States wishing to marry their first cousins, because of migration and changing conditions of family structures, provides an impetus to reconsider the laws against such marriages. One factor that must be taken into account in reconsidering cousin prohibitions is the genetics of consanguinity. Before investigating this matter, however, I want to examine why the belief in the deleterious effects of cousin marriage became widely accepted in the United States even though there was no clear scientific evidence to support it. Why did Americans accept the idea that cousin marriages produced unfit offspring while Europeans did not? To explore this, the next two chapters examine the European roots of the prohibition against cousin marriage in the United States and the nature of a debate in Great Britain that led the British to take a very different legal position on cousin marriage.

3

European Laws Prohibiting the Marriage of Relatives

> . . . concepts about what inbreeding and outbreeding actu-
> ally are, and whether they are good or bad, depend on
> one's conceptual history.
>
> —William M. Shields, *The Natural and*
> *Unnatural History of Inbreeding*
> *and Outbreeding*

According to Hammurabi's Code, a nearly four-thousand-year-old Baby-lonian list of forbidden marriage partners, a man could not marry his moth-er, daughter, and daughter-in-law, but no consanguineal collateral relatives were prohibited from marrying (Danby 1940:108). The ancient practice in the Middle East and the Eastern Mediterranean of allowing marriage be-tween close collateral relatives is consistent with this set of regulations. The Old Testament mentions sibling marriage—Abraham married his sister Sarah, for example—and nonreligious sources provide substantial histori-cal evidence for this type of union. Sibling marriage existed among ancient Egyptian royalty and was extended outside of the royal family during the Middle Kingdom (Černy 1954). It was noted during the Ptolemaic period in Egyptian census returns from the first and second centuries A.D. The Ro-man governor of Egypt ordered district officials to carry out a household census of the whole population every fourteen years for taxation purpos-es, and from nearly three hundred of these returns it has been possible to ascertain that at least one-third of the families in the first and second cen-turies with marriageable children of both sexes had brother-sister marriages. These marriages between full siblings in Egypt were like any other kind of marriage, publicly celebrated with wedding invitations, marriage contracts, and dowries. They resulted in children and sometimes ended in divorce (Hopkins 1980; Shaw 1992).

Marriages between siblings were also permitted in ancient Greece. The Athenians allowed marriage between children of the same father and different mothers, while the Spartans permitted siblings of the same mother but different fathers to marry. After Alexander, a Macedonian Greek, conquered Egypt, the Greco-Macedonian rulers took up the Egyptian practice of full brother-sister marriage. Two-thirds of the kings' fifteen marriages were with their full siblings (Shaw 1992:283). Ptolemy II, for example, divorced his first wife and married Arsinoe, his full sister, who became known as Arsinoe Philadelphus, Arsinoe the Brother-Lover (Hopkins 1980:311). Later, Cleopatra "immortalized by Shakespeare, Shaw, and Elizabeth Taylor" married her brothers (Bixler 1982:271–72). Brother-sister marriage legally ended with the implementation of a Roman law in A.D. 212. Although siblings were forbidden to marry, first cousins could marry under Roman law.

Cousin marriage had existed in ancient "Greece, where it was actually prescribed for an heiress, an epiklerate, . . . in Ancient Israel where it was permitted in the levitical rules, . . . in the Palestine of Jesus Christ, who was himself, according to one legend, the offspring of just such a marriage" (Goody 1983:53; see also Dugard 1673:24–25, and Huth 1875:33). The Roman prohibition in the third century A.D. against sibling marriage did not affect the legality of marriage between first cousins. As Shaw and Saller (1984) point out, "There is no doubt that marriage between cousins was not only legal but also carried no social stigma in Roman society of the late Republic and early empire" (433). There is some evidence to suggest that marriage between children of first cousins was forbidden in ancient Roman law, but by the first half of the first century B.C. it is certain that marriage between first cousins was permitted (Watson 1967:39). Westermarck (1922) writes, "In ancient Rome marriages between persons under the same *patria potestas,* that is *cognati* related within the sixth degree (the degree of second cousins), were considered immoral and unlawful—they were *nefariae et incestuae nuptiae.* These prohibitions were gradually relaxed: from the time of the Second Punic War [begun in 218 B.C.], at least, first cousins were allowed to intermarry, and subsequently marriage with a brother's daughter was declared legal" (1:149). Thus, prior to the fall of the Roman Empire, the marriage of consanguineal collateral kin, including cousins, was not prohibited around the Mediterranean. Today first cousin marriage continues to be a well-known feature of social life in the Mediterranean area and the Middle East. Legal under Islamic law, it is a preferred form of union in a number of societies in many areas of the world (Pasternak 1976). Following the fall of the Roman Empire, however, prohibitions against the marriage of a wide range of relatives, including cousins, spread throughout Europe. The major instrument of this spread of cousin prohibitions was the Roman Catholic church.

The early Roman Catholic church at first followed Roman custom and did not prohibit cousin marriage. Emperor Constantine adopted Christianity and made it the official religion of the Roman Empire during the first half of the fourth century and also married his children to the children of his half brother. Prohibitions against cousin marriage appeared only in the waning years of the Roman Empire, toward the end of the fourth century. "The Emperor Theodosius I," according to Goody (1983:55), "condemned unions between cousins in a law made in 384 or 385. It was still possible to effect such a marriage by imperial dispensation, a means of avoiding its own prescriptions that the Church was not slow to use." Theodosius's son Honorius (A.D. 395–423), emperor of the western half of the Roman Empire, mitigated the penalties for disregarding the ban but maintained the prohibition and the right of granting dispensations. An Irish Catholic council of the mid-fifth century was reported to have prohibited marriages within four "joints" of the Germanic system of reckoning distance. This would have included first cousins (Herlihy 1990:5).

At the Council of Agde (A.D. 506) after the fall of the Roman Empire, marriages between first cousins and between second cousins were forbidden (Gies and Gies 1987:52). The late seventh century Penitential of Theodore, however, forbade only first cousins from marrying and recognized those already married as legitimate (Gies and Gies 1987:53). Councils in Rome in 721 and 743 reaffirmed the prohibition against marriage between collateral relatives of the fourth degree. According to the Roman method, that meant relatives up to and including first cousins. A series of councils were then held that eventually settled on extending the prohibition against marriage of collateral relatives to six degrees, or second cousins, calculated by the Roman method. By the time of Pope Alexander II (A.D. 1062–73) the prohibitions had been extended to the seventh degree. They included many affinal kin and spiritual kin, such as godparents and godchildren, as well as cousins (Esmein [1891] 1968, 1:339–43; Herlihy 1985:61; Bouchard 1981:270–71; Huth 1875:44–47; Gies and Gies 1987:83; Goody 1983:135).

Roman law calculated the distance between relatives by summing the number of links from each related individual to a common ancestor. A parent and child are related in the first degree according to this method of reckoning. A brother and sister are related in the second degree. Counting up from the brother to the parent is one degree and counting up from the sister to the parent is also one degree, making a total of two degrees of relatedness. Their children, first cousins to each other, are related in the fourth degree according to this method of calculation. There are a total of four links from cousin to cousin through their common grandparent. Uncle and niece or aunt and nephew are related in the third degree. This is calculated from the one link between the uncle/aunt and common ancestor and the two links between the niece/nephew and the common ancestor. The Roman method of reckoning is still used today by the Greek Orthodox church. It is also used in European and American civil courts.

A different method of calculating the degrees of distance between relatives, the Germanic (or Canonic) method, was adopted in the eleventh century by the Roman Catholic church. It differs markedly from the Roman or civil law method of reckoning. Instead of counting up from both relatives to a common ancestor and summing the number of links, the Germanic method counts the number of links between just one of the relatives and the common ancestor. Thus, brother and sister are first degree relatives in this method of reckoning rather than second degree relatives using the Roman method. There is only one filial link between either sibling and the parent. The children of siblings, first cousins, are related in the second degree. Second cousins, the children of first cousins, are related in the third degree. If there is an unlike number of links between two relatives and their common ancestor, only the longest connection to the common ancestor is used to determine the degree of relatedness between them. For example, uncle and niece are calculated to be related in the second degree by this method. There is one filial link between the uncle and the common ancestor, while there are two links between the niece and the ancestor. By the Germanic method of reckoning degrees of relatedness, the longest number of links, two in this case, determines the degree of relatedness between the relatives. (See figure 2 for a comparison of the methods.)

With the Roman Catholic church's official adoption of the Germanic method for calculating the degree of relatedness in the eleventh century, the range of filial kin prohibited from marrying in the church suddenly increased dramatically. Under the Roman system of reckoning, the prohibition against seventh degree relatives' marrying meant that relatives up to, and including, second cousins once removed could not marry without dispensation. Third cousins, being in the eighth degree of relationship, could freely marry. With the shift to the Germanic method, third cousins were now fourth degree relatives. The interdiction against marriage within the seventh degree of consanguinity now required people related as distant as sixth cousins to get dispensation to marry. Relatives as distant as the great-great-great-great-great-grandchildren of an individual were now forbidden to marry and had to request dispensation if they wished to do so.

This sudden extension of the range of forbidden relatives because of the change in the method of reckoning had several consequences for European family and social life. One outgrowth of extending the prohibitions to very distant relatives was an increase in the production of family trees among European nobility. Bouchard (1981) found that French nobles in the late tenth and eleventh centuries often drew up lists of their family ancestors to try to comply with the church's extensive prohibitions and to avoid marrying anyone that might fall within the prohibited degrees. Likewise, in England King Henry I drew family trees to compare his daughters' proposed spouses and "decided against at least two marriages because both partners were descended from a forester whose name was not even remembered" (Bouchard 1981:272). Not everyone wanted to avoid marriage with someone within the degrees of the prohibitions, however. Marriage between cousins frequently occurred among townspeople, and "marriage between

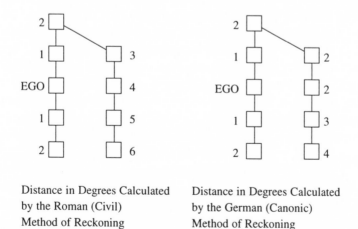

Distance in Degrees Calculated   Distance in Degrees Calculated
by the Roman (Civil)   by the German (Canonic)
Method of Reckoning   Method of Reckoning

Figure 2. Comparison of the Roman and German Systems for Calculating Kinship Distance

blood relatives was so common in some communities that they were granted permanent dispensations" (Segalen 1986:16).

Another consequence of the extension of the range of forbidden relatives was that many more couples were married within the forbidden degrees who, if they did not receive dispensation from the church, were provided a legal means to break their marital tie. Divorce was otherwise extremely difficult or impossible to obtain. European royalty used the prohibition against marrying consanguineal kin as early as the ninth century as a means for breaking marriage relationships. Marriages, otherwise sacrosanct, could be broken for a number of reasons, including simply a desire to provide a heir to the throne, by claiming that the couple was too closely related. Gies and Gies (1987) point to an example: "In 858 Lothair II, king of Lotharingia (Lorraine), wanted to divorce his barren wife, Theutberga, in order to marry his former concubine, Waldrada, who had given him children that he now proposed to legitimize," and to accomplish this, Lothair made an issue of the consanguineal relationship with his wife and accused her of incest to nullify the marriage (88–89).

The extended range of the marriage injunctions of the eleventh century made it easier to claim consanguinity as a reason for breaking a marriage, and it became a commonly used escape clause from the church's prohibition against divorce. As Duby (1983) points out that among the aristocracy "genealogical inquiries, which could be counted on to uncover some sort of dubious relationship, were the surest means of ending marriage they had tired of" (173). One side effect of this aspect of the marriage prohibition was the development of an industry based on corrupt practices. Many people began to buy genealogical inquiries that "found" kin ties between spouses. Witnesses were also paid to swear to evidence of an illicit link between couples so that divorce would be granted.

The prohibitions against cousin marriage now threatened the stability of marriage (Esmein [1891] 1968, 1:355). The extended range of prohibitions and the buying of genealogies showing some forbidden relationship between spouses made divorce relatively easy. This was enhanced by the fact that affinal and spiritual ties could be used along with consanguinity in determining forbidden relationships in order to break a marriage one or both partners no longer desired. Affinal relations between a man and his brother's wife, son's wife, stepmother, and uncle's wife are mentioned in Leviticus and were forbidden early in church history. Prohibitions of marriage between spiritual kin appeared in the Roman Catholic church beginning in the sixth century and were given greater emphasis by the eighth century (Goody 1983:197; Brundage 1987:193; Lynch 1986:219–20). The spiritual prohibitions forbade marriage between people with a relationship of compaternity, the "relationship linking spiritual sponsors at baptism or confirmation with those receiving the sacrament" (Herlihy 1990:1). A person was forbidden to marry a godchild, the child of a godparent, or the parent of a godchild as well as the spiritual kin established through baptism: the person baptized, the parent of the person, or the child of the person. The child of the baptizer likewise was forbidden to marry these individuals (Lynch 1986:233). The range of prohibited individuals was thus extended well beyond those related by marriage or common ancestry. People used these prohibitions against fictive kin in imaginative ways to break marital ties. A woman would become a godmother to her own child and request separation from her husband. She could now get the marriage nullified—otherwise nearly impossible for her to do—since the spiritual prohibition meant that the new relationship between her, her child, and her husband made the marriage incestuous. As early as the ninth century the church recognized there was a serious problem with these prohibitions. Divorces by reason of incestuous relations through spiritual connections became so numerous in the Frankish Kingdom that, according to McNamara and Wemple (1976), the "bishops assembled at the Council of Châlons were obliged to prohibit women from standing as godmothers to their own children or as sponsors to their confirmation in order to have an excuse for separating from their husbands" (102).

To resolve the problems created by the increased range of marriage prohibitions, the church instituted reforms. At the Fourth Lateran Council in 1215, less than 150 years after the forbidden degrees were extended as a result of the formal acceptance of the Germanic means of reckoning distance of kin, the church reduced the number of prohibited degrees. Computed in the Germanic (or Canonic) method, the degrees were reduced from seven to four. This meant that now only third cousins and closer collateral relatives were required to get dispensation to marry.

The range of the degrees of relatives prohibited from marrying was reduced further in 1537 for Indians of South American origin and in 1897 for blacks (Goody 1983:144). Pope Benedict XV reduced the degrees for all Roman Catholics to three in May of 1917 through canons that became effective on Pentecost Sunday, May 19, 1918. Dispensation is thus no longer necessary for marriages between second cousins once removed or any more distant collateral relatives (Siegle 1979:127). Only first cousins, first cousins once removed, and second cousins or relatives of lesser degree of collateral consanguinity, reckoned by the Canonic method, require dispensation to establish a valid marriage in the Roman Catholic church.

These reforms, however, were not sufficient to meet the criticisms of people opposed to the many prohibitions and the practice of providing dispensation from forbidden marriage relationships for a fee. Dispensation was one of the major complaints about the church during the Protestant Reformation. Martin Luther thought of them simply as an unnecessary means for accruing capital. Similarly, a British parliamentary statute in 1540 accused the Roman Catholic church of administering the prohibitions "for their Lucre" (quoted in Fry 1756:97). Dugard (1673) called the prohibitions "a matter of Mony" (preface, n.p.). This materialistic view of the church's prohibitions and practices has been revived and refined in a provocative work by Jack Goody. In *The Development of the Family and Marriage in Europe* (1983), Goody explains that the church adopted cousin marriage prohibitions as a means to receive monetary benefits. These benefits accrued by the church's involvement into the heart of domestic matters. Its marriage prohibitions and dispensations meant that "the whole world was sinning and paying for it" (Goody 1983:45). The church also gained financially by interfering with the traditional patterns of familial inheritance established through cousin marriage and redirecting the wealth of family estates to itself. Goody's main thesis is that the marriage prohibitions broke the continuity of European family estates and maneuvered property into the church.

That pecuniary interests of the church were the basis for the prohibitions is questionable (Davis 1985; Verdery 1988). But whatever the reason the church had for them, the dispensations and prohibitions plainly disturbed many Europeans during the sixteenth century. Reforms in the marriage laws of the Catholic church beginning in the thirteenth century did not do enough. They had reduced the prohibitions against collateral consanguineal relatives to four degrees by the sixteenth century, but much more drastic changes were demanded and fashioned in the Protestant Reformation. The sixteenth-century revolt against the church by Martin Luther bitterly opposed the papally declared prohibitions against marriage and the system of dispensations that had developed. Protestants discarded any financial mechanism for avoiding the prohibitions and greatly reduced the range of relatives forbidden to marry. Luther denied that spiritual kinship should be a barrier to marriage and accepted only those prohibitions mentioned in Leviticus. Marriage, in the words of Lyman (1978), "was rightfully prohibited to one's mother, stepmother, full sister, half-sister, granddaughter, father's sister, mother's sister, daughter-in-law, brother's wife, wife's sister, stepdaughter, and uncle's wife" (69). Andreas Osiander, one of Luther's followers, thought several more relatives should be included in the list of prohibited marriages, however. John Calvin included more relations in his list of prohibited degrees than those listed in the eighteenth chapter of Leviticus. Both reasoned that the list was incomplete and that rationality called for including other relationships. Daughter, for example, is not mentioned in Leviticus, but Calvin thought it was implied—since granddaughter is mentioned—and should be included in a list of prohibitions. Likewise, from the listing of the father's sister and mother's sister it was inferred that the brother's daughter and the sister's daughter should be included. Calvin considered the twelve females mentioned in Leviticus only as illustrative and reasoned that any relationship of the same degree or closer than those twelve should be prohibited.

The reforms in marriage law instituted by the Protestants on the Continent quickly spread to England, where they became embroiled in hotly debated political matters. Arguments over the prohibitions of marriage in England became involved with issues of succession to the throne. King Henry VIII had received dispensation from the Roman Catholic church to marry his first wife, his brother's widow, Princess Catherine of Aragon. He lived with her for more than twenty years, had two sons that died young, and fathered a daughter, Mary Tudor, who was later to become queen of England. When Mary was twelve, Henry arranged with the French king to marry her to the duke of Orleans, the French king's second son. But a question about Mary's legitimacy was raised at that time, which led Henry to investigate the legality of his marriage (Fry 1756:84–85). Or, perhaps as some have suggested, Henry simply wanted another wife. In either case, scholars at several universities were asked for an opinion on the legality of the marriage. They answered in the spirit of the Reformation that since marriage with a brother's widow was not lawful and since the pope's dispensation contravened ecclesiastical law and was not recognized, Catherine was not a legitimate spouse. Faculty members from different universities made clear that dispensation did not absolve the invalidity of the marriage:

> "After frequent meetings," say they, "having most diligently and conscientiously examined the sacred Scriptures, with the most approved Expositors, together with the General and Synodical Decrees of the councils of the Church, established, received, and approved by long usage—we do unanimously answer, assert, and determine, that a mar-

riage with a sister-in-law is equally prohibited by the law of nature and of God; and that the Pope cannot grant a dispensation for such a marriage." The Faculty of the University of Bononia, at the same time, and if possible, even in stronger language, testified their abhorrence of such marriages. "Nor can the Pope," say they, "upon any consideration, dispense with the contraction of such marriage." (Milledoler 1843:32)

The king and queen were consequently divorced by the archbishop, their marriage declared null and void, and Henry remarried. In 1533 he took as his new queen Anne Boleyn. Parliament then passed an act that year establishing the heirs to the throne as those of the new marriage, making it high treason to speak against the new marriage, confirming the succession by requiring an oath of the king's subjects, and averring that certain degrees of consanguinity and affinity were to be forbidden in marriage. The prohibited degrees followed those of the Reformation on the Continent, using the Old Testament rather than papal decree as a source and omitting any prohibition against cousins. The act, in affirming the illegality of marriage with the brother's wife, ensured that Henry's first marriage was void and that Mary was not a legitimate heir to the throne. Amidst the ensuing struggles between Catholics and Protestants in England and the conflicts over succession to the throne, this act would be repealed by two subsequent acts. A major collection of statutes published in 1735, however, included the act and omitted the two acts that repealed it (Fry 1756:84–87).

The king's new wife provided Henry with a child (Elizabeth, who would become queen), but Anne Boleyn was soon accused, tried, condemned, and beheaded in the Tower of London. Immediately after her death in 1536 Henry VIII married Lady Jane Seymour, and Parliament passed a series of acts that year repealing the first statute and declaring the king's two former marriages void and his daughters Mary by Catherine and Elizabeth by Anne illegitimate. It was high treason for either of them to claim any right to the crown and for anyone to affirm they had that right. The king's marriage to Jane Seymour was confirmed, her heirs recognized, and the forbidden degrees of kinship "forbidden by God's law" spelled out:

the Son to marry the Mother, or the Stepmother, carnally known by his Father; the Brother the Sister; the Father his Son's Daughter, or his Daughter's Daughter; or the Son to marry the Daughter of his Father, procreat and born by his Step-mother; or the Son to marry his Aunt, being his Father's or Mother's Sister; or to marry his Uncle's Wife carnally known by his Uncle; or the Father to marry his Son's Wife

carnally known by his Son; or the Brother to marry his Brother's Wife
carnally known by his Brother; or any Man married and carnally knowing his Wife, to marry his Wife's Daughter, or his Wife's Son's Daughter, or his Wife's Daughter's Daughter, or his Wife's Sister. (Quoted in
Fry 1756:91–92)

The acts also declared that the prohibitions were to be maintained for
persons who had intercourse even if they were not married. Thus, if any man
was to "know carnally" a woman, he was forbidden to marry any of her relatives listed above. Furthermore, no dispensations were to be recognized for
any of the forbidden relationships; if any persons had been married within
the degrees, they were to be separated; and if already separated because of
an illicit relationship, the separation was to be legally recognized. All marriages before November 3, 1534, that were not prohibited by parliamentary
law were declared legitimate without concern for the impediments of canon
law, and any children arising from them were to be considered legitimate.
This meant that children produced by first cousin marriages, for example,
were now legally recognized whether or not their parents had received dispensations from the church. Parliament's enactment of these statutes established the legal precedent of prohibiting only those relationships mentioned
in the Scripture. It also denied the legitimacy of Mary, whose right to the
throne depended on the Catholic law recognizing the dispensation from the
prohibition, which made her mother's marriage to Henry legitimate.

In 1540 Parliament passed another act defining the range of kin permitted to marry, which would become the standard for determining legitimate partners in marriage in the English-speaking world for a long time.
The act denounced the range of prohibitions held in the Roman Catholic
church as means of acquiring "Lucre" and declared that beginning July 1,
1540, all marriages in the Church of England would be contracted between
lawful persons, defined as those "not prohibited by God's Law to marry."
This phrase would define legitimate marriage partners not only in England
but also in many states across the Atlantic until the third quarter of the
nineteenth century. It permits the marriage of cousins.

The act of 1540 was repealed during the reign of Mary, Queen of Scots.
Mary acceded to the throne in 1553, after the death of Henry VIII and his
successor, Edward. She immediately affirmed her legitimacy, annulled
Henry's divorce from her mother, and rejected any statements in previous
acts of Parliament that declared her illegitimate. The legislators under Mary
now averred

that Process of Time had brought *Truth to Light,* and that they then understood the *very true State* of the Marriage in the Act mentioned (which was a Marriage betwixt the King and his Sister-in-law, *viz.* his Brother *Arthur's* Widow;)—that the said Marriage *in very Deed was not prohibited by God's Law,* and therefore could not by any Reason or Equity be *so spotted*—but—to be taken for a *most just, lawful,* and to all respects, a *sincere and perfect Marriage,* that could not, nor ought, by any Man's Power, *Authority or Jurisdiction be dissolved, broken or separated.* (Quoted in Fry 1756:107–11)

Parliament repealed the prohibited degrees of marriage established in the acts of 1536 and 1540, the Roman Catholic church again became the state church of England, and over three hundred Protestants were executed.

After Mary's death, Elizabeth acceded to the throne, and in the first year of her reign, 1558, Parliament reestablished the Protestant regulations of marriage in the 1540 act. Marriage was once more permitted between those not "prohibited by God's law." Furthermore, the Second Act of Supremacy in 1559 reinstituted the Anglican church as the official church.

From King Henry VIII's first divorce until Queen Elizabeth's reign, a tumultuous period in England's history, the marriage laws were changed back and forth. One could tell whether Catholic or Protestant interests controlled the state simply by knowing whether cousins were prohibited from marrying. Citizens, however, could never be sure whether cousin marriages would be recognized and whether the offspring of such unions would be considered legitimate. Queen Elizabeth's reign put an end to this uncertainty. Marriage law became firmly established under the Church of England, and cousin marriage was permitted. However, it was still uncertain exactly which relationships were prohibited by "God's law." To clarify this, Matthew Parker, the archbishop of Canterbury, published a table spelling out the relatives forbidden to marry.

Matthew Parker's Table of Kindred and Affinity was first printed in 1560. It was revised in 1563, received authority by the ecclesiastical courts of the Church of England in 1603, and introduced into civil law by a parliamentary act in 1835 (Goody 1983:175; Huth 1875:55). The table specified the forbidden relationships for the Anglican church and established conformity in English marriage law. The revised edition was printed at the end of each Book of Common Prayer and was displayed in churches after 1681 to ensure that people would be aware of the prohibitions. Evidently many people had not known about them or had paid little attention to them (Ingram 1988:246–47). The revised table of 1563 spelled out thirty relatives prohibited to a man and the same number for a woman. The prohibited relatives for a man were his grandmother, grandfather's wife, wife's grandmother, father's sister, mother's sister, father's brother's wife, mother's brother's wife, wife's father's sister, wife's mother's sister, mother, stepmother, wife's mother, daughter, wife's daughter, son's wife, sister, wife's sister, brother's wife, son's daughter, daughter's daughter, son's son's wife, daughter's son's wife, wife's son's daughter, wife's daughter's daughter, brother's daughter, sister's daughter, brother's son's wife, sister's son's wife, wife's brother's daughter, and wife's sister's daughter. The corresponding thirty relatives of a woman were also listed (Commission Appointed by the Archbishop of Canterbury 1940:44).

The table's list of prohibited relatives went well beyond the relatively small list in Leviticus. The consanguineal kin forbidden to a man were his grandmother, aunt, mother, daughter, sister, granddaughter, and niece (corresponding relatives were forbidden to a woman). This was a small increase over those mentioned in the Old Testament (mother, sister, granddaughter, and aunt), but Archbishop Parker's table contained more than twice the number of affinal kin. The prohibited affinal relationships in the table had been extended to all primary consanguineal relations of a spouse or sibling. Thus, a man could not marry his wife's sister, daughter, or mother. Nor could he marry his brother's wife.

A man's secondary affinal relatives were not forbidden in the table. A man, for example, could marry his brother's wife's sister. But the courts prohibited marriage between a man and his deceased wife's mother's sister in the nineteenth century (Hammick 1887:41, note d, citing Butler v. Gaskell, Bilbt. 156).

The list of relatives in the table was the result of calculating, by the civil method of reckoning, second degree consanguineal kin of the opposite sex in the direct line of an individual and the opposite sex third degree collateral consanguineal kin. To these were added the spouses of all those just calculated and the spouse's kin likewise calculated. The table was also understood to imply that all consanguineal relations in the direct line were prohibited and that half relationships were to count as full relationships (Hammick 1887:37–38).

While Protestants, both in England and the United States, for the most part accepted the archbishop's table, some did not. The Puritans, for one, were not satisfied with the list of prohibitions. They were particularly opposed to cousin marriage and brought their opposition to this union to the United States in 1629 (Howard 1904, 2:212–13). Similarly, the Quakers in England were opposed to cousin marriage and carried their opposition with them to the colonies. The Society of Friends in England, in spite of the fact that the chief justice of England had declared in 1669 that marriages between cousins were legitimate (Trumbach 1978:19), maintained a prohibition until the 1880s. It was not until 1883 that the English Society of Friends rescinded its regulations against cousin marriage. The Friends did so reluctantly at their meeting, after having considered the matter several times. They remarked, "In coming to this judgment, we would record our strong feeling that such marriages are highly inexpedient, and ought to be, as far as practicable, discouraged among us" (quoted in Hammick 1887:366).

Whereas the Puritans and Quakers found the table too permissive, others found it too restrictive. In particular, the marriage between a man and his wife's sister was thought to be a relationship with positive social benefits that should not be forbidden. It was said that "the Consequences of [marriage between a man and his sister-in-law] . . . may be not only conducive to their own personal Satisfaction and Felicity, but likewise intimately connected with the National Security, and the Establishment and Enlargement of the Protestant Interest" (Fry 1756:viii–ix). A major controversy arose over the legitimacy of the marriage between a widower and his wife's sister, however, which raged in England until the early decades of the twentieth century.

In the eighteenth century writers who disagreed with the list of relatives in the table did not use only scriptural or ecclesiastic sources to draw up their list of relatives to be prohibited from marrying. They utilized information from contemporary families and attempted to discover a natural law of marital relationships. Such investigations laid the foundation for the evolutionary approaches to human social relationships that were to flourish a century later. Fry (1756), for example, argued that only consanguineal relationships in the direct line and siblings should be prohibited from marrying. To justify his list of forbidden relatives, Fry critically reviewed the Scripture and searched for a law of nature that could be rationally deduced from the existing roles and duties in families. Uncovering the natural law of marriage meant discovering the fitness of different marital relationships. *Fitness* meant, for Fry, the ability of a relationship to meet the functions of marriage. For him, the primary purposes of marriage were the procreation of children, mutual aid, and support. He concluded that these ends are much more likely to be achieved when the partners in marriage were people familiar with each other. Close kin, such as cousins or in-laws, are the most likely to be so acquainted. Thus, their marriage would be the fittest and should not be prohibited (Fry 1756:79).

Throughout the eighteenth and nineteenth centuries opposition to the prohibition of marriage between a widower and his deceased wife's sister increased in England. This opposition was manifested by the number of couples who married despite affinal prohibitions. In-laws would marry, and "many couples enjoyed long marriages free from official interference" (Morris 1992:143). Public opposition was also expressed as early as the first half of the nineteenth century by "thousands of middle- and upper-class couples who had taken advantage of their wealth and the more lenient laws of other countries to contract affinal marriages abroad" (Morris 1992:141; see also Anderson 1982). Attempts to change the law and remove the sister-in-law from the list of prohibited marriages repeatedly failed, however. Throughout the nineteenth century in England, a sexual relationship between these affinal relatives continued to be considered incestuous. It was treated very seriously in the courts, and a woman could get a divorce in case her husband had sexual relations with her sister. In 1801 the first divorce case secured by a woman in England resulted from her husband's adulterous relationship with her sister. Since intercourse as well as marriage established the prohibitive relations, the resumption of intercourse with her husband after his adultery was considered incest by the courts, and divorce was granted (Wolfram 1983:314).

A debate in Parliament over the prohibition against the marriage of a man and his deceased wife's sister was begun with Lord Lyndhurst's Act of 1835 (Wolfram 1987:30–40). This fierce, prolonged debate about the legitimacy of marriage between these in-laws continued in Parliament for decades. The original intention of the act was to "guarantee the legitimacy and inheritance of the son of the seventh Duke of Beaufort, who had married his deceased wife's half-sister" (Anderson 1982:67). The law, however, had a much greater impact. It made all marriages within the prohibited degrees of affinity that had been celebrated before its passage secure by guaranteeing that they could not be annulled. Marriages of persons within the consanguineal degrees prohibited were not affected. It also made all marriages between consanguineal or affinal kin within the prohibited degrees after its passage null and void. Its passage reaffirmed the injunction against marriage between a man and his wife's sister. More important, it changed the nature of family relationships under the law.

Since the time of James I all marriages within the prohibited degrees were considered valid by the ecclesiastical courts until a decree nullified them. Such a decree could only be pronounced while both parties to the marriage were alive. This prevented children from becoming illegitimate heirs after the death of their parents in case the parents were related in some way prohibited by the table. After the passage of Lord Lyndhurst's Act all marriages within the affinal prohibitions that had taken place prior to the passage of the law were to be recognized and could not be annulled. However, marriages after the passage of the law were automatically null and void: "They no longer needed to be brought before a court in order to be voided and for any children of the union be declared illegitimate" (Lord Bramwell 1886:403). Lord Lyndhurst's Act meant that, in the case of property left by the death of a husband and wife married within the forbidden degrees of relationship, a relative of one of the spouses rather than the children could now obtain the estate since the marriage would not be recognized and the children would not be considered legitimate and proper inheritors. One of the stated goals of Lord Lyndhurst's Act was to eliminate the uncertain status of children during the lifetime of the parents. It did that.

Lord Lyndhurst's Act was also designed to put an end to marriages with a deceased wife's sister. At that time in England many unmarried women were living with their married sisters, and when the sister died, they took over rearing the children. It was common for the widower to marry his wife's sister in these situations, in spite of the church's prohibition. Conservative Englishmen expressed great consternation about this since they felt these relationships threatened the entire structure of prohibitions. If these marriages were permitted, so it was argued, the way was opened to unbridled incest and the subsequent destruction of the family. A royal commission was appointed in 1847 to look into the issue of marriage between affinal relatives and to investigate the impact of Lord Lyndhurst's Act. The commission reported that marriage between a man and his dead wife's sister was by far the most frequent type of affinal marriage relationship and that it had become the primary focus of their inquiry: "In fact it formed the most important consideration in the whole subject; and that as these so-called marriages will take place, especially among the middle and poorer classes, when a concurrence of circumstances gives rise to mutual attachment, the commissioners were of opinion [that Lord Lyndhurst's Act] had failed to attain its object" (Howard 1904, 2:97, quoting from the report of the commission). The commission also was of the unanimous opinion that no prohibition would be effective in regulating these marriages. The commissioners reported, "We are not inclined to think that such attachments and marriages would be extensively increased in number, were the law to permit them; because, as we have said, it is not the state of the law, prohibitory or permissive, which has governed or, as we think, ever will effectually govern them" (quoted in Commission Appointed by the Archbishop of Canterbury 1940:7).

The royal commission's conclusions that Lord Lyndhurst's Act did not have any impact on the incidence of marriage between a man and his wife's sister and that any legislation concerned with prohibiting such marriages would be ineffectual were followed by several attempts to do away with the prohibition. The act was, according to Hammick (1887), "more frequently and earnestly debated and disputed than any other point connected with our marriage laws" (33–34). Each attempt during the nineteenth century to do away with the prohibition against marriage between a man and his dead wife's sister failed.

Two of the major fears often expressed in opposition to any bill attempting to legitimize marriage between these affines was that it would lead to the abolishment of all affinal prohibitions and inevitably to the destruction of the family. To prove the point, Bishop J. F. Oxon (1886:677) referred to the rising divorce rate in the United States. The increased number of divorces, he thought, was the direct result of the disappearance of the prohibitions against the marriage of the wife's sister.

Opposition to the abolishment of the civil affinal proscriptions in marriage was also raised because the legislation was seen as the state's encroachment into church affairs. It was considered a threat to the fundamental religious notion that marriage was the union of husband and wife into "one." Opponents also argued that such a bill would increase the disruptive force of sexuality in the family and would threaten society's right of moral control over individual action (Anderson 1982). Today it may be difficult to imagine the emotions that were raised in the fierce debates over whether marriage with the wife's sister was incestuous and whether it should be legally permitted. But to some in the nineteenth century it was such a grave issue that "one gentleman, who had been Lord Chancellor of England, more than once declared that if marriage with a deceased wife's sister ever became legal 'the decadence of England was inevitable,' and that, for his part, he would rather see 300,000 Frenchmen landed on the English coasts" (Howard 1904, 2:101). The controversy spanned several generations, and "it was only after many futile attempts and in the face of very strong opposition that an Act legalising marriage with a deceased wife's sister in the United Kingdom was passed in 1907" (Westermarck 1922,

2:152). Even then, intercourse with a living wife's sister continued to be considered incestuous and was grounds for divorcing a husband (Wolfram 1983:312).

England's staunch defense of its laws forbidding the marriage of affinal kin that had been first defined in Archbishop Parker's sixteenth-century table continued throughout the nineteenth century. In contrast, most states in the United States dropped prohibitions against the marriage of affinal kin from the list of forbidden marriages by the end of the nineteenth century. Legislation in the eastern states discontinued the prohibitions against the marriage of affinal kin by the middle of the 1800s, and most of the western states never adopted any such prohibitions. By the late nineteenth century legislators in the United States concerned about the dangers of marriage between close relatives began prohibiting cousins from marrying. Concerns about cousin marriage were raised in England as well. Both the Americans and the British examined the impact of cousin marriage on the health of offspring and questioned its effect on society, but the results were quite different.

4

European Views
of Cousin Marriage

Not to love your cousins is to be devoid of natural affec-
tion—to show a cold, callous, and bad heart.
—*Saturday Review*, 1862

The early nineteenth century saw scholars in the United States and Europe argue whether marriage between a man and his dead wife's sister was incestuous and jurists on both sides of the Atlantic debate whether the moral fiber of a nation would be threatened with the passage of civil laws permitting the marriage of close affinal kin. The fundamental premises for these arguments were that a man and a woman became one in marriage, family and marriage were the primary institutions for maintaining social order and morality, marriage was the arena within which sexual activity was undertaken, and the Scripture was the source for answers to questions about proper marriages. Those in favor of the proscription interpreted the pertinent passages in Leviticus to support their conclusion that marriage between in-laws threatened the tranquility of the family and ultimately the social order of civilized society. Those opposed to the prohibition also referred to Leviticus to argue their position that in-law marriage was proper under contemporary conditions. The conclusion to this debate was not achieved by any interpretation of Leviticus or by any argument based on biblical exegesis.

Toward the middle of the nineteenth century a new framework for understanding the role of marriage in human behavior emerged: "In place of Jehovah, the new Victorian God of Science was called on to prove that it was incestuous to marry a wife's sister. The 'one flesh' argument from Genesis, for example, was transmuted into biological theory, with the contention that sexual intercourse causes an actual physiological change in the marriage partners that makes them blood relations" (Anderson 1982:75). The new "Victorian God" settled the argument, but not by determining that there was some biological basis for in-law prohibitions. It bypassed the debate over the scriptural basis for forbidding the conjugal relationship between a man and his wife's sister by establishing an evolutionary framework in which affinal relationships no longer were of concern.

In England human evolutionary progress based on biological factors in a process of natural selection became the framework for evaluating the propriety of marital relationships. The acceptance of this framework eventually led to the elimination of the prohibition in England against marriage with the widower's wife's sister (Anderson 1982:83; Wolfram 1987:142). In 1907, nearly three-quarters of a century after the introduction of Lord Lyndhurst's Act, Parliament removed the prohibition against the marriage between a man and his dead wife's sister.

The focus on human bioevolutionary progress shifted the concern with the regulation of marriage from the maintenance of morality in the family to the regulation of breeding. This change reduced affines from a position of central importance to a position of little significance. They became negligible because they were not important to the inheritance of physical characteristics by individuals, now considered the chief concerns of incest and the major factors in the advancement of a race or civilization. With this change in perspective, the affinal prohibitions no longer made any sense. The range of affinal relationships in Archbishop Parker's table ceased to be a matter for serious debate. Concerned individuals now turned to the range of the deleterious physical effects of consanguineous marriages. This transformation is clearly reflected in the Punishment of Incest Act, establishing criminal penalties for incest, passed by Parliament in 1908. This act defined criminal penalties for incest solely in terms of consanguineal relationships (between a man and his granddaughter, daughter, sister, or mother).

The new framework for understanding marriage, found scattered among the writings of the authors of the eighteenth century, clearly emerged in the first half of the nineteenth century. In spite of the fact that Lord Lyndhurst did not intend to draw any distinction between relationships of affinity and consanguinity, his act introduced this difference into law. For the first time in English courts these two types of relationships were to be treated differently. The act declared that marriages of forbidden degrees of affinity contracted before the law was enacted were not to be annulled, whereas marriages of consanguinity were to be annulled. Lord Lyndhurst had not meant to introduce this distinction between the two types of relationships: "His Bill, as he afterwards said, had nothing to do with annulling marriages; it had no other end in view than the condition of children, which the existing law left in an unsettled state during their parents' lifetime. In its passage through Parliament the distinction (retrospectively) between consanguinity and affinity was introduced" (Oxon 1886:676).

The distinction in Lord Lyndhurst's Act between consanguinity and affinity was accompanied by an emphasis on consanguinity in marriage law and a rising concern with cousin marriage. Cousin marriage was a centuries-old practice in Great Britain (see, for example, Pryce 1993), and a regular, though small, percentage of aristocratic marriages, at least since the end of the seventeenth century, was between first cousins (Trumbach 1978:21). In the nineteenth century the rate of marriage between cousins was estimated to be 4.5 percent among the aristocracy and 3.5 percent for the middle classes. For all classes in London it was figured to be 1.5 percent (George Darwin 1875:162–63). In the twentieth century the general population in England has been estimated to marry cousins at a rate less than 1 percent (Fox 1983:223).

Although there has been some opposition to the practice of cousin marriage in England for some time, there is no evidence that, as Trumbach (1978:33) suggests, the greater part of English society disapproved of it since the Middle Ages. Cousin marriages became illegal early in British history with the acceptance of canon law, but they were made legal again at the time of Henry VIII, when the Roman Catholic canons were replaced by parliamentary acts affirming "God's law" for determining the legitimate marriage relationships. Cousin marriage has been permitted since the time of Queen Elizabeth, affirmed in common law court since the seventeenth century, and accepted among wealthy families since the eighteenth century (Anderson 1986:285–86).

Physicians began to question the propriety of marriage between cousins in England at the beginning of the second half of the nineteenth century. One doctor noted that in "writings upon medical and hygienic subjects we constantly find the marriages of blood relations enumerated, as a matter of course, among the causes of degeneration of race, sterility, insanity, scrofula, &c." (Child 1862:461). This nineteenth-century physician took exception to the argument that illness resulted from cousin marriage. He pointed out that these fears were not based on careful research, a clear understanding of the inbreeding of domesticated animals, or proper statistical analysis. He noted that domesticated animals are inbred and that the closeness of the relationships far exceeds anything that happens in human marriage. Dr. Child recounted that a well-known, nineteenth-century prize bull, named Comet, was the result of breeding a pair from the same cow, then breeding the female offspring with its father, and then breeding the offspring of that pair with its mother. No breeder of cattle would speak of cousin unions as close breeding.

After analyzing the "Herd-book," which contained a careful record of generations of cattle breeding, and discussing the matter with cattle breeders, Dr. Child concluded that the only potentially negative aspect of consanguineal unions is "that where very close and continued through many generations, close breeding has a tendency to diminish fertility, and seems to do so by lessening the generative power of the male sex" (465). He also thought that close breeding intensified individual characteristics but did not, unless the parents were diseased, produce disease in the offspring. Considering heritability and human marriage, the doctor reasoned that it would be safer to marry a cousin than a nonrelative. Since heritable characteristics, not close marriage, produce ill effects, marriage with a cousin of known healthy parentage is more likely to produce healthy offspring than one with a stranger of unknown parentage. His general conclusion was that "the effects of consanguineous marriages are not of a character to afford support to the general opinion that such marriages are in themselves contrary to some law of nature, and calculated to lead to degeneration of race" (469).

A very different opinion was expressed by the deputy commissioner for lunacy in Scotland, Arthur Mitchell. The Scottish believed that cousin marriage produced injurious results (Mitchell 1866:409). In 1858 Mitchell began a systematic inquiry into the relationships of the parents of lunatics. After reading a report in a 1859 Liverpool medical journal that 10 percent of the cases involving deafness in the city were due to cousin marriage, he broadened his research into the detrimental effects on the offspring of consanguineal marriages (421). The deputy commissioner now looked for any deleterious effects of cousin marriage and in 1860 recorded forty-five cases of cousin marriage from a district of Scotland. These cases confirmed his belief that cousin marriage led to the injury of the offspring, but he was unsure whether this was the result of close marriage itself or some trait that was being transmitted from parents to children. He opted for the former: "Given a man and woman not cousins both predisposed say to x, and a man and woman similarly predisposed who are cousins, the chances of transmitting x to the offspring will be greater in the last case

than in the first; in other words, that the kinship will not be altogether si-
lent" (411).

In the spirit of the new social scientific methods of the times, Mitchell
collected more empirical data and prepared statistical tables to prove his
case. He investigated the possibility that deaf-mutism was the result of
cousin marriage by gathering data on the parentage of inmates in institutions of the deaf and dumb. These investigations also confirmed his belief
in the dangers of cousin marriage, but to establish its general harmfulness
even more clearly, he decided to collect data from isolated Scottish communities on islands, such as St. Kilda and the island of Lewis in the Outer
Hebrides. He had been told that marriages between consanguineal relatives
were common on these small islands, and he expected to find numerous
offspring with health problems. To his surprise, he found that St. Kilda
"does not realise the disastrous results which one would expect to find in
a community where more than one-third of all the married couples are
related by blood" (426). Furthermore, on Lewis, "instead of finding the
island peopled with idiots, madmen, cripples and mutes," Mitchell found
that "not one such person is said to exist in it" (434). In the face of these
unexpected results, however, Mitchell did not give up the idea that cousin
marriage was dangerous. Instead, he speculated that the dangers of consanguinity might be overcome by proper living:

> [The results of inbreeding are] least grave, when the parents are living
> in tolerable comfort, without ambitions, anxieties, or much thought of
> the morrow; when they follow healthful open-air occupations, living
> by their muscles but not overworked, and easily earning enough to
> procure good food and clothing; when they lead routine but not indo-
> lent lives, working but not struggling for existence; when they have a
> fair education, but are without pretence of refinement; when they steadi-
> ly adhere to sobriety; when, in short, they have good constitutions and
> are able to manage these wisely after marriage. (447)

Mitchell's belief that the well-behaved upper classes would not have to
worry about consanguineal marriage—only the sinful and poor would—
touches on an important consideration that would not be scientifically investigated for another hundred years. Not until after World War II, when
the United States Atomic Energy Commission investigated the impact of
consanguinity on Japanese children, would anyone carefully consider the
socioeconomic factors involved in cousin marriage (Schull and Neel 1965).
Mitchell's work indicates that some of the illnesses found in groups that

practiced cousin marriage were because of poor living conditions rather than marriage practices. But this was ignored, even by Mitchell, except for the brief moment noted above. He simply believed that close kin marriage produced bad effects and that these could be overcome by correct living.

Mitchell's general survey of cousin marriage did not find sufficient support for his hypothesis that cousin marriage was harmful to offspring. Rather than discard the hypothesis, however, Mitchell searched for an explanation of its failure. Not only did he speculate that proper living could counter cousin marriage's harmful effects, but he also thought that its effects, not found in his data, may emerge in subsequent generations. He also surmised that the harmful nature of consanguineal relationships would turn up as a general deterioration of the group rather than as any specific detectable abnormality (447–48). That way, even if no significant injurious results could be detected in his data, Mitchell could maintain that cousin marriage is harmful.

Mitchell concluded from one of his studies that "illegitimacy itself tends to produce defective children" (416). Morality was evidently a factor in determining his views about the dangers to the offspring of cousin marriages. He shared his Scottish contemporaries' belief that cousin marriage was immoral and, as a physician, sought to justify his belief through empirical investigation into the health of the offspring. His work illustrates how research about the ill effects of cousin relationships can be the vehicle for expressing the investigator's values and beliefs rather than simply the impassive unearthing of results through unbiased analysis of data.

Westermarck (1922) pointed out that the relationship between the supposed detrimental effects of close marriage and the institution of its prohibition was not what was usually stated. He argued that sex between relatives has been "considered harmful because it is disapproved of, and it is not in the first place disapproved of because it is considered harmful. This appears from the fact that other forms of illicit love, such as adultery and fornication, are supposed to produce the same disastrous effects" (Westermarck 1922, 2:182). Westermarck's point is illustrated in Arthur Mitchell's publications.

Less than a decade after Mitchell's work in Scotland, an English study reported that in "respect to deaf-mutes, the proportion of offspring of first cousin marriages is precisely the same as the proportion of such marriages for the large towns and the country, and therefore there is no evidence whatever of any ill results accruing to the offspring in consequence of the cousinship of their parents" (George Darwin 1875:172). George Darwin was careful to use appropriate samples to draw conclusions. He was also one of the first to note that although there was increased mortality with inbreeding, first cousin marriages had a slight advantage over nonconsanguineous unions in terms of net fertility. Modern estimates of the risks to the offspring of cousins in general populations "appear to be in remarkably close agreement with the levels calculated by Darwin 1875" (Bittles and Makov 1988:164).

In refuting Mitchell's work, George Darwin used Mitchell's speculations to compare their homelands. Darwin suggested that "perhaps the apparent invalidation is due to the fact, that a large majority of Englishmen live under what are on the whole very favourable circumstances" (George Darwin 1875:175–76).

Darwin was not alone in criticizing Mitchell. Other researchers found results contrary to Mitchell's and concluded that consanguinity, by itself, was not a factor in producing abnormalities in offspring. A growing number of English investigators in the last half of the nineteenth century were becoming aware that inheritable factors, not simply consanguinity, were responsible for congenital problems. An example of this growing awareness can be found in an English physician's letter to George Darwin: "As regards insanity, my own impression is, that unless there exists a hereditary predisposition the marriage of cousins has *no effect* in producing it" (quoted in George Darwin 1875:169).

While there was growing opposition in England to Mitchell's thesis and numerous publications were providing evidence contradictory to his conclusions, Mitchell was being uncritically accepted in the United States. An American physician, for example, used passages from his work to provide support for the thesis that consanguineous marriage leads to the deterioration of the race (Stern 1891). The whole issue of the possible deleterious effects of consanguineal marriage had aroused great interest on both sides of the Atlantic, and numerous investigations were undertaken. Published studies of the possible deleterious effects of consanguineal marriage "abounded from the 1850s onwards" (Wolfram 1983:309).

One of the contributors to the debate about the possible deleterious effects of close relatives' marrying was Charles Darwin. In the first edition of his *Various Contrivances by Which Orchids are Fertilized* (1862) he mused about the probability that marriage between close relatives is injurious, but in the 1877 edition he removed the comment. In *The Effects of Cross and Self Fertilization in the Vegetable Kingdom,* also published in 1877, he reaffirmed that cousin marriage does not represent any evolutionary risk. He pointed out, reminiscent of Mitchell, that any evil arising from marriage between healthy, somewhat closely related individuals would be counterbalanced in civilized nations by the habits of its upper-class individuals (1877a:461). Charles Darwin had married his first cousin, and the couple produced ten excellent offspring so his conclusion that close marriage did not necessarily lead to ill effects may come as no surprise. His concern about close relatives' marrying in the original edition of his book on orchids indicates he had considered the issue, however. His conclusion that it was not a problem came after his son George had studied the possible deleterious effects of consanguineal marriage on offspring and had concluded that there was no danger in cousin marriages. Charles Darwin's later views were probably due to his son's research.

In the 1860s and 1870s a large number of publications presented data and discussed the merits and dangers of cousin marriage. Alfred Huth (1875) critically examined the various arguments for and against cousin marriage. He first listed the numerous afflictions thought to be brought about by marriage between close consanguineal relatives. His list included dwarfism, cretinism, idiocy, insanity, epilepsy, deaf-mutism, sterility, rickets, and leprosy. He then searched the literature for evidence supporting the claims that these disorders were caused by consanguinity. Finding no convincing evidence that there was any causal relationship, he concluded there was insufficient support for the argument that close marriage of kin resulted in detriments to the offspring.

Huth carefully distinguished between marriages of close relatives and marriages between people of any relationship who possessed unwanted genetic traits. He argued that the transmission of traits in the parents to the children, not the parents' consanguineal relationship, caused unwanted characteristics in the offspring. Huth stated, furthermore, that marriage with close relatives not only was harmless but also could even be advantageous: "In mankind, at least, a cross is always a dangerous thing, since if he marries into a family not related to him, he knows, as a rule, nothing whatever of the pathological history of its members, while he can avoid intermarriage in his own family if there is the least suspicion of hereditary disease" (308). Huth's book was widely reviewed in Europe.

British legislators agreed with Huth and did not see any threat from cousin marriage. Those activists who called for legislative action were ignored. The attitude in England toward those who claimed that there were dangers in cousin marriage and that this danger required legislation was exemplified by Parliament's reaction to the scientists who requested legislative approval to gather census data about cousin marriage. When Sir John Lubbock and others attempted to obtain more needed data about cousin marriage by adding a question to the Census Act of 1871, the request was not taken seriously. It was rejected in the House of Commons "amidst the scornful laughter of the House, on the ground that the idle curiosity of philosophers was not to be satisfied" (George Darwin 1875:153). The scientists who desired the information were deemed "meddling animals" (Huth 1875:355).

England has never added cousins to its list of forbidden relatives, but in a series of marriage acts between 1907 and 1986 it has removed several of the affinal relationships from the list of kin originally published in Archbishop Parker's sixteenth-century table and permitted exceptions to those relationships that remain. The wife's sister was removed from the list of prohibited relatives in 1907, the brother's widow in 1921, all relatives of a deceased spouse except those in the direct line in 1931, and all relatives of a divorced spouse except those in the direct line in 1960. In 1980 and 1982 a man's deceased wife's daughter and a man's father's widow were also eliminated. The remaining affinal prohibitions express the traditional concerns with marriage as a social institution that incorporates individuals into a family and needs governmental protection. In the former colonies different courses of action have been taken. Australia, for example, abolished all prohibitions based on affinity in 1975.

The archbishop of Canterbury appointed a commission in 1937 and charged it with reconsidering the list of forbidden degrees in the Anglican church. The archbishop noted that the parliamentary acts between 1907 and 1931 had put English civil law at variance with Archbishop Parker's table of forbidden degrees and that many people were distressed and confused. He asked for a comprehensive consideration of the matter: "For us Anglicans the reconsideration of the subject must have a special reference to Archbishop Parker's Table, but I should be glad if the treatment of the subject by the Commission went behind this Table to the ultimate principles which ought to underlie any Table of Prohibited Degrees, and included the consideration of the bearing of anthropology and biology on the subject" (Commission Appointed by the Archbishop of Canterbury 1940:6). The commissioners, following the archbishop's request, utilized the expertise of people from a wide range of disciplines, including biology, anthropology, medicine, psychoanalysis, and law. They also received input from the more traditional sources used by religious commissions: the Bible, the history of the Roman Catholic church, and practices in the contemporary

Christian churches of England. The commission concluded that only marriages of consanguinity closer than first cousins should be prohibited. This required no change in the table's list of prohibited degrees of consanguinity. The report also concluded that relationships of collateral affinity should no longer be prohibited in the churches in England but granted the possibility that Anglican churches outside of the country may prohibit them (Commission Appointed by the Archbishop of Canterbury 1940:83). Finally, the report recommended that the list of forbidden degrees be changed so that the Anglican list would conform to the relations prohibited by English civil law.

In 1982 the archbishop of Canterbury constituted another group to review the marriage prohibitions. Its report, published in 1984, contained a majority recommendation that the legal impediments to marriage between all affines be removed, subject to certain restrictions. A minority recommendation suggested that only those legal impediments between stepparents and stepchildren be removed. In 1986 a bill was introduced in Parliament that offered a compromise between the two views expressed in the report.

The Marriage (Prohibited Degrees of Relationship) Act of 1986 permitted marriage between a man and his wife's mother or son's wife (corresponding relations for a woman) if both parties are over twenty-one years of age and if both previous spouses are deceased. If a man wishes to marry his wife's mother, for example, he can do so if both his wife and his wife's father have died. Likewise, a woman may not marry her son-in-law unless both her daughter and her daughter's father are dead. In the case of marriage with a man's son's wife (woman's father-in-law) it is permissible if both the mother of his son and his son (woman's husband and husband's mother) are dead. The inclusion of the death requirements was in response to opponents' fears that permitting these in-law marriages would encourage sexual relations and divorce within the family circle (Ross 1987:21). The 1986 act also established that marriage with the wife's mother, wife's daughter, father's wife, grandfather's wife, or wife's granddaughter (corresponding relations for a woman) is not void if both husband and wife are over twenty-one at the time of their marriage and neither was treated as a child by the family of the other while under eighteen years of age (Mcknorrie 1992:217). This last provision is to ensure that no marriage will occur between individuals who have previously been in a parent-child relationship. This indicates the continuing concern in England with the regulation of social order within the family. The Marriage Act of 1986 also eliminated the grandparent-in-law and the grandchild-in-law from the previously forbidden degrees of relationship in Scotland. This effectively established that in Scotland "no relationship by affinity will by *itself* constitute a bar to marriage" (Ross 1987:20). The relatives forbidden to marry in England today include those consanguineal kin in Archbishop Parker's table and a much reduced list of affinal kin (see table 4).

The changes in marital regulations in England were accompanied by a secularization of marriage, which occurred throughout Europe. Prior to

Table 4. Prohibitions in England Today

Relatives Men Are Forbidden to Marry	Relatives Women Are Forbidden to Marry
mother (also adopted)	father (also adopted)
daughter (also adopted)	son (also adopted)
father's mother	father's father
mother's mother	mother's father
son's daughter	son's son
daughter's daughter	daughter's son
sister	brother
wife's mother*	husband's father*
wife's daughter (wife alive)*	husband's son (husband alive)*
father's wife (father alive)*	mother's husband (mother alive)*
son's wife*	daughter's husband*
father's father's wife*	father's mother's husband*
mother's father's wife*	mother's mother's husband*
wife's father's mother	husband's father's father
wife's mother's mother	husband's mother's father
wife's son's daughter*	husband's son's son*
wife's daughter's daughter*	husband's daughter's son*
son's son's wife	son's daughter's husband
daughter's son's wife	daughter's daughter's husband
father's sister	father's brother
mother's sister	mother's brother
brother's daughter	brother's son
sister's daughter	sister's son

*Marriage between relatives over twenty-one is not void if neither was treated as a child of the family of the other while under eighteen.

Source: Martindale-Hubbell 1995:ENG-11.

1857, except for France, which had established civil control earlier in the century, ecclesiastical courts throughout Europe had responsibility for marriage. By 1889 civil courts had been given exclusive jurisdiction (Wright 1889:981–82). The English civil court for divorce and matrimonial causes was constituted by a statute passed in 1857, and the Irish court of matrimonial causes and matters was established by law in 1871. In Austria marriage jurisdiction was taken from the ecclesiastical courts and given to the civil courts in 1868. In Switzerland a federal law regulating marriage took effect in 1876 (Wright 1889:981). Prior to the passage of the federal law in Switzerland each canton had its own regulations, codified or customary, regarding marriage. Some regulations were based on popular law (voted in), the civil code (based on French law), Roman Catholic common and canon law, Protestant common law, and Austrian law. The federal law established that "marriage is prohibited between persons already married; between blood relations of all grades in ascending or descending line; brothers and sisters of the whole or half blood; uncles and nieces or aunts and nephews, whether the relationship is legitimate or illegitimate; between parents-in-law and children-in-law; step-parents and stepchildren; adopted parents and adopted children" (Wright 1889:1063). These prohibitions remain today.

The secularization of marriage and the emerging concerns about the deleterious effects of close consanguineal unions during the nineteenth century in Europe were not accompanied by any notable adoption of laws against the marriage of first cousins. Only Russia, Austria, Hungary, and Spain banned cousins from marrying during the nineteenth century. Austria's list of prohibitions was typical of these countries. It included marriage "between blood relations in ascending or descending line; between full or half brothers and sisters, or between their offspring; between uncles and nieces, or aunts and nephews, whether the relationship arises from legitimate or illegitimate birth" (Wright 1889:983). The listed relatives of one's spouse were also forbidden. In Spain and Hungary, following the centuries-old pattern of the Roman Catholic church, dispensations were available from the government (Westermarck 1922, 2:101). The prohibitions against first cousin marriage have since been removed in each of these countries. Thus, today no European country forbids cousin marriage.

During the second half of the nineteenth century several countries witnessed an increase in first cousin marriages in spite of the concerns some voiced about the possible deleterious physical effects of cousin marriage. Studies of church records have revealed that the predominantly Catholic

Mediterranean countries saw a relatively high increase in marriage rates between consanguineal relatives during the nineteenth century and then witnessed a steep decline in these types of marriages after 1900 (McCullough and O'Rourke 1986:364). By the 1950s only 0.45 percent of all marriages in Italy were between first cousins; the highest incidence of this type of union (1.65 percent) was in Sicily (Fraccaro 1957:36). Some have speculated that the nineteenth-century increase was because of the loss of primogeniture rights during the Napoleonic period (1796–1815) (Pettener 1985; McCullough and O'Rourke 1986). Some have reasoned that when changes were made to permit all children to have equal rights to a father's property, the viability of traditional landholdings was threatened, and cousin marriages increased to keep agricultural property from being overly subdivided. Others have suggested that the rise in cousin marriages may simply be related to an increase in population during that time, which provided more available cousins (Pettener 1985). Still others have put forth the idea that the increase was because of the "relaxation of Catholic authorities in granting dispensations for close-relationship marriages" (Pettener 1985:286). In support of this last notion, Pettener points out that the Italian Kingdom, created in 1861, required no dispensation for civil marriage between first cousins. When parish priests in the Upper Bologna Appennine solicited dispensations from higher church authorities, they often mentioned that "the spouses could have recourse to so-called civil marriage" (Pettener 1985:286).

From after the Reformation until 1680 the Swedish church prohibited first cousin marriage unless a dispensation was obtained. The incident of first cousin marriages was extremely low in Sweden during this period. From 1680 until 1828 dispensations were granted for a high fee, and there was only a slow increase in first cousin marriages, to about 1 percent (Alström 1958:302–4). After the high fee for obtaining a dispensation for first cousin marriage was abolished in 1828, however, first cousin marriage quickly increased by 50 percent, to 1.5 percent (Jorde and Pitkänen 1991: 137). In 1844, after several unsuccessful attempts earlier in the century, the prohibition against first cousin marriage was removed.

The argument that the relaxation of restrictions, the increase in population, or the reduction in fees could have resulted in an increase in cousin marriages assumes that people in Europe aspired to this kind of union. These mechanisms would then have allowed this desire to be met. The primogeniture argument, however, suggests that the change in rights created an increased interest in cousin marriage. At this point there is insufficient evidence to be certain about the reasons for the increase in first cousin marriages in Europe during the latter part of the nineteenth century. Whatever the reasons for this increase, the number of first cousin unions in Europe has since declined. Furthermore, marriages between cousins have been no more than 3.63 percent of all marriages, even though there were no civil impediments against these unions (Lebel 1983:549–51).

The consanguineal relatives currently prohibited from marrying in all European countries are ascendants/descendants and brother/sister. Sweden is an exception in that it does permit the marriage of half siblings. In France and Italy uncle-niece and aunt-nephew marriages are forbidden, but the president of France and government officials in Italy can grant special permission for them to marry. European countries still prohibit a few affinal relatives from marrying. England's prohibited kin have been noted earlier. In France, Germany, and Norway marriage between primary affines related through lineal relatives cannot marry. A man can not wed his father's former wife or son's former wife, for example. Sweden at one time forbade marriages to one's parents' siblings, but these unions were made legal in 1937 (Fraccaro 1957:38). In France and Italy brother-in-law/sister-in-law marriages are prohibited, but people can get special permission from the government. In the Netherlands no affinal relationships are prohibited. Adopted siblings are proscribed in marriage, but the Crown may grant dispensation. In the countries that made up the Soviet Union, affinal relatives have no proscription (Farber 1968:59).

Changes governing the marriage of relatives have taken place over the centuries in both the United States and Europe. Since the middle of the nineteenth century both have been affected by the secularization of marital regulation and the emergence of a bioevolutionary framework for viewing social life. But there is a major difference between European and American laws. In European countries the range of prohibited kin has been significantly reduced. The lists of prohibited affinal relationships, in particular, have been severely reduced or eliminated, and prohibited relationships of consanguinity have either remained the same or have diminished. Consanguineal relatives prohibited to marry in European countries today are lineal relatives and collateral kin more closely related than first cousins. Furthermore, sexual intercourse between blood relations will probably soon cease to be a crime (Group Appointed by the Archbishop of Canterbury 1984:146). It has been suggested that "the laws prohibiting incest and forbidding relatives from marrying serve no useful purpose in a modern society, and that the rules ought to be scrapped forthwith" (Mcknorrie

1992:219). While the range of affinal kin has also been reduced or eliminated in the United States, the range of prohibited consanguineal kin has been extended in a majority of states to include first cousins. Europe and the United States have both seen marital regulation become a matter of civil law, bioevolutionary factors replace biblical exegesis and social order as a framework for marital law, and legislative bodies eliminate or reduce the range of the prohibitions against affinal relatives. But only in the United States has first cousin marriage become tainted by a fear of genetic defects and prohibited. Why? The reasons for this difference will be made apparent in the following chapters.

5

The Evolutionary Factor

Malinowski, Rivers,
Benedict and others
Show how common culture
    Shapes the separate lives:
Matrilineal races
Kill their mothers' brothers
In their dreams and turn their
    Sisters into wives. . . .
—W. H. Auden, "Heavy Date"

Why the Roman Catholic church adopted proscriptions against the marriage of cousins nearly two thousand years ago has puzzled scholars for generations. The prohibitions were based on neither Roman nor Mosaic law, the two most likely precedents of church law. The Romans had put an end to the Ptolemaic practice of sibling marriage, but they did not prohibit the marriage of cousins at the time the church was formed. The Mosaic law likewise contained no cousin marriage proscriptions. The passages in Leviticus that have defined the marriage prohibitions over the centuries specify that a man shall not "uncover the nakedness" of his mother, stepmother, sister and half sister, granddaughter, father's sister, mother's sister, father's brother's wife, son's wife, wife's mother, wife's daughter, stepson's daughter, and stepdaughter's daughter. The brother's wife and wife's sister are also mentioned, but it is generally argued that these relatives are forbidden to a man only while his brother and wife, respectively, are alive (Mielziner 1901:45; Danby 1940:109). The only consanguineal relationships mentioned are a man's mother, sister, granddaughter, and aunt. There is no mention of first cousins.

One of the earliest explanations of the Roman Catholic church's adoption of the cousin prohibitions is that they provided a benefit by forcing an increase in social ties. This notion was put forth by the North African

Catholic philosopher Saint Augustine. Kin marriage was a prominent feature of the fifth-century Mediterranean world of Saint Augustine, and the church's adoption of a prohibition against the marriage of close relatives required some justification. Augustine provided one by combining a functionalist view of marriage with a fundamental myth of the church.

Saint Augustine accepted the biblical myth of human origins. Consequently, he took for granted that humans descended from one divinely created couple and that the natural continuation of the human population for at least two generations after the divine origin had to be the result of mating between close relatives. In defending the church's prohibitions, Augustine had to justify the ban against marrying close kin, while at the same time recognizing that this type of relationship occurred in the Old Testament and was even necessary according to the church's myth of human origins. He argued that the prohibition against marriage with close kin served the positive social function of increasing social ties. He then explained that close kin marriage, while functionally disadvantageous, was unavoidable at the beginning of human history. Earliest humans had to marry their close relatives since they had no other choice. But once choice was possible, Augustine contended, advanced societies would opt for the natural advantages of avoiding close kin, and they would institute prohibitions against the marriage of close relatives.

This functional view of marriage was used earlier by Plutarch, the second-century Greek biographer and essayist, in his reflections on Roman customs. Plutarch, aware of the Greek custom of sibling marriage, wondered why the Romans did not follow this practice and marry their nearest kin. He speculated that they wished to increase their alliances through marriage and acquire more kin by giving and receiving wives from outside their kindred (Jevons 1892:158). This structural-functional view of marriage prohibitions as a mechanism to extend relationships beyond the family has had a long history. It continued to be used in analyses of marital law during the Middle Ages and still plays a central role in the speculations of evolutionist and alliance theorists, nearly two millennia after Plutarch's analysis of Roman customs.

Augustine's notion that cousin marriage is a result of limited possibilities also has had a long history. It exists today in evolutionists' writings and not just among those who accept the Genesis myth of human origins. Some believe that cousin marriage is a function of reduced marital choices that came about, for example, through decimation of a population by disease (Ember and Ember 1983). The assumption that humans descended from a single aboriginal pair forces the conclusion that the individuals in the immediate following generations mated with close relatives. But it does not follow that individuals in societies with small populations (because of disease, emigration, warfare, or whatever) would necessarily marry their first cousins, nor is there any empirical evidence to support this.

"Contrary to common expectation," Bittles (1993) noted, "the highest rates of inbreeding are not necessarily found in small, isolated groups. Rather, the observed levels depend on the degree to which consanguinity is preferential in the community" (4). Studies of a Swedish-speaking minority in Finland indicated that first cousin marriage rates were "unlikely to be due primarily to a lack of available mates" (Jorde et al. 1992:25). Isolated communities with small populations, such as those on the Åland Islands in the Baltic and Tristan da Cunha in the southern Atlantic, have many people related to each other through multiple lines, but even then the average inbreeding coefficient for the population is generally low (Jorde et al. 1992; Roberts 1992).

Ottenheimer (1992) analyzed the minimum number of couples necessary to sustain a pattern of marriage in a society in which no individual marries a first cousin or any closer relative. The number is surprisingly low. With only four couples per generation it is possible to sustain a marriage system with a first cousin prohibition. For the society to continue to exist under these conditions, each couple needs to produce only one son and one daughter. Thus, individuals in diminished populations, unless the group is reduced to less than four eligible mates of each sex, need not marry first cousins. If random mating occurs in the group, the probability of first cousin unions will be inversely related to the size of the population. Humans rarely marry randomly, however.

The ancient practice of cousin marriage in the Mediterranean area was an anachronism for Saint Augustine. It was left over from the earliest period of human history when it was necessary because of limited choices. Contemporary societies had sufficient populations and could prohibit cousin marriages to take advantage of the positive social effects of marrying out. For Augustine, the church's adoption of the prohibition was thus a progressive social action undertaken in recognition of its natural beneficial results. Society would benefit from maximizing external social relationships.

"It is very reasonable and just," wrote Augustine, "that men, among whom concord is honourable and useful, should be bound together by various relationships; and that one man should not himself sustain many relationships, but that the various relationships should be distributed among several, and should thus serve to bind together the greatest number in the same social interests" (Saint Augustine [c. 420] 1950:500). Were a man to marry his sister, he would combine the two potentially distinct relationships of sister and wife into one. Their children would restrict even more relationships if they married. The children's union would combine the potential distinct relationships between father, father-in-law, and uncle into one relationship. The husband, furthermore, would be married to a woman who is both cousin and sister as well as wife. In the next generation even more relationships would be restricted between individuals. According to Augustine, if this form of marriage had been prohibited, "the social bond would not have been tightened to bind a few, but loosened to embrace a larger number of relations" (501).

The notion that the prohibitions enhanced the extension of a person's social relationships applied to affinal and fictive kin as well as consanguineal kin. Close in-laws, adopted relatives, and godrelatives were all prohibited from marrying (Esmein [1891] 1968, 1:336). Forbidding all these relatives from marrying forced individuals in the church to make marital ties with persons well outside their own immediate family, thus engendering widespread social interconnections. Herlihy (1985) suspects that the "Church's insistence on exogamy must have forced a freer, wider circulation of women through society" (61). It also "helped reduce abductions and with it the level of violence in early medieval society" (Herlihy 1990:12).

The eighth-century expansion of the prohibition against collateral marriages among the Franks has also been explained as a case in which cousin prohibitions served as a mechanism for expanding social ties outside a closely related group. Gies and Gies (1987) have argued that Pepin, the Frankish king, viewed noble connections through kin marriage as a threat to his power. Consequently, he backed St. Boniface, an English missionary acting as papal legate to the Frankish church, in extending the marriage prohibitions. Boniface, after consulting with the pope, recommended that the prohibition against cousin marriage be extended to the seventh degree, and this became part of Frankish law. The church also adopted the vastly expanded prohibitions. Gies and Gies concluded that "the extended prohibitions were, in their origin, not solely the invention of the Church, but the product of a convergence of religious ideology and royal self-interest" (86).

While propounding positive functions for the canon law and attributing dysfunctional aspects to close relative marriage have been mainstays of the literature explaining or justifying the Roman Catholic prohibitions against the marriage of close relatives, including cousins, there has been little consensus among authors about which functions were essential (Wolfram 1987:184). In the thirteenth century Thomas Aquinas augmented Augustine's historical and functionalist arguments by stating that close kin marriages would threaten the honor due family members, increase lust, and encourage licentiousness (Goody 1983:57). This fear that close kin marriages would threaten the moral fiber and structure of the family has been maintained for a considerable time. In 1910 the Indiana Supreme Court averred, "Family intermarriages and domestic licentiousness would inevitably confuse parental and filial duties and affections, and corrupt the moral sentiments of mankind" (State v. Tucker, 174 Ind. 715). This position became well known in anthropology through the writings of Bronislaw Malinowski (1927).

Other explanations for the prohibitions have involved a belief in dire biological consequences of cousins' mating. Pope Gregory's "experience that no offspring can come of such wedlock" (quoted in Gies and Gies 1987:53) was the early medieval church's explanation for the prohibition against first cousin marriage. Assertions that unwanted physical characteristics appear in the offspring of consanguineal unions are rare until much later. The common American belief today that prohibitions against cousin marriage are a reaction to the tendency for parents with consanguineal ties to produce offspring of lower intelligence or less fitness is a relatively recent development in the history of the concerns about cousin marriage.

A materialistic explanation for the church's prohibitions became popular at the time of the Protestant Reformation. Protestants saw the prohibitions and their accompanying dispensations as means for the papacy to obtain "Lucre." Goody (1983) published a modern expression of this idea. As discussed in chapter 3, he contended the prohibitions were adopted to weaken the family estate so that the church could acquire greater wealth and power.

In the seventeenth century the justifications for not allowing first cousin marriage were:

1. Their being against Nature: 2. Their being forbid by Scripture. 3dly their hindering of the spreading of Society, and Friendship, which is enough among Naturall Relations already. 4. The ill prospering of them. 5. Their being forbid by Theodosius and Arcadius Christian Emperours, with severe Punishments to Offenders in this kind. 6. Their not being in use with the Primative Christians. 7. Their being prohibited by Apostles Canons, and the canon law. 8. It being unlawfull for Second Cousins

to marry, and therefore First may not. 9. However, if they are not un-lawfull, yet a wise man upon the account of Credit will abstain from them. (Dugard 1673:6)

One author has suggested that the prohibitions arose in the church sim-ply "from a [human] habit of making rules for conduct" (Darlington 1960:300), but most writers have tried to specify some underlying ratio-nale for them. One specific justification proposed for the adoption of the cousin marriage prohibitions in Roman Catholic canon law, aside from those listed above, has been that they were a reaction against local customs of close marriage (Howard 1904). The adoption of the prohibition was thought to be a reaction specifically against Germanic kindred marriage (Goody 1983:59).

Jeremy Taylor (1660), a seventeenth-century British biblical scholar and politician, presented a different cultural interpretation for the church's adoption of the prohibitions. He thought the injunction against cousin marriage was a cultural pattern introduced by the Goths. Taylor's notion is a reasonable deduction based on the facts that the prohibition against cousin marriage was derived from neither Roman nor Mosaic law and that the Visigoths became an important element in the population of the Ro-man Empire during the time the prohibition was instituted. It was, after all, following the capture and sacking of Rome by Germanic Visigoths under Alaric I in A.D. 410 that the marital regulations of cousins became well established and were greatly amplified.

Taylor's cultural-historical analysis of cousin marriage proscriptions in the early church also offered an explanation for dispensations from the prohibitions. As noted in chapter 3, dispensations were offered by the Roman emperors who adopted Christianity. Their action can be seen as a syncretic response to the issues before them. It has been noted that Europe has been the juncture of two basic cultures: Mediterranean and European (in Goody's terms), or Oriental and Occidental (in Guichard's terms). In the Mediterranean/Oriental culture a pattern of marriage with close rela-tives is the norm. The European/Occidental culture prohibits marriage with close relatives. The invasion of the northern European Visigoths of Italy and Spain and their presence in the Roman Empire forced the early church political leaders and social reformers to confront the two patterns of mar-riage. To deal successfully with this problem, they would assimilate the two cultural practices. By making close kin marriage illegal, the church would meet the cultural demands of the Goths. It would not matter that there were few cousin marriages in the western Roman Empire at the time (Shaw and Saller 1984:438). (The number of unions seems to have little to do with the passage of laws against them. There was not a significant number of cousin marriages in Maine, for example, when it passed its prohibition in 1985.) At the same time, dispensations enabled the Mediterranean pattern of close kin marriage to continue in the face of the prohibition. The injunction against cousin marriage accompanied by dispensations can thus be viewed as a masterful political maneuver. It was a syncretic device that successfully met the need to accommodate two distinct cultures at the crossroads of Europe. That the church was later to benefit financially from the prohibitions and dispensations would be simply a reward—a result, not a cause, of its actions.

As scholars have pointed out, the Germanic Goths had a tremendous impact on the church's marriage laws. Howard (1904) noted, "During the period preceding the Teutonic invasion, speaking broadly, the church adhered to the Roman law and custom; thereafter those of the Germans, even when the marriage consisted in the formal sale and tradition of the bride, were accepted" (1:291). "Remarkably," commented Herlihy (1985), "over the centuries of the late empire, by measure of both marital terms and ages, the Roman marriage was converging toward the barbarian model" (73; see also Esmein [1891] 1968, 1:344). One of the noteworthy changes in the church was the adoption of the Germanic method of reckoning the degrees of kin distance.

At one time it was thought that as early as Pope Gregory I (A.D. 590–604) the western church began to diverge from using the Roman method of calculating the degree of relatedness (Huth 1875:44). Scholars now believe it was later in the eighth century (Herlihy 1985:61; Esmein [1891] 1968, 1:347) or ninth century (Bouchard 1981:270) that the Latin church began to adopt the Germanic method. The church continued to employ the Roman method as late as the first half of the eighth century (Gies and Gies 1987:84), and both Roman and Germanic methods of calculating the degrees of relatedness were in use in Europe through the eleventh century. With Alexander II's canon of 1076, however, the church formally shifted from the Roman to the Germanic, or "popular," system of reckoning (Esmein [1891] 1968, 1:346; Goody 1983:136–37). The civil courts in Europe and the United States, in contrast, use the Roman method of reckoning kin.

The Greek Orthodox church, unaffected by this Germanic influence, has also maintained the Roman method. Consequently, it is possible for prospective spouses who are from the different churches to discover that if they are related to each other, under one set of canon laws the marriage is not prohibited, while under the other set it would be valid only with dispensation. As Siegle (1979) pointed out, "Interritual marriages frequently take place and hence a situation might take place where a Latin would plan to marry an Oriental to whom he might be related in the fourth or fifth degree of consanguinity often in the collateral line. According to his own law, the Latin may contract marriage validly whereas the Oriental could be disqualified from contracting a valid marriage without a dispensation" (138).

At the time of the Reformation, Protestants argued for the jettison of papal authority as a basis for marriage regulations and for the removal of all prohibitions against cousin marriage. They constructed a new list of prohibited relatives and sought their own justifications for their marriage laws. At first the Old Testament (Leviticus, in particular) was the single guiding standard for Protestant marriage law. This biblical source was found to be insufficient for delineating the degrees of forbidden relationships, however, and scholars were forced to spend a great deal of time and energy trying to deduce which set of relationships should be prohibited. The list of prohibitions in Leviticus was problematic for primarily two reasons: it appeared to be incomplete, and it was not consistent with the marriages recorded elsewhere in the Old Testament. The first problem was manifest by the absence of the daughter in the list of relatives. Scholars were certain that daughter should have been included in any list of a man's prohibited relatives. It made little sense to them to prohibit a granddaughter, which is mentioned in Leviticus, but not a daughter. The other major problem was the appearance in the Old Testament of valid marriages between relatives specifically mentioned in the list of prohibited relations in Leviticus. Augustine had argued away the disparity between the prohibitions and the close relative unions in Genesis, but others remained. For example, a half sister was expressly mentioned in Leviticus and thus should be a relationship forbidden to a man. Yet Abraham married his half sister Sarah. Because of these difficulties, any scholar who attempted to discover the reasons for the prohibitions in the Bible was warned that he "will by Experience find it be too hard for his Head" (Bishop Jeremy Taylor, quoted in Fry 1756:77). In spite of the bishop's warning, Protestants made many attempts to make sense of the scriptural material and use it to construct a coherent set of marriage regulations.

In lieu of papal authority and with an incomplete or insufficient biblical basis, Protestants sought a rational justification for marital prohibitions. Three justifications for forbidden relatives became prominent from the

Reformation until the nineteenth century. Writers postulated that the prohibitions served to prevent roles in the family from becoming confused, status relations among family members from being upset, and the household from being disrupted by sexual promiscuity and rivalry (Wolfram 1987:162–68). These functions of the prohibitions were deduced from contemporary assumptions about the nature of European family relationships or derived from comparative data of the practices found in different societies around the world. By the end of the eighteenth century an unprecedented amount of information about the marriage practices of different peoples around the world had been brought back to Europe.

One example of the attempt to derive the proper list of forbidden relatives is the analysis of the eighteenth-century writer John Fry. He tried to make sense of the prohibitions in Leviticus and to determine precisely who should or should not marry by turning to the recently collected information about peoples around the world. For the propriety of marriage between a man and his deceased wife's sister, for example, Fry referred to Montesquieu's 1748 work, *The Spirit of Laws,* in which an Indian marriage custom is described. The custom permitted a man to marry his deceased wife's sister. Several eighteenth-century British groups had contested the Anglican church's prohibition of this marriage relationship, and Fry argued their case by pointing out that the Baron de Montesquieu viewed this as "'*extremely natural,*' for his new Consort becomes the Mother of her Sister's Children, and not a cruel Step-mother" (Fry 1756:80).

Fry searched for the fundamental nature of marriage by comparing cross-cultural material. His analysis led him to conclude that the major purposes of marriage were procreation and mutual support and that "those Matches must be the *fittest* that are contracted between such as are most likely to answer these Ends" (Fry 1756:79). This approach, in which marriage is thought to serve natural ends, the fitness of a relationship is measured in terms of its ability to meet those ends, and the ends are sought by comparative analysis of distant marriage practices, is a direct precursor of modern structural-functional social analysis.

By the middle of the nineteenth century the "fitness" of close kin marriages became the central issue of civil regulations of marriage. Empirical investigations into the health of offspring and comparative analyses of marital practices of different peoples around the world became the ways to determine the fitness of a marriage type. The question of whether there was "a law of nature" (Milledoler 1843:17) governing the marriage of relatives was now investigated by lawyers using comparative analysis and physicians examining empirical data. Physicians provided statistical analyses of the physical conditions of the offspring of cousin marriages that had been derived from data obtained by surveys. The Bible was no longer the primary source for determining civil law concerning marriage. Biblical exegesis, formerly the standard means for providing rationales for prohibiting close kin relationships, was replaced by comparative analysis of social data made available from the expansion of European overseas activities, empirical investigations of people in asylums, and examinations of the medical records of the offspring of cousin marriages. The results of these nonbiblical approaches were not used for improving the exegesis of Mosaic law. Instead, they became part of a natural theory of social evolution that would determine its own set of close relative prohibitions.

The changes in determining the basis of forbidden relatives are evident in publications of the 1860s: Henry Sumner Maine's *Ancient Law* (1861), Johann Jakob Bachofen's *Das Mutterrecht* (1861), Numa Denis Fustel de Coulanges's *La cité antique* (1864), and John Ferguson McLennan's *Primitive Marriage* (1865). *Primitive Marriage,* in particular, was a revolutionary book. McLennan ignored biblical exegesis and canon law in determining the basis of proper marriage regulations. Instead, he turned to a cross-cultural analysis of social behavior. His work clearly marks the change that had occurred in the search for the basis of the marital prohibitions. McLennan took the search from a quest for God's truth and biblical exegesis to an inquiry into the natural law of marriage and the comparative analysis of cultural data. Not surprisingly, McLennan's work was controversial and received considerable criticism. Furthermore, his radical departure from traditional views cost him half of his law practice (Tylor 1881:9–10).

In his departure from the traditional search for a rationale for marital relationships, McLennan analyzed material written by travelers, merchants, soldiers, and administrators about marriage practices of different peoples outside of Europe, especially reports filled with intimate details about marriage in the caste systems of India and the clan systems of North America. People in the caste system did not marry outside of their particular group. In the clan system, by contrast, people were forbidden to marry within their group. McLennan saw something essential to human social organization in these two different systems. He introduced the terms *endogamy* and *exogamy* to denote each of the two different types of marriage practices. *Endogamy* meant the marriage between individuals of the same kinship group; *exogamy* meant marriage between individuals from different descent groups.

McLennan defined these terms by referring to groups delimited by the kinship ties of descent. Although these terms are still widely used today, their meanings have changed. Today, instead of just referring to the descent group, *endogamy* often means marriage within a group, and *exogamy* means marriage outside of the group, no matter how the group is defined.

With his newly coined terms, McLennan divided up the "less advanced portions of mankind" into seven divisions ([1865] 1970:59). These divisions were grouped into two major categories, based on whether the groups were exogamous or endogamous. Subgroupings within these categories were determined by whether it was the tribe as a whole or the segments of it that were marrying in or marrying out. The first five groups were listed together within the category in which exogamy occurs. Marriage was prohibited between members of the whole tribe in the first group. In the second through fifth groups the tribe was subdivided into units, such as clans, and marriage was forbidden within these units but could exist between them. The sixth and seventh groups were endogamous. In the sixth group members were forbidden to marry outside of the tribe. The last group McLennan categorized was one in which the tribe had subgroups, such as castes, and their members had to marry within their subgroup.

McLennan did not accord the seven groups any temporal order. He did not think either exogamy or endogamy appeared in the earliest stages of human social development (compare Trautmann 1987:198). McLennan thought that either could have arisen from the most primitive state, one in which there were only indiscriminate matings. He explicitly states:

> Although these tribal systems may be arranged as above so as to *seem* to form a progression, of which the extremes are pure exogamy on the one hand, and endogamy—transmuted into caste of the Mantchu and Hindu types—on the other, we have at present no right to say that these systems were developed in anything like this order in tribal history. They may represent a progression from exogamy to endogamy, or from endogamy to exogamy; or the middle terms, so to speak, may have been produced by the combination of groups severally organised on the one and the other of these principles. The two types of organization may be equally archaic. Men must originally have been free of any prejudice against marriage between relations—not necessarily endogamous, *i.e.,* forbidding marriage except between kindred, but still more given to such unions than to unions with strangers. From this primitive indifference they may have advanced, some to endogamy, some to exogamy. (McLennan [1865] 1970:60)

Although McLennan was uncertain whether exogamy or endogamy occurred first in human history, he was convinced that the earliest stages of human history did not have either. The earliest periods of human development were characterized by groups in which individuals did not recognize any kinship relationships. He also believed that individuals at that time mated indiscriminately with anyone, related or not. The recognition of kinship ties emerges in a later stage of human development, and it is only with this recognition that exogamy and endogamy emerge. McLennan's definitions of *endogamy* and *exogamy* proffer that they cannot exist unless there are recognizable kinship ties. The change in usage from McLennan's definitions of *endogamy* and *exogamy* was accompanied by a change in their temporal associations. Exogamy was preceded by endogamy, and endogamy became associated with the earliest stages of human social development.

Nineteenth-century evolutionists did not think the earliest stage of human life began with the direct descendants of a primordial pair created by divine intervention, but they still viewed the beginnings of human life as a time in which people had sexual relationships with their closest relatives. The ancient notion that early social life was characterized by close kin marriage found a place in evolutionary theory with the idea that endogamy characterized primeval conditions of social organization.

A fundamental notion of nineteenth-century evolutionary thought was that the earliest peoples lived in undifferentiated groups, without recognizing kinship ties, without marital prohibitions, and without rules governing sexual conduct. Herbert Spencer, for example, proposed that civilization emerged through a process in which societies became less uniform, more specialized, and more complex. He wrote, "Primitive hordes are without established distinction of parts" (Spencer 1897, 1:593). According to Spencer, their development into the higher forms of tribes and eventually civilized nations was accompanied by differentiation of parts: "Unions of tribes are followed by more unlikenesses, governmental and industrial—social grades running through the whole mass, and contrasts between the differently occupied parts in different localities. Such differentiations multiply as the compounding progresses. They proceed from the general to the special" (593).

The idea that society evolves from homogeneity to heterogeneity, from an undifferentiated collection of individuals to a differentiated set with subgroups, or from a level in which there is close kin marriage to one in which there are prohibitions against the marriage of cousins dovetailed into other ideas expressed during the nineteenth century. As noted earlier, the biblical view of the creation of human beings that evolutionists were trying to replace had the species developing from an original male-female pair. In this schema there were no other choices for the earliest humans but to "know" their kin. This simple conceptual scheme provided an explanation for not only the origin of human beings but also the marriage of relatives. Close kin marriage was an essential feature of earliest social interaction. Social groups that married their close relatives were thus analogous to, or even a holdover from, the earliest stages of human life.

Although the evolutionists rejected Genesis as a literal description of the early history of human development, they maintained the assumption that close breeding was associated with earliest human existence. What they changed was the underlying reason for this behavior. According to Lewis H. Morgan, for example, early peoples married their kin because of their animal ancestry rather than out of demographic necessity due to miraculous creation. In this naturalistic view early peoples had low intellectual abilities. Furthermore, marriage practices from their animal past kept them in a stage of savagery and prevented them from achieving a level of civilization. Only after their groups became internally differentiated by descent and they adopted exogamy were early groups of humans able to develop the intellectual capacity to progress to the higher stages of human development. From this lofty perspective they were then able to recognize the inherent dangers in close kin marriage (those the nineteenth-century social evolutionists supposed existed) and pass laws forbidding it.

The idea that complex social organization rose out of homogeneous primeval human groups paralleled a prominent idea in a very different arena of nineteenth-century science. A popular natural explanation for the origin of celestial phenomena was the Kant-Laplace cosmological theory, developed in the previous century. In this theory the solar system coalesced out of undifferentiated matter, gradually accreting individuality out of sameness. Herbert Spencer, very influential in making evolution a popular concept, saw this relationship. As early as 1855 Spencer wrote that the rise of complexity in human beings was similar to the development of the universe. He maintained that intelligence

> presents a progressive transformation of like nature with the progressive transformation we trace in the Universe as a whole, no less than in each of its parts. If we study the development of the nervous system, we see it advancing in integration, in complexity, in definiteness. If we turn to its functions, we find these similarly show an ever-increasing inter-dependence, an augmentation in number and heterogeneity,

and a greater precision. If we examine the relations of these functions to the actions going on in the world around, we see that the correspondence between them progresses in range and amount, becomes continually more complex and more special, and advances through differentiations and integrations like those everywhere going on. And when we observe the correlative states of consciousness, we discover that these, too, beginning as simple, vague, and incoherent, become increasingly-numerous in their kinds, are united into aggregates which are larger, more multitudinous, and more multiform, and eventually assume those finished shapes we see in scientific generalizations, where definitely-quantitative elements are co-ordinated in definitely-quantitative relations. (Spencer 1900:627–28)

Spencer defined evolution as "change from a state of relatively indefinite, incoherent, homogeneity to a state of relatively definite, coherent, heterogeneity" (quoted in Carneiro 1967:xvii).

Many nineteenth-century thinkers concerned with the natural development of human society shared the view that human social development was a movement from the simple to the complex, from a condition in which society was characterized by isolated, homogeneous groups to one in which complex societies with interactive divisions existed. They believed families originally lived in a state of undifferentiated primeval sexual promiscuity, then passed through a period of marriage with brothers and sisters, and finally arrived at the modern state of monogamous marriage with nonimmediate family members (see, for example, Bachofen 1861; Fustel de Coulanges [1864] 1980; Lubbock 1870; McLennan [1865] 1970; and Morgan [1877] 1958). Although they differed in their descriptions of the precise paths societies took in the progression toward civilization, the nineteenth-century evolutionists assumed that the earliest stages of society were characterized by small, homogeneous, isolated groups. Fustel de Coulanges ([1864] 1980), for example, spoke of the early Aryans' being composed of innumerable numbers of small groups: "These thousands of little groups lived isolated, having little to do with each other, having no need of one another, united by no bond religious or political, having each its domain, each its internal government, each its gods" (108).

Another characteristic of the nineteenth-century evolutionists' picture of the earliest stage of human interactions was that individuals did not follow rules governing sex or marriage or distinguish between consanguines, affines, and mates. Each human social group consisted of an undifferentiated mass of females and males at this stage. Siblings, for example, could simultaneously be spouses and in-laws, and, at the same time, an offspring was both child and nephew (or niece) to them. A parent was both mother (or father) and aunt (or uncle) to the child. Only after a period of development did natural forces operate to establish marital relationships outside of the family. With the establishment of marriage outside of the group, parental, collateral, and other relationships became clearly differentiated. Larger social units were then formed from the bonds holding together the smaller units. This subsequently led to the creation of injunctions against marriage between close relatives. Essential to the progression was the change in marital practices from endogamy to exogamy. The final result was the emergence of civilization.

Endogamy for the nineteenth-century evolutionists meant simplicity, homogeneity, primevalness, and uncultured life. It was viewed as an integral part of human society at the beginning of social evolution, something that had to be overcome in society's progress toward civilization. These notions became central tenets of Western marriage theory, cornerstones of comparative social research, as well as accepted elements in the evolutionists' schema. The ancient notion that close kin marriage was a primeval form of social organization, which we first saw in the writings of Saint Augustine, now had a modern expression and was, as McLennan stated, easily understood. Similarly, McLennan's proposition that exogamy was the key to human social interaction was also widely accepted. In cosmological theory gravity was the force by which the solar system developed from an undifferentiated mass of matter. In evolutionary theory exogamy was the force that moved human social units from undifferentiated small groups of individuals into complex, highly differentiated societies. It forced individuals from their primary units to establish linkages with other units to form larger aggregates, which eventually developed into the modern forms of highly differentiated social organization. Exogamy deserved detailed analysis. One of the most prominent social evolutionists of the nineteenth century, Lewis Henry Morgan, provided one.

Morgan published an influential work, *Ancient Society,* in 1877 in which he wrote that close consanguineal unions and endogamy were characteristics of earliest human social life. He wrote about the horde, the earliest form of human social grouping, as a group of people living in "Promiscuous Intercourse." The horde was "the lowest conceivable stage of savagery—it represents the bottom of the scale" ([1877] 1958:507). This stage, characterized by indiscriminate relationships, was replaced by another stage, in which the first form of human family, the "Consanguine Family," appeared.

This family was characterized by brothers and sisters marrying in a group. In Morgan's evolutionary scheme this social group had a "Malayan System" of consanguinity and affinity, in which cousins were terminologically equated with siblings. Morgan theorized that cousins would be termed the same as siblings since the group marriage of siblings would imply that siblings would not be distinguished from cousins. Your father, for example, would be married not only to your mother but also to his sisters and his spouse's sisters, and their children would therefore be your siblings.

Morgan was intimately aware of the behavior of several North American Indian groups and had gathered detailed information about the family practices of different peoples around the world (Morgan 1871). Although there were several cases of groups in which siblings and cousins were called by the same kinship terms, his comparative analysis of the data did not reveal anything like the horde. No society appeared to live in a state without marital or sexual regulations or had group marriages of siblings. Nonetheless, he determined that the data implied this state of affairs. He decided that "the consanguine family and the Malayan system of consanguinity presuppose antecedent promiscuity" ([1877] 1958:507). Primeval promiscuity could only be theoretically deduced since its empirical verification "lies concealed in the misty antiquity of mankind beyond the reach of positive knowledge" ([1877] 1958:509). The conditions of promiscuity and close kin marriage of the earliest stage of human social organization were constructed, not discovered, by Morgan.

Writers in geography, biology, and anthropology criticized the idea that early humans lived in a stage of sexual promiscuity. Peschel (1876) argued that ethnographic cases, such as that of the Hawaiians, in which marriage took place between siblings should be considered local variations and not examples of a primitive stage of human social behavior (231). He also thought that close kin mating could not mark any general condition of early humans since such unions would not produce any offspring (232). Charles Darwin also took issue with the notion that the earliest stage of human social organization was universally characterized by indiscriminate sexuality in small groups. Aware of the research on animal behavior, Darwin wrote:

> [I] cannot believe that absolutely promiscuous intercourse prevailed in times past, shortly before man attained to his present rank in the zoological scale. . . . Therefore, looking far enough back in the stream of time, and judging from the social habits of man as he now exists, the most probable view is that he aboriginally lived in small communities, each with a single wife, or, if powerful, with several, whom he jeal-

ously guarded against all other men. Or he may not have been a social animal, and yet have lived with several wives, like the gorilla. . . ." (Charles Darwin [1874] 1901, 2:759–60)

Wake (1874) also faulted the idea that there was a stage of human history in which there was sexual promiscuity and criticized as unjustifiable Morgan's inference from classificatory kinship terminological systems. He pointed out that there was no ethnographic evidence to support such an inference. He also showed that the existence of such a stage was not necessary to explain the classificatory kinship systems that Morgan had posited. He suggested that the grouping of kin into terminological classes was due to "the operation of marriage regulations" (204). These produced the classification of kin into marriageable and nonmarriageable groups. If a mother's sister's daughter was referred to as a sister, for example, it was because, like a sister, she was not a marriageable individual in the society.

It is not clear whether the notion that promiscuity was a feature of human behavior was put to rest because of published criticisms or the recognition that no cases existed in the ethnographic record. Whatever the reason, it was dropped from the professional sociocultural literature. With it went the notion that primitive promiscuity was responsible for the classificatory systems of kinship terminology. The notion that endogamy was primitive and that exogamy was intricately involved in the rise of civilization remained, however.

The ethnographic literature contained plentiful examples of endogamy and exogamy. Morgan placed these into a temporal sequence in which the former was associated with earliest social life. Trautmann (1987) has argued that the Rev. Dr. Joshua H. McIlvaine, "Morgan's closest friend and intellectual companion," was largely responsible for this evolutionary pattern (61, 62–72). Trautmann is likely correct. McIlvaine was more than simply Morgan's companion in Rochester, New York. He was also his minister. McIlvaine was one of the nineteenth-century "Presbyterian scholar-educators who held very positive attitudes toward science, and promoted scientific education" (Trautmann 1987:67). McIlvaine saw science as a means to uncover God's truth and Morgan's work as a method to vindicate his religious convictions. In particular, McIlvaine was opposed to cousin marriage and saw it as "promiscuous intercourse." He spoke of the degradation and inferiority of the American Indian as "the deleterious consequences of their practice of intercourse among cousins, as a species of inbreeding" (Trautmann 1987:244).

Morgan did not completely agree with McIlvaine's point of view. He could not accept the pejorative evaluation of the American Indian and did not see cousin marriage as simply a matter of inbreeding. Morgan did place endogamous marriages in the earliest stages of human social development and exogamy in those later stages associated with the rise of civilization, but he used these concepts in the sense that McLennan had introduced. Endogamy was not simply a matter of inbreeding. It was intimately involved with the process of kinship reckoning. Morgan was familiar with North American Indian practices of not marrying a member of one's clan. He knew about the Iroquois, for example, and referred to exogamous marriages specifically in terms of the prohibition of marriage with members of one's unilineal descent group (which Morgan referred to as a "gens"): "As intermarriage in the gens was prohibited, it withdrew its members from the evils of consanguine marriage and thus tended to increase the vigor of the stock" (Morgan [1877] 1958:68). For Morgan the crucial factor in the emergence of exogamy is the avoidance of intermarriage within the "gens," not simply the avoidance of close consanguineal marriage. Cousin marriages outside of the descent group are thus separate from the other, more primitive types. The more primitive types are endogamous. They occur between members of the same descent group. Only the endogamous marriages kept human society in the lowest levels of development. Morgan did not consider marriage between a man and his mother's brother's daughter or between a man and his father's sister's daughter (Tylor [1889] was to soon label these "cross-cousin" marriages) endogamous unions. In unilineal descent systems these kind of marriages are between individuals of different descent groups.

The distinction between endogamy and exogamy in terms of descent lines was important to Morgan. Morgan had married his mother's brother's daughter in 1851 (Trautmann 1987:243), and he could view his marriage (Charles Darwin's marriage as well) to his cousin as nonendogamous and thus not involved with the "evils of consanguine marriage" (Morgan [1877] 1958:68). Morgan's marriage was exogamous in the original sense of the term since it was between cross-cousins, not between members of the same "gens." Morgan could consider his marriage neither endogamous nor primitive.

The formation of unilineal descent groups and the adoption of exogamy were the crucial factors for human social progress for Morgan. They produced the great social changes in history, moving human society from savagery to civilization (Morgan [1877] 1958:48). This evolutionary progress was caused by increased hybrid vigor within a population through the systematic marriage of individuals outside of their descent groups. Interbreeding raised the intellectual and physical capabilities of its participants. It also led to an increase in population. These changes produced by exogamy provided the impetus for humans to move along the road of progress. In Morgan's words:

> The influence of the new practice, which brought unrelated persons into the marriage relation, must have given a remarkable impulse to society. It tended to create a more vigorous stock physically and mentally. There is a gain by accretion in the coalescence of diverse stocks which has exercised great influence upon human development. When two advancing tribes, with strong mental and physical characters, are brought together and blended into one people by the accidents of barbarous life, the new skull and brain would widen and lengthen to the sum of the capabilities of both. Such a stock would be an improvement upon both, and this superiority would assert itself in an increase of intelligence and numbers. ([1877] 1958:468)

By inference, those groups that did not adopt exogamy but continued the endogamous marriages of the early stage of human existence would remain underdeveloped or even cease to exist.

Milledoler's question about the dangers of close kin marriage was now answered. Morgan had responded with the idea that those groups in which individuals married solely within their kin group would not progress as well as those who married outside of their kin group. They would be left behind as the society evolved toward civilization or be eliminated in the struggle for survival. Morgan assumed that outbreeding increased the physical and intellectual development of human beings and that natural selection ensured the successful development of groups that practiced it. In this scheme marriage within the kin group represented an evolutionary danger. It threatened the physical and intellectual development of generations of individuals and the subsequent stultification of society at the stage of savagery.

Morgan's bioevolutionary view of human social development put much weight on human physical characteristics and biological inheritance. He even spoke of human thoughts and experiences being "handed down as transmitted systems, through the channels of the blood" (1871:vi; see also 4–13). Kinship, in particular, was primarily a matter of consanguineal relationships, and marriage was a secondary relationship, whose main function was to serve the natural order by continuing bloodlines and perpetuating the species (Morgan 1871:10). Schneider (1968) has pointed out that these views are common in American society today. For many Americans kinship is defined as a biogenetic relationship, with blood a distinctive feature of this relationship. Blood signifies the natural order of life. Marriage is a secondary relationship, based on law rather than blood (Schneider 1968:26–27). In this American kinship scheme, cousin marriage has become primarily an inbreeding mechanism rather than a social relationship. It is treated as a unitary phenomenon, with no reference to the social categories of descent. Cousin marriage is a biological matter, not a social one, and the difference between cross- and parallel-cousins, which is important in Morgan's distinction between exogamy and endogamy, is lost. All cousin marriages threaten the social progress of the United States. It is against the background of this view of cousin marriage that the laws in the United States prohibiting the marriage of first cousins were passed.

The supposed evolutionary danger of first cousin unions was widespread in the United States at the time Morgan published his work (Withington 1885:2–3). States prohibiting cousin marriage were thus doing more than simply preventing the production of unwanted offspring; they were protecting the foundation of modern civil life. The laws against cousin marriage in the United States are mythical symbols in a struggle to maintain civilization. They were enacted because of a belief that cousin marriage threatened the status of the United States as a civilized society, not because there was evidence of genetic risk to offspring.

Early in the last half of the nineteenth century the inheritability of traits began to be understood. It was already clear to some that the fundamental concern with cousin marriage went beyond the potential for undesirable characteristics in offspring. The *Westminister Review* (1863) criticized those who maintained that the danger in cousin marriage was a matter of inherited defects: "the fact remains that such defects or peculiarities, once acquired, are, as a rule, transmitted to the offspring; and if the writers of whom we are speaking had contented themselves with showing that the marriages of blood relations are more likely, *ceæteris paribus,* to produce unhealthy offspring than others where an hereditary taint exists, they would have made an assertion which, though neither very novel nor very interesting, could not well have been disputed" (94–95).

Herbert Spencer warned in 1851 that colonists become barbaric when living under aboriginal conditions: "The back settlers of America, amongst whom unavenged murderers, rifle duels and Lynch Law prevail—or, better still, the trappers, who leading a savage life have descended to savage habits, to scalping, and occasionally even to cannibalism—sufficiently exemplify it" (quoted in Peel 1972:20). Cousin marriage was another feature of savage life. If Americans were afraid of becoming savages or, at the very least, fearful of being viewed as savages (the lowest form of human life on the evolutionists' developmental stages) and if they were to avoid dropping into this lowest stage of human social development, they must not only bring the rule of law to the settlement of their disputes and cease cannibalistic behavior but also desist from marrying their cousins. This concern with becoming uncivilized and being seen as savages provided the major impetus to the passage of the laws against cousin marriage in the United States.

The passage of laws against cousin marriage in a number of states in the nineteenth and early twentieth century was one of several reactions to the fear that American society might degenerate. The eugenics movement sanctioned restricting the marriage of diseased individuals, and several states passed laws prohibiting individuals with various disorders from marrying for much the same reason (Ludmerer 1972; Kevles 1985). Another reaction was the prohibition of polygamy. In 1862 the U.S. Congress passed "An Act to Punish and Prevent the Practice of Polygamy in the Territories of the United States and Other Places, and Disapproving and Annulling Certain Acts of the Legislative Assembly of the Territory of Utah" (37th Cong., 2d sess., chap. 126). This act, specifically aimed at the practices of the Church of Jesus Christ of Latter-day Saints, was signed into law by President Lincoln, and monogamy became the only form of legal marriage in the United States. The ramifications of this legislation for Mormons and non-Mormons alike were immediately recognized. Opponents of the legislation protested that the ban against polygamy was a breach of the country's constitutional guarantees of personal and religious freedom. The law was enforced, and the cases were immediately appealed. The appeals went to the Supreme Court.

The Supreme Court upheld the right of the federal government to suppress polygamy in a series of cases beginning with *Reynolds v. United States* in 1878 (Grossberg 1985:123–26). In one case, *Maynard v. Hill* in 1888, the Court specifically noted its rationale for supporting the federal law and establishing the government's right to control marital relations and prohibit polygamy. The Supreme Court saw marriage as a cornerstone of civilization and a key to social progress that required protection by law: "[Marriage] is an institution, in the maintenance of which in its purity the public is deeply interested, for it is the foundation of the family and of society, without which there would be neither civilization nor progress. . . .

Marriage, as creating the most important relation in life, [has] more to do with the morals and civilization of a people than any other institution" (quoted in Chotiner 1974:29). In this context, the Court viewed polygamy as a barbaric practice, comparable with human sacrifice and prostitution, and feared it threatened civilization.

Since the Court considered polygamy a practice that threatened civilized society, all appeals were dismissed, the right of the government to outlaw polygamy was upheld, and monogamy was firmly established as the legal form of marriage in the United States. Not until 1946, over a half a century after the landmark cases, did a Supreme Court justice express a dissenting opinion. After World War II, Justice Frank Murphy disagreed with the majority opinion that polygamy was comparable with prostitution and expressed a modern social scientific view recognizing that polygyny is one of a number of legitimate forms of marriage rooted in the culture of the society in which it is found (Chotiner 1974:41; Glendon 1989:53). But this had little effect, and in spite of how faulty or biased the nineteenth-century Supreme Court's view of marriage appears now, the decisions affirming the constitutionality of the ban against polygamy still stand. Thus, even though the justification for the prohibition is no longer considered valid, the law still remains. This is also the case with the prohibition of first cousin marriage.

The emergence of a bioevolutionary framework in the United States for understanding human history put cousin marriage into the position of being a threat to the civilized status of the country. Laws forbidding first cousin marriage were thus passed to protect the status of American society. They are symbols of a bioevolutionary view of human social development in which inbreeding is assumed to be a condition of savagery.

6

Biogenetics and First Cousin Marriage

> Although directly contradicted by current scientific knowl-
> edge of genetic inheritance, common knowledge continues
> to teach that incestuous unions cause mentally and/or
> physically defective offspring.
>
> —Carolyn S. Bratt, *Incest Statutes*
> *and the Fundamental Right of*
> *Marriage: Is Oedipus Free to Marry?*

The American myth of cousin marriage, ingrained in the popular culture of the United States today, assumes that offspring of cousins will be defective and that the legislative prohibitions were passed to prevent the offspring from suffering and the society from degenerating. These ideas are "common knowledge" and are expressed in different ways (Bratt 1984:259). Record sales by the popular country musician Jerry Lee Lewis reportedly declined after he married his first cousin once removed in 1958 (Stephen Thompson, personal communication). In the film *Brighton Beach Memoirs* one of the protagonists exclaims, "You can't marry your first cousin, you get babies with nine heads!" When the French film *Cousin, Cousine* was remade for an American audience the relationship between the lead characters was changed. In *Cousins,* the American version of the film, the lovers are cousins-in-law rather than the first cousins of the original French version. A cartoon by Mike Smith ("Ratz") was published in the June 1994 *Memphis Entertainment Monthly* in which one rat tells a very stupid joke and then laughs loudly at it. Another replies to this obviously dumb behavior by asking the joke teller, "Are your mom and dad cousins?" The myth of cousin marriage can even be found in gardening magazines. The editor of *Organic Gardening,* Mike McGrath, described his garden bed as containing carrots whose pretty flowers "should attract the same bene-ficial insects as Queen Anne's lace because the two plants look like cous-ins close enough that they shouldn't marry" (McGrath 1993:5).

The myth about the dangers of cousins' marrying is often expressed in twentieth-century fiction (Anderson 1986:297). It can also be found in sec-ondary school textbooks. A high school biology text, for example, states, "Harmful, recessive genes may be brought together by inbreeding and thus be expressed. This is why close relatives are prohibited from marrying in most states" (Schraer and Stoltze 1983:430). Many readers will probably be able to recall the references in their school textbooks to European royalty marry-ing close kin and having serious physical problems. I can still recall that my high school textbook over thirty years ago contained a reference to hemo-philia among the ruling families of Europe as an example of the results of close marriages. Several people have also communicated to me this same linkage between hemophilia and cousin marriage among European royalty. Hemophilia, however, is the result of a sex-linked (X-linked, to be specific) recessive gene. If a gene is X-linked, the incidence among male descendants has nothing to do with inbreeding. As Levitan and Montagu (1977) put it, "The idea that hemophilia was prevalent in the royal houses of Europe as a result of so-called 'inbreeding' is, therefore, quite erroneous" (490).

Queen Victoria arranged for the marriage of four of her five daughters into different royal houses of Europe. She was a carrier of hemophilia, unfortunately, probably due to a mutation in one of her parents' genes. It became manifest in her eighth child and fourth son, Leopold, Duke of Al-bany, and in ten of her grandchildren and great-grandchildren. The best known of her affected descendants was her grandson Czarevitch Alexis, the son of the last tsar and tsarina of Russia, Nicholas II and Alexandra, and the brother of Anastasia. He received the gene through his mother. Because hemophilia is caused by a sex-linked recessive gene, females with the gene will normally simply be carriers. If they are married to a normal male, half of the male children will likely be hemophiliacs, and half of the females will be carriers. If a male hemophiliac marries a noncarrier woman, all of the daughters will be carriers, and none of the sons will be hemophiliacs. The disease thus manifested itself in a number of the royal houses of Eu-rope in which the children of Queen Victoria married. The disease would have occurred regardless of whether the rulers had married their cousins. The present royal family in England is free of the gene even though Queen Elizabeth married Prince Philip Mountbatten, Duke of Edinburgh, and they are slightly more closely related than third cousins.

In spite of the modern understanding that hemophilia is caused by a sex-linked gene, it seems that in American texts and minds the two separate issues of hemophilia and cousin marriage have become entwined. This mistaken relationship between inheritable diseases and kin marriage seems to obscure the number of cousin marriages in Europe that have resulted in healthy offspring. One case is the family of Charles Darwin. The famous evolutionist married his first cousin and had ten children, none of whom suffered from any unwanted inherited defects and a number of whom proved to be exceptional. This is rarely pointed out in American literature.

Anecdotal evidence, like that about European royalty, continues to justify the American myth of cousin marriage in the minds of many Americans and confirms for them an exaggerated threat from cousin marriage. They consequently uphold the idea that the prohibitory laws are necessary to protect those who would marry their cousins from the health hazards to their offspring. It is therefore not surprising to find that, in the words of Bratt (1984), "a commonly articulated state purpose for incest statutes is that they serve a hereditary-biological function in which the state has a legitimate interest. This function is based upon certain misconceptions of the hereditary process and unexamined attitudes reflecting negative eugenics theory entertained by legislators, jurists, and the public" (267).

Not all Americans have shared the misconceptions of cousin marriage, however. White (1949) pointed out that a danger in close breeding "is so plausible as to seem self-evident, but it is wrong for all that. In the first place, inbreeding as such does not cause degeneration; the testimony of biologists is conclusive on this point. To be sure, inbreeding intensifies the inheritance of traits, good or bad. If the offspring of a union of brother and sister are inferior it is because the parents were of inferior stock, not because they were brother and sister" (305). Similarly, some legislators have recognized the shortcomings of the popular explanation for the injunctions. In Illinois, for example, a legislative committee examined the state's criminal code concerning incest and looked into the possible genetic basis for the statutes. Members evidently were aware of modern genetic theory and research. "Thus, it appears," they wrote, "that genetics does not provide a very convincing scientific rationalization for broad ranging prohibitions against intra-family matings" (Illinois Annotated Statutes 1972, chap. 38, §11-11, Committee Comments).

The fear of cousin marriage now found in the United States did not originate during the nineteenth century. It is simply a modern expression of the millennia-old prejudice against close kin marriage. What was added to the age-old distaste of cousin marriage in the nineteenth century was a bioevolutionary theory and empirical research for evidence to support the prejudice.

In the United States during the nineteenth century, bioevolutionary theory rather than biblical exegesis became the dominant framework for marital legislation, and natural law became the foundation for the regulation of marriage. Lewis Henry Morgan's fundamental tenets that kin marriage is a form of inbreeding that represents a primeval period of human social history, results in less intelligent offspring, and had to be overcome for society to progress to a civilized state clearly expressed the widespread concern about the dangers of cousin marriage. Consanguineal marriage threatened the developing country's status as a civilized nation. Legislators quickly responded.

One empirical avenue to verify that offspring of cousin marriages would not be as intelligent or healthy as offspring of those parents who were not related and that societies with consanguineal marriage would devolve into savagery was undertaken through comparative analysis of worldwide social organizational data. It was assumed that isolated tribes had social practices from the oldest stages of human development or, at least, that their social organization allowed direct inference about the earliest type of human behavior. It was also believed this information would confirm that close consanguineal unions were a fact of early human social organization. This was never confirmed.

Morgan and other evolutionists had assumed that peoples furthest removed from the centers of Western civilization retained practices from the earliest times of human history and would therefore provide clear examples of primeval behavior. They expected to find endogamous marriages among peoples in the most remote areas of the world, but their investigation of the data did not confirm the evolutionists' belief that the marriage of close kin was a primeval marital practice. Instead, they uncovered a bewildering assortment of practices. Cousin marriage, in particular, proved far more complex than expected. Even the most rudimentary societies offered no consistent pattern. Some prohibited first cousin marriage, while others permitted it. Some distinguished between different types of cousins, permitting one type to marry yet prohibiting others. The data did not admit to any simple conclusions. Although the data did not indicate that early peoples married their close kin, the evolutionists were not deterred from their convictions. Sir James Frazer, for example, examined the published descriptions of North American Indian behavior and found only one clear case of marriage between first cousins. This did not lead him to re-consider his conviction that early peoples permitted the marriage of cousins, however. After discovering that a group did not have cousin marriage, he concluded that

> the case is so typical and it fits in so well, as we shall see presently, with the classificatory system of relationship which appears to be universally observed by the American Indian, that it is hardly rash to conjecture that such marriages are or were formerly very much commoner among the Indian tribes of America than appears from such a meagre record, and that they have only escaped observation because inquirers have not attended to the fundamental distinction between the classes of marriageable and not-marriageable cousins. Hence we may legitimately receive with distrust the statements even of otherwise competent observers as to the general prohibition of marriage between cousins in certain tribes. (Frazer 1919, 2:146–47)

This is a classic example of the sarcastic adage that if the data do not support your hypothesis, ignore the data. Frazer's rationalizing away the North American data demonstrates the power of culture in research. Frazer was certain that early peoples married their cousins and that the North American Indians would demonstrate this. Like Arthur Mitchell before him, who studied Scottish consanguineal marriages, Frazer found a way to justify disregarding the data when the empirical information not only did not confirm his belief but clearly contradicted it. He overcame the fact that the data did not support the idea that American Indians practiced cousin marriage by arguing their terminological systems indicated it had existed in the past. His belief in the primeval existence of cousin marriage thus remained intact.

Other attempts to verify empirically the supposition that kin marriage was a threat to human progress commenced during the nineteenth century in medical research. Genealogical and health studies of the period were undertaken to reveal what physical defects befell the offspring of cousins. A large number of empirical studies during the middle of the nineteenth century examined the pedigrees of people in institutions and under physicians' care. These data were biased, as noted above, and influenced the results of the work. But this was not the only problem with the nineteenth-century empirical research into the potential hazards of cousin marriage. Poor samples were used, data were collected with defective techniques, genetics was poorly understood, analytical methods were inadequate, and little attention was paid to the social and cultural factors that could affect the offspring of cousin marriages. All sorts of misfortunes were blamed on cousin marriages. What was attributed to consanguinity, however, could often be explained by a lack of access to adequate health services, poor living conditions, or other sociocultural factors, such as lower age at the marriage of first cousins. When Schull and Neel (1965) began their classic investigation of the effect of inbreeding on Japanese children after World War II, they found that "despite the great interest in consanguinity in the Western world down through the ages, . . . we have been unable to locate any publications containing reasonably valid statistics on mortality in relation to consanguinity in Caucasian populations prior to the twentieth century" (105). Recent research has been more careful, the data much more balanced, and the results more reliable.

The debates about the potential deleterious effects of cousin marriage in the nineteenth century may have heightened interest in the whole field of the inheritance of traits and contributed to the rediscovery of Mendelian genetics in 1900. Once Mendelian genetics was rediscovered, a new era began in the study of cousin marriage. Mendelian genetics offered a fresh understanding of the processes underlying the inheritance of traits and their possible effects on the offspring of cousin marriages. The consequent development of modern genetic theory, advances in statistical analysis, recognition of the involvement of sociocultural factors, and better data-gathering methods now meant considerable improvement in understanding the role of close kin relationships in the inheritable risks to health. Especially since the middle of this century the quality of scientific investigation into the potential consequences of cousin unions has significantly improved. Contemporary research has begun to draw a clear picture of the impact of inbreeding on the health and well-being of people around the world.

According to modern genetic theory, parental consanguinity can increase the risk of death for offspring. This increased risk is caused by two factors: (1) the existence of rare, recessive forms of a gene that in the homozygous condition can produce fatal results for the phenotype and (2) a distribution of these in a population that makes the offspring of related individuals more likely to be homozygous for them than the offspring of nonrelated individuals are. The various forms that genes at a specific locus may take are called *alleles,* and if there are no deleterious recessive alleles in a population, there will be no difference in the risk for the offspring of related parents and nonrelated or randomly selected parents. Likewise, if everyone in a population is heterozygous for the same recessive allele of a gene, then the difference in the probabilities for hymozygosity at the locus of the gene in the offspring of parents who are related and those randomly selected will also be zero. Neither of these extreme cases is likely in any sizable human population. But these examples do illustrate that the difference between the probabilities that the offspring of related parents and the offspring of nonrelated parents would have the recessive alleles of a gene at a locus is related to the distribution of the allele in the larger population to which the parents belong.

The probability that a child will be born homozygous for a rare, recessive form of a gene (a) is a function of the frequency (q) of that form of the gene in a population. For a given q, the probability that a person selected at random will have a at a locus is $2q$. The probability is twice the frequency since there normally will be two genes at a given locus and a can be either one or both. If the frequency of a is one in twenty, for example, then the probability that a person will have the gene at a locus is $2 \times \frac{1}{20} = \frac{1}{10}$ (10 percent). If the frequency is $\frac{1}{100}$ (1 percent), then the probability the person will have the gene at a locus is $\frac{1}{50}$ (2 percent). There is a simple relationship here. The less frequent the gene in the population, the less likely a person will have it. If two people chosen at random marry, then the chance that their child will be homozygous for the gene is $(2q)^2 \div 4$ (or q^2). The result, q^2, is derived from the probability for a parent ($2q$) multiplied by the other parent's probability times the chance that their offspring will be homozygous for the gene $\frac{1}{4}$. For a gene frequency of $\frac{1}{100}$, the probability that a random marriage will produce a child homozygous for the gene is thus $\frac{1}{10,000}$ (0.01 percent). Again, the relationship is a simple, direct one. The lower the frequency, the less the chance for homozygosity in the offspring of a random marriage.

If one parent is a carrier—that individual is heterozygous for the gene—and marries an unrelated individual, the chances their child will be homozygous for a recessive gene is one-fourth of $2q$. This results from the probability that the spouse will also carry the gene ($2q$), making it possible for the child to be homozygous and the odds it will inherit the recessive gene from each parent $\frac{1}{4}$. There are four possibilities for the genotype of a child. If both parents are carriers of a recessive form of a gene and each has the genotype Aa, for example (A representing the dominant form of the gene and a representing the recessive form), their child will have one of the following four possible combinations of genotype: AA, Aa, Aa, and aa. The probability that a child will be homozygous for a rare, recessive gene (aa) when the population frequency for the gene is $\frac{1}{100}$ is 0.5 percent ($\frac{1}{200}$, which is the result of $\frac{1}{4} \times 2 \times \frac{1}{100}$). If the individual heterozygous for a recessive gene has inherited it from a grandparent and marries a first cousin, the chance that their offspring will be homozygous increases to 3.125 percent ($\frac{1}{32}$). This probability derives from the $\frac{1}{8}$ chance that the spouse will also have inherited the gene from the common ancestor and the $\frac{1}{4}$ chance of homozygosity for their child ($\frac{1}{8} \times \frac{1}{4} = \frac{1}{32}$). Thus, if we assume the frequency for a to be $\frac{1}{100}$ in the general population and that one parent has inherited a from a grandparent, then the child of that person is 6.25 times more likely to be homozygous (aa) at the locus of the gene if the parents are first cousins than if the parents are not related (3.125 percent versus 0.5 percent).

If, however, it is assumed that the grandparents have the same opportunity as any other individuals in a given population to be carriers, then the probabilities for the offspring of cousins and those of randomly chosen parents change. The probability for the offspring of cousin marriage to be homozygous for a recessive form of a gene in this case is the sum of the probability that the child is homozygous because of inheritance from a common ancestor and the probability that the genes were inherited independent of the common ancestor. If the population frequency for the gene is again assumed to be $\frac{1}{100}$, then the probability that a child will be homozygous for the gene because it was inherited from one of the parents' common ancestors is 0.0625 percent ($\frac{1}{1,600}$, which equals the result of the probability of being homozygous because of inheritance [$\frac{1}{16}$] times the gene frequency [$\frac{1}{100}$]). Adding this to the probability that the cousins may have the same form of the gene but received it independently of their common ancestor ($\frac{1}{10,000}$), the overall probability of their offspring being homozygous in the genotype for a rare, recessive gene is $\frac{116}{160,000}$ (0.072 percent).

When the frequency of a recessive form of a gene in a population is small, the probability that a child will be homozygous for the gene will be relatively larger when the parents are first cousins than when they are not related. With a gene frequency of $\frac{1}{100}$, for example, if the parents are first cousins, the 0.00072 probability that a child will be homozygous for a recessive gene is approximately seven times as large as the $\frac{1}{10,000}$ (0.0001) chance that a random mating will produce a homozygous offspring. While the difference is relatively large, the probability that an offspring of first cousins will be homozygous for a recessive gene is still very small.

If the incidence of a recessive form of a gene in a population is large, $\frac{1}{20}$, for example, the expected percentage of homozygous progeny from first cousin marriages will be relatively large (26.5 percent), but the percentage from random marriages will also be large (25.0 percent). The difference between the two will therefore be small. In general, when the gene frequency is high, there is little difference between the frequency of homozygous offspring resulting from first cousin marriage and those from nonrelated marriages. When the gene frequency is small, the difference between the two cases is large, but the overall frequency of offspring that will be homozygous for the gene is small.

Another factor affecting the probability for recessive homozygosity in offspring is the closeness of the relationship between the parents. The probability that an offspring will have at a given locus two genes that are identical by descent is known as the coefficient of inbreeding (F). The greater the coefficient, the greater the probability that an offspring will be homozygous for a rare, recessive gene and the greater the probability that the individual will be at risk. (See table 5 for the coefficients for the offspring of different relatives.)

Guided by these theoretical considerations and by the knowledge that human populations have some frequency of recessive, deleterious genes lethal in the homozygous condition, studies over the past fifty years have examined populations with cousin marriages to determine if inbreeding produces significantly higher rates of mortality in the offspring of related parents than in those of unrelated parents. This research has provided the clearest evidence for the relationship between consanguinity and mortality, although the results have not always been internally consistent. Theoretical genetics leads one to expect a direct relationship between the risk of health dangers to the offspring of close consanguineous marriages and the coefficient of inbreeding. That is, the closer the parents are related, the greater the risk should be for the children. The data, however, have sometimes indicated the risk is greater for second or third cousins than for first cousins or first cousins once removed. This lack of internal consistency in the data has been noted for some time. Bemiss's tables (1858) showed a higher percentage of defective children for third cousins than for second and first cousins. While his data are clearly suspect for several reasons, including his methods of gathering evidence, this pattern has been repeated in carefully conducted modern studies. Schull and Neel (1965), for example, recorded the same results in their study of the consanguinity among the Japanese. A recent survey of thirty-one studies of consanguinity in marriage indicated that "offspring of first cousin once removed and second cousin marriages had median relative risks of 1.16 and 1.26, respectively" (Khoury et al. 1987:251; see also Jorde 1991:439). The increased

Table 5. Coefficient of Inbreeding (F)

Parental Relationship	F of Offspring
Parent-child	.5 (½)
Sibling	.25 (¼)
Grandparent-grandchild	.1250 (⅛)
Aunt/uncle–niece/nephew	.1250 (⅛)
First cousin	.0625 (1/16)
First cousin once removed	.0312 (1/32)
Second cousin	.0156 (1/64)

risk for the offspring of third cousins over second cousins and for second cousins over first cousins once removed does not conform to theoretical expectations and has been left unexplained. I will ignore this internal inconsistency here and simply point out that the overall results of modern research do conform to theoretical expectations.

A full-scale investigation of the potential genetic effects of the atomic bomb in Japan after World War II led to the first modern investigation of the impact of consanguinity on offspring. It was the first scientific large-scale attempt since the beginning of empirical explorations of the question a century earlier (Schull and Neel 1965:1). Recognizing the potential effects of socioeconomic factors, using sophisticated statistical techniques, having a good grasp of modern genetics, and making use of a large sample, investigators collected and analyzed data about Japanese women who had married their relatives. Since the early 1960s the percentage of consanguineal marriages in Japan has steadily declined, but prior to that time it had one of the highest frequencies of consanguineous marriages in the world (Imaizumi 1987). Schull and Neel (1965) estimated the overall percentage of first cousin marriages to be between 4 and 5 percent (11). Studying the effects of inbreeding on Japanese children from Nagasaki and Hiroshima, they examined 4,476 children of consanguineous parentage. This group was then compared with 4,817 children of unrelated parents in the cities. One conclusion of their study was that "the range of variation in regression values observed in Japan is readily compatible with the range of values set by recent studies on Caucasians, Indians, and Negroes. Thus, there is no convincing evidence that the effects of inbreeding on mortality differ in the major racial groups nor that these effects are large" (113).

The Atomic Energy Commission supported the Japanese study and a study of the offspring of consanguineal relationships in the Chicago area (Slatis et al. 1958). One hundred and nine first cousin marriages were located through records of dispensations offered by the Roman Catholic church. These were compared with 83 families in which the parents were not cousins but one of the spouses was related to at least one of the cousins of the 109 families. Both groups were found to have the same average number of offspring (2.3 children per fertile family), with no significant differences between the two groups in stillbirths and miscarriages. "Thus," as the Argonne National Laboratory reported (1957), "in contrast with what has generally been expected, there appears to be but little indication from these indices that there are genetic factors capable of affecting the fertility of consanguineous marriages or the viability of their offspring up to the time of live birth" (29).

In a study of the offspring of consanguineous couples in rural Sri Lanka, Reid (1976) found "no significant decrease in offspring viability" (144). He pointed out that studies of the impact of inbreeding on offspring revealed that "generally, though not always, the effects on birth rates and fetal loss have not been statistically significant" (139). Others have also found that first cousin marriage does not mean significant genetic risks. The *British Medical Journal* (1981) reported that "the risks to the children of father-daughter and brother-sister unions, in contrast to those of first-cousin marriages, seem unacceptable" (250). Thus, first cousin marriages do not appear to be as genetically dangerous as once feared. Mortality clearly does not appear to be the factor of two once thought to be the result of such unions (Newton Morton 1961:274).

The results of the most recent studies, where sociocultural factors are taken into consideration, generally agree with those from Japan. There is a measurable effect of consanguinity on prereproductive mortality (death before age twenty), but it is small. The survey of thirty-one studies of the effect of consanguinity on mortality mentioned above concluded that there is higher risk of prereproductive mortality with first cousin offspring than with the offspring of unrelated parents (by a factor of 1.4), but the "overall impact of inbreeding on prereproductive mortality is shown to be minor" (Khoury et al. 1987:252). "Even in areas with first cousin marriages in the range of 5–15 per cent," Khoury et al. (1987) point out, "only about 5 per cent or less of prereproductive mortality can be prevented by eliminating such practices" (258; see also Jorde 1991:439). Research recently undertaken in Pakistan indicated that "prereproductive mortality was significantly associated with the reported degree of inbreeding" (Bittles 1993:17), but there was an absence of socioeconomic controls to allow any definite conclusion that consanguinity was the cause of the increased mortality.

The fertility of the parents as well as the mortality of the offspring must be considered in evaluating the overall impact of consanguinity on the viability of offspring. Since the nineteenth century, population studies have generally reported a modest increase in fertility for the offspring of related parents. The greater fertility of these families may be because of the "lessened frequency of maternal-fetal antigenic incompatibility in consanguineous marriage" (Schull and Neel 1965:349). In cousin marriages the common ancestry of the couple may ensure better chemical compatibility between mother and child and therefore decrease the risk of a spontaneous abortion. It is also possible that the increased fertility is a compensation for the moderately increased mortality associated with cousin marriages.

Increased fertility in cousin marriages may also result from some of the social advantages that cousin marriage offers. The marriage of cousins can bring the wife into a household of familiar or related women who will provide her with support (Bittles et al. 1991:790). Consanguineal unions may also be undertaken at an earlier age than those between unrelated spouses. The earlier age of betrothal may account for the increased family size associated with cousin marriage, and, at the same time, it may be an important factor in the increased mortality and morbidity rates noted in cousin marriages in some areas of the world. Overall, when fertility and family size are taken into consideration, there is no measurable advantage or disadvantage to this type of marriage. In particular, when compared with marriages of nonrelatives, first cousin marriages do not result in any significant decrease in the number of a couple's offspring.

Besides mortality and family size, morbidity has also been used to measure the impact of consanguinity on offspring. It is difficult to assess the overall results of the research in this area because morbidity does not have an exact definition. Even when defined as the disease rate in a population, morbidity has included illnesses of considerable variation, with questionable diagnostic accuracy (Jorde 1991:439–40). When morbidity is restricted to congenital malformations, there does appear to be a significant risk associated with consanguinity in parents (Bittles et al. 1991:791). It should be pointed out that this risk is with inbreeding, not with first cousin marriage. While first cousin marriage implies consanguinity, the reverse is not true. This difference is important, especially for our purposes here, but it apparently is rarely made in the public's mind. For example, it is not uncommon for people in the United States to have heard about abnormalities among the Old Order Amish—for instance, the group has a relatively high number of cases of Ellis van Creveld syndrome, a form of dwarfism that is one of four suspected autosomal recessive genetic abnormalities appearing among them—but most do not realize that although they rarely marry outside of their group, the Amish do not marry their first cousins. The cause of the higher frequency of the disorders has been attributed to the founder effect and genetic drift. According to McKusick (1978), "A population derived from a small number of founders will be likely to have an unusually high frequency of the particular rare recessive genes carried by the founders . . . further enhanced by chance events subsumed by the term *drift*" (517).

A much higher than normal frequency of a rare bleeding disorder (von Willebrand disease) was discovered in the Åland Islands, a Finnish archipelago in the Baltic Sea. This autosomal dominant disorder occurs in one of the islands with a frequency of 20 percent, while it occurs only once in 20,000 individuals (0.005 percent) in larger European populations (O'Brien et al. 1988:477). Other genetic disorders that rarely appear elsewhere are also found in the islands. Since the islanders have relatively small and isolated communities, the high incidence of autosomal recessive disorders—taporetinal disease (an eye disorder) among others—was first suspected to be the result of inbreeding or, possibly, genetic drift. A recent and extensive study of inbreeding on Sottunga, one of the smaller, remote islands of the archipelago, revealed that "the high incidence of some autosomal recessive disorders in Sottunga is likely the result of founder effects and drift rather than nonrandom inbreeding" (O'Brien et al. 1988:485; see also Jorde et al. 1992:31).

Studies in Great Britain, Pakistan, Japan, Tristan da Cunha, and Canada have indicated there can be significant genetic risks to offspring in small, isolated communities. Small, inbred populations may have an increased number of genetic problems in their offspring, but this is more likely due to the founder effect and genetic drift than first cousin marriage. Unfortunately, as Harper and Roberts (1988) point out,

> There is a strong tendency to attribute any disorder seen in a member of an inbred community to the inbreeding that has occurred. But many inbred communities are small, have existed in isolation from other populations perhaps for a prolonged period, and other possible explanations for the occurrence of high frequencies of some disorders include enhanced drift that comes with small population size, the founder principle and subsequent expansion from a small group, possibly selection.

One needs to eliminate such variables before attributing the high frequency of disorders to consanguinity or inbreeding in a population as
a whole. (180)

The founder effect occurs when a population isolate is created by a
small group of people with one or more individuals carrying a specific gene.
Their descendants will have an unusually high frequency of that gene as a
result. In the case of the Amish, immigrant groups of as few as two hundred individuals founded isolated colonies in Pennsylvania. Some of these
individuals are suspected to have brought with them the genes for the four
autosomal recessive conditions found in high proportion among the Amish:
Ellis van Creveld syndrome, pyruvate kinase deficiency, cartilage-hair
hypoplasia, and Troyer syndrome. A small group can carry recessive genes
when leaving a larger population, with the result that there is a significant
difference between the frequency of the genes in the small group and the
frequency of these genes in the parent population. For example, 10,000
people with a frequency of 0.02 percent for a specific autosomal recessive
gene will have 200 genes in the population. If 200 people emigrate from
the original population and only 10 persons of the immigrant group carry
the gene (I am assuming heterozygosity), the change in frequency for the
parent population is small. The parent population would now have 9,800
people, 180 individuals with the gene, and a gene frequency of 0.018 percent. This is a small drop from the 0.02 percent of the original group.
However, the 200 immigrants with the 10 carriers of the gene would have
a frequency of 0.05 percent for the gene, more than two-and-one-half times
that of the parent population. If the migrating group has only 10 people
and 2 have the gene, the resulting difference in frequencies would be even
greater (over ten times larger). The new population with a markedly higher frequency of the gene would have a higher number of offspring with an
autosomal disorder than would the larger group from whence it came. This
difference may be maintained and even increased if the new group remains
isolated and geographically inbred. This may occur even if no one marries
a first cousin. As pointed out earlier, it is possible for groups with less than
a dozen people to reproduce without having unions between first cousins
or closer relatives. Groups may have an aversion to or taboo against first
cousin marriage and still have a relatively high incidence of autosomal
recessive disorders because of the founder effect and genetic drift. Conversely, recessive disorders may not be any more frequent in small groups
practicing first cousin marriage than it is in the larger population. It is not

the marriage of first cousins that is important for genetic concerns, it is the frequency of particular genes in the population and, for individuals, the likelihood that a couple will produce a child homozygous for a specific condition.

The founder effect can be responsible for an especially high frequency of a gene in a population in a number of ways. A small group of individuals who have left a larger population will not be the only one to feel its effect. In the Saguenay-Lac-Saint-Jean region of Quebec province there is an exceptionally high prevalence of a form of muscular dystrophy, myotonic dystrophy, which is an autosomal dominant disorder that has been associated with a founder effect (Veillette et al. 1992). Sociological analysis of the population suggests that the individuals affected may have experienced genetic isolation and increased the frequency of the disorder without having migrated. The affliction affects individuals' living conditions, which, in turn, affects spouse selection. People with the disorder tend to have a lower educational level, to be less well off economically, and to be residentially immobile. This places them in a separate social category, with lower chances of marrying out of the category. This illustrates that it is possible for a subgroup to have a higher proportion of a genopathy because of self-selection in the larger population.

The founder effect can also be a significant factor when a group faces a sudden decrease in population through disease or war. The present population of the Aland Islands can be traced back to the survivors of the Great Northern War in the beginning of the eighteenth century. The islands, inhabited for seven thousand years, were densely settled prior to 1721, when war reduced the population by approximately one-half (O'Brien et al. 1988:478).

Isolated populations, such as those on small, remote islands, have afforded an excellent opportunity for studies of medical genetics, and since Mitchell's study of Scottish islanders (see chapter 4) they have attracted interest as potential sources for determining the impact of inbreeding on offspring. Over the years anecdotal reports have attributed a variety of maladies in these isolated populations to close kin marriage. Only in recent genetic studies has it become clear that the rare, recessive disorders in isolated populations more often involve genetic drift and the founder effect than close kin marriages. Yet the public continues to believe that consanguinity, especially first cousin marriage, is the primary mechanism for genetic pathologies in small populations. Furthermore, this posited relationship in small, isolated groups is often mistakenly extended to general populations. As several human biologists have said:

Many general impressions as to the effects associated with inbreeding stem from studies conducted on population isolates and minorities. But even in the absence of preferential consanguinity, genes rare in large populations can increase to high frequency in small groups within a few generations, because of genetic drift in a breeding pool of restricted size. Representative examples of this phenomenon are Ellis van Creveld syndrome in the Amish and von Willebrand disease in the population of the Åland Islands. To extrapolate from these atypical groups, in which founder effect and genetic drift may be predominant, to continental populations is of questionable validity and little practical use. (Bittles et al. 1991:791)

Jorde (1991) points out that "at least a dozen studies of inbreeding and IQ have been published, and all indicate that the average IQs of the offspring of first-cousin mating are several points lower than those of matched controls" (440), but it is uncertain what these and other anthropometric studies mean in terms of human behavior and development. What is clear is that when the processes of genetic inheritance are utilized correctly, when the founder effect and genetic drift are recognized as potent factors in isolated breeding communities, and when sociocultural conditions are considered in evaluating the risks of consanguinity, modern research does not confirm the common notion that first cousin marriage represents a significant physical threat to the offspring. "Thus," according to Bittles and Makov (1988), "the overall conclusion must be that, with the exception of incest and families known to carry deleterious recessive mutants, the risks to the offspring of inbred unions generally are within the limits of acceptability" (164).

First cousin unions are certainly not the threat to civilization or the impediment to social progress put forth in the nineteenth century by such writers as Lewis Henry Morgan. Neither are they the horrendous health hazard imagined in American folklore. The real concern for couples who wish to marry and have children is not whether they are first cousins but whether their genetic history indicates a potential to produce offspring with congenital problems. Genetic tests and counseling can play an important role here. The high incidence of autosomal recessive diseases among Pakistani immigrants in Birmingham, England, is a clear example of the increased genetic risks to a small, inbreeding population. As Bundey (1992) puts it, "These incidences which are ten to twenty times those in Europeans must be due to the parental consanguinity which is often closer than first-cousin relationships" (152). The need for genetic counseling is especially important here, and people should be made aware of the risks they take when inheritable defects are known to exist in their family.

The laws against cousin marriage, however, do little to promote appropriate reactions to any latent genetic hazards and, in fact, may even be counterproductive in achieving genetic goals. They may hinder effective communication of the real concerns to potential parents. In the case of the Pakistani immigrants in Great Britain, for example, in spite of their many consanguineous relations and an excess of malformations and chronic handicaps, Darr and Modell (1988) warned against simply trying to prevent their kin marriages. The investigators recognized that it was necessary to provide adequate information and appropriate genetic counseling rather than simply impose an archaic prohibition against cousin marriage. They also warned that trying to impose a prohibition against cousin marriage can be detrimental to meeting fundamental cultural needs: "It is even more important to avoid giving inappropriate advice. Consanguineous marriage has important social functions, compared with which its genetic consequences are relatively minor, and attempts to discourage it systematically on genetic grounds would certainly do more harm than good" (189). For the immigrant Pakistani, the practice of marrying one's cousin was beneficial in providing extended support and friendship in an alien country, and its positive value outweighed its potential harm (Bundey 1992:153).

Biologists have recognized the importance of cultural factors in understanding inbreeding for some time (see, for example, Freire-Maia 1957: 127), but those concerned with human population genetics have only recently begun to pay serious attention to the cultural aspects of cousin marriage. Human biologists evaluating the risks or benefits of consanguinity now recognize that, along with an understanding of the genetic processes, "the social, cultural and economic benefits of consanguineous unions also need to be fully considered" (Bittles et al. 1991:793).

The results of a recent study of consanguinity in Finland pointed out that a large number of economic, demographic, and cultural factors influenced human breeding patterns. In fact, the investigators found the best predictors of first cousin marriage were cultural factors. The study concluded that specifically in regard to first cousin marriage "*cultural* factors such as ethnicity and social class are much more important factors than many of the more commonly studied variables such as population size, geographic distance, population density, and urban/rural residence" (Jorde and Pitkänen 1991:138).

Both the genetic and the cultural import of first cousin marriage must be grasped before the consequences of this form of union can be fully understood or any conclusion can be derived about whether legislation against it is warranted. Marriage is at the nexus between genetics and culture, and cousin marriage must be examined from both perspectives to provide a properly balanced evaluation. Modern genetic research indicates there is no basis to the fears about the disastrous consequences to offspring of cousins that produced the legislation against first cousin marriage in the United States. From a biological perspective, there appears to be no need to forbid the marriage of first cousins. But are there cultural factors that would support a prohibition?

7

Culture and Cousin Marriage

Why do many social scientists still pose cultural and genetic determinants of behavior adversatively when both theory and experiment affirm their complementarity?

—Ray H. Bixler, *Incest and Avoidance*
as a Function of Environment
and Heredity

Spuhler and Kluckhohn (1953) recognized two meanings in the concept of mating: the social and the biological. "Socially speaking, we may refer to *endogamic* mating, that is, to mating which occurs within the limits of a socially-defined category, such as a community, a clan, a caste, or a class. Biologically speaking, *inbreeding* refers to the mating of individuals with one or more common biological ancestors. Inbred individuals are offspring of genetic relatives and inbreeding is the mating of genetically related individuals" (Spuhler and Kluckhohn 1953:295). The distinction is important to understanding the contrast in European and American social evolutionary thought over the past century and a half, especially when comparing the writings of the two most influential evolutionists in the last century, Sir Edward Tylor and Lewis Henry Morgan.

The English anthropologist Sir Edward Tylor had interests and ideas that were similar to Lewis Henry Morgan's. Both were concerned with describing the nature of human social development over time and were innovative thinkers, combining ancient assumptions about the nature of marriage with contemporary evolutionary theory. Both accepted the time-honored idea that endogamy was a prominent feature of early human social life, both sought natural laws of human social development, and both saw exogamy as the pivotal mechanism of change. Exogamy, once simply the means for extending personal relationships—the view Saint Augustine expressed nearly two millennia earlier, which dominated thinking prior to the nineteenth century—became for Morgan and Tylor the crucial instrument of natural law and the key to understanding human social evolution. For both, exogamy was the mechanism by which humans developed beyond the primitive stage of animal-like behavior. But whereas Morgan understood exogamy as a mechanism for breeding more intelligent offspring, Tylor saw exogamy as a sociocultural mechanism. Each writer saw exogamy as operating in a different way to bring about human social evolution, and this difference sheds light on the reasons cousins have not been treated the same in American and European law. It also makes clear a bias in the analysis of cousin marriage.

Morgan characterized human social evolution by stages. The first, and lowest, stage was one in which humans had indiscriminate sexual relationships. This was followed by a second stage, in which there were endogamous marriages, and then the highest and latest stages of human history followed as a result of exogamy. In this view of social progress, outbreeding is the primary mechanism of social change. By improving the physical characteristics (especially intelligence) of offspring, it enabled individuals to create the technology that carried their group beyond the stages of savagery and barbarism. In this scheme marriage is a matter of breeding; reproduction is its primary function. Exogamy is desirable because it promotes improvement in the physical characteristics of offspring and, consequently, the progress of the society. Endogamy is undesirable because it does not increase the fitness of offspring and stultifies the evolution of the society. I will refer to this position in the following pages as the American view of marriage.

Contrasting sharply with the American view of marriage is Tylor's sociocultural analysis of the import of marrying out. His argument centered on marriage as a means to create intergroup alliances and the way these ties were the key to human social development. Exogamy was the mechanism that enabled groups of humans to survive in a hostile environment.

Tylor was uncertain, at first, whether anyone not versed in civil law could do justice to the subject of cousin marriage (Tylor 1878:279), but by the publication of his "On a Method of Investigating the Development of Institutions; Applied to Laws of Marriage and Descent" in 1889, he had developed a significant thesis on the topic. His ideas became extremely influential. They essentially outlined the basic principles several generations of social anthropologists used in the study of social organization.

Tylor believed that both endogamy and exogamy existed during the earliest periods of human social life. Early humans, he thought, originally lived in small groups and practiced both forms of marriage. Exogamy did not suddenly appear in a later stage of human history, as Morgan thought, but existed from the beginning of human existence and then developed as a key factor in the evolution of human societies when ecological conditions deteriorated. Cousin marriage was not a means for ensuring the perpetuation of bloodlines through mating related individuals (as it was for Morgan) but an exogamous mechanism for establishing intergroup alliances. Primeval groups that practiced cousin marriage in circumstances of scarcity enjoyed an important advantage over endogamous groups because exogamy could foster political interrelationships. This sociocultural aspect of marriage is the key to human social progress for Tylor. The notion that cousin marriage is a form of exogamy and that exogamy's principal function was to create intergroup alliances became the cornerstone of twentieth-century anthropological analysis of social structure.

Sir Edward Tylor had broadened McLennan's definitions of endogamy and exogamy beyond the descent group. Tylor defined endogamy in terms of marriage within the local group as well as the descent group. Similarly, exogamy meant marriage outside of the local group rather than simply outside the descent group. Thus, exogamy was an institution that could establish and maintain relationships between people in different localities. It therefore would play a central role in the development of humankind by helping groups survive in adverse environmental conditions. Societies were more likely to survive during periods of limited resources and intergroup conflict if exogamy had established intergroup alliances. In developing his thesis, Tylor alluded to a "maxim of Mohammed" that matrimonial alliances increase friendship, cited a passage from the Bible in which the exchange of daughters implied the mixing of two people into one to argue for the naturalness of marrying out, and referred to the concepts of "survival of the fittest" and "natural selection." Survival of the fittest was fundamental to Tylor's idea that exogamy was a means to effect human social change. He declared, "Again and again in the world's history, savage tribes must have had plainly before their minds the simple practical alternative between marrying-out and being killed out" (Tylor 1889:267). This phrase, well known among anthropologists, is a concise expression of Tylor's evolutionary view of marriage.

Tylor presumed that the earliest humans lived in a bountiful environment. In this Eden-like scenario, both endogamy and exogamy could be practiced with little risk. Living in small groups in this plentiful environment that had a low population density, humans had sufficient resources to maintain themselves. No conflicts arose between the small, independent groups since each human population was sufficiently sustained. All could easily survive, even those with endogamous marriages. During this early period of human society exogamy brought no special advantage. Over time, however, population increased, producing significant changes: "tribes begin to adjoin and press on one another and quarrel, [and] then the difference between marrying-in and marrying-out becomes patent" (Tylor 1889:267). Under the pressures of increased population, resources became limited, conflicts arose between tribes, and natural selection began to have an impact on human social development. Humans who married only within their group were politically weak relative to those who practiced exogamy. Marrying outside the group established intergroup alliances and consequently produced groups of expanded social and political complexity and power. These more powerful groups, through violent struggles brought about by the pressures on resources, eliminated the weaker, endogamous tribes or forced them to retreat into more hostile environments. A preference for exogamy or a rule prohibiting endogamy thus produced more complex societies and ensured their survival in the face of the process of natural selection.

A twentieth-century sociobiologist summarized Tylor's position this way: "Throughout history, alliances have been forged by arranging marriages between the offspring of different social networks. It works, because much as we might bicker with our in-laws, we are disinclined to make war against them" (Barash 1979:151). Tylor, however, recognized that marrying out did not necessarily mean violent conflicts between the groups would be prevented. He specifically mentioned cases where interclan strife and bloodshed were not ameliorated by intermarriage (1889:268), and he must have been well aware of the history of royal intermarriages in Europe. For ten generations of non-Catholic European royalty, for example, 29.9 percent of the marriages were between cousins (Fleming 1973:240–41). Yet there is no evidence that those political states with marriages between royal families had any fewer political and military conflicts than did those in which the royal families did not intermarry. Tylor realized that marrying out "cannot be claimed as absolutely preventing strife and bloodshed" (1889:268). He merely postulated that exogamy established alliances, thereby increasing chances for survival by lessening the probability of conflict between groups.

Tylor also recognized that exogamy was practiced most often between individuals from different segments of a society, such as clans or lineages, rather than between individuals from different societies. Most peoples are endogamous with respect to the larger group in which they hold membership—marrying within their tribe, for instance—and are exogamous solely with respect to a particular subgroup within the tribe. Matrimonial alliances thus served primarily as mechanisms of cohesion between subgroups in a population rather than as a means to create larger, intergroup alliances. "Still," Tylor maintained, "by binding together a whole community with ties of kinship and affinity, and especially by the peacemaking of the women who hold to one clan as sisters and to another as wives, it tends to keep down feuds and to heal them when they arise, so as at critical moments to hold together a tribe which under endogamous conditions would have split up" (1889:268). Exogamy served as the primary mechanism ensuring survival in a hostile environment by providing cohesion in a society composed of different subgroups through the activity of women.

Tylor considered cousin marriage a form of exogamy. Cousins were not treated as a unitary phenomenon, however. He distinguished between cross-cousins and parallel-cousins (see figure 3). Cross-cousin marriage is often an exogamous form of union. In a society with patrilineal descent groups, for example, if a man marries his father's brother's daughter, the marriage is endogamous. The marriage partners are from the same lineage. In contrast, marriage between a man and his mother's brother's daughter in the same society likely means the spouses are not from the same lineage. Likewise, if a group practices patrilocal residence, the daughter of a father's brother would be from the local group, while the daughter of a mother's brother would likely be from a different group. In either case, cross-cousin marriage could be between individuals of different groups, while the parallel-cousin marriage would be an intragroup one. Since the two types

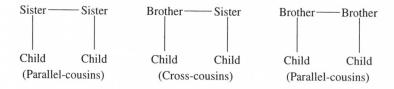

Figure 3. Parallel- and Cross-Cousins (Descendants of same-sex siblings are parallel-cousins. Descendants of opposite-sex siblings are cross-cousins.)

of marriage serve these different functions, they are treated differently by Tylor. Cross-cousin marriage played the essential and positive role as a mechanism for establishing intergroup alliances in the development of human society.

Tylor's fundamental tenets that exogamy is an important mechanism of social cohesion and that cross-cousin marriage is exogamous became widely accepted in anthropology by proponents of "alliance theory." His premises achieved their greatest prominence in the work of the French structural anthropologist Claude Lévi-Strauss. Lévi-Strauss's first major analytical work, *The Elementary Structures of Kinship,* published in French in 1949, was an attempt to demonstrate that human behavior is formally organized and explicable in terms of scientific laws. His analysis rested on the assumption that the incest taboo is the foundation of all human social behavior. Like most of the nineteenth-century evolutionists who had examined the social organization of non-Western peoples, he viewed the development of human social behavior in terms of a prohibition against unions with close relatives. For Lévi-Strauss it was the central feature of humanity, the foundation of cultural behavior. If this was the case, however, how could one explain that many societies exist today with cousin marriage? Since approximately 50 percent of contemporary societies permit cousin marriage (Pasternak 1976:68), how could a rule against sexual intercourse within the group be a universal mark of human culture? Lévi-Strauss responded to this critical question by contending that "the analysis of cross-cousin marriage [is] the crucial experiment for the problem of the incest prohibition" (Lévi-Strauss 1969:177). In his analysis of the marriage practices of non-Western societies Lévi-Strauss examined how cross-cousin marriage acted as a form of exogamy and thus explained how cousin marriage does not contradict the notion that the incest taboo is the basis of human cultural behavior.

In societies with unilineal descent reckoning, especially if one looks at the way marriage serves to maintain alliances between descent groups, cousins cannot be treated as a unitary group. One must distinguish between cross-cousins and parallel-cousins. Their marriages do not have the same structural organization with respect to intergroup alliances. A descent group is an association of people in which membership is determined by filial links to a common ancestor. In a patrilineal descent group an individual belongs to the group to which the father belongs. The father belongs to his father's group and so on. In a matrilineal descent group a person belongs to the group of one's mother, who belongs to her mother's group, and so on. In a double descent system a person may belong to both the father's group and mother's group. This is not the same as simple filial reckoning, in which one is considered related to all of one's ancestors. In double descent one does not belong to the descent group of one's father's mother or mother's father. They are in different groups. So are one's cross-cousins.

If you lived in a society with unilineal descent reckoning, the children of your father's brothers or the children of your mother's sisters (your parallel-cousins) belong to one of your unilineal descent groups. The children of your father's brothers belong to your patrilineal descent group, and those of your mother's sisters belong to your matrilineal descent group. But your cross-cousins, the children of your mother's brothers and the children of your father's sisters, do not. Thus, when you marry your cross-cousin, your marriage is exogamous. If the incest taboo applies to people only within the descent group, the consummation of your marriage to your cross-cousin would not violate the taboo.

Examining cross-cousin marriage in detail, Lévi-Strauss noticed that societies with marriage between a man and his mother's brother's daughter (matrilateral cross-cousin marriage) largely outnumbered those societies with marriage between a man and his father's sister's daughter (patrilateral cross-cousin marriage). He explained this quantitative difference in cross-cousin marriage types by the ability of a marriage system to produce solidarity of groups within a society. More societies have matrilateral cross-cousin marriage, he argued, because marriage with the mother's brother's daughter is a more efficient mechanism for creating and maintaining alliances between the exogamous groups of a society. The matrilateral cross-cousin marriage pattern is more efficient because it unites any number of subgroups of a generation within a society into a single integrated exchange system. Marriage between a man and his father's sister's daughter marriage, however, is not as eloquent; it shares some characteristics with simple exchange systems, which tend to maintain separate intermarrying subgroups in a society and thus can not serve to integrate the society as a whole.

While Lévi-Strauss, like Tylor, viewed marriage in terms of its ability to keep social units together, there is a significant difference between Lévi-Strauss and Tylor. In a subtle shift, Lévi-Strauss removed women from the central political role they had played for Tylor in the management of social cohesion. For Lévi-Strauss marriage is a social mechanism controlled by men. They trade sisters or daughters for wives as a means of establishing or maintaining group solidarity among different descent groups. Women are social goods, objects to be exchanged by men in establishing sociopolitical alliances. In much of this century's structuralist-functionalist's discussions of marriage, consequently, women have been pawns in a male game (Sacks 1979).

Denigrating women to mere exchange tokens to be used by men in structural manipulations of society does little justice to marriage. The failure to provide an appropriate place for women in sociomarital relationships is a serious drawback of Lévi-Strauss's approach to marriage. Another failure is its inability to pass the "truth test" of parallel-cousin marriage (Bourdieu 1977:30). Lévi-Strauss's analysis of marriage as a mechanism for establishing alliances across descent groups in a society has become a virtual paradigm for social science research, but it fails to explain parallel-cousin marriage.

Tylor's premise that marriage is a political mechanism, which Lévi-Strauss also used, emphasizes external relations in marriage and views exogamy positively. For Tylor it engendered human social evolution, and for Lévi-Strauss it established alliances promoting social cohesion. Endogamy, in contrast, is assumed to be dangerous to the social development or to the maintenance of a society. Consequently, Lévi-Strauss focused discussion of consanguineal marriage almost exclusively on cross-cousin marriage, which is exogamous. Endogamy and parallel-cousin marriage, however, are virtually ignored.

Lévi-Strauss (1969) defined endogamy as "the obligation to marry within an objectively defined group" (45), and he distinguished between two types: "true" and "functional" (45–46). The first type is "merely the refusal to recognize the possibility of marriage beyond the limits of the community" (46). It defines the group within which marriage is possible. Every society has some limit within which marriage is possible. Every society consequently has some form of "true" endogamy. The range of possible spouses may be defined as those people in the same religious group, ethnic group, or racial group. It may also simply be defined as those who are human. Functional endogamy, in contrast, is the practice whereby marriage occurs between potential spouses within a group defined by excluding everyone else from marriage. "It is only a function of exogamy, or the counterpart of a negative rule," he maintained (47). Functional endogamy occurs, for example, when people are expected to marry collateral relatives but not siblings, and parallel-cousins are classified as siblings. The parallel-cousins are therefore ineligible as marriage partners. This leaves cross-cousins as the only group from which marriage partners can be chosen. In this case cross-cousin marriage is a form of functional endogamy.

Lévi-Strauss's distinction between forms of endogamy is no more than a semantic maneuver that allows him to treat cross-cousin marriage as a form of endogamy. Thus, by investigating cross-cousin marriage, he can claim he is dealing with both endogamy and exogamy, and he can ignore parallel-cousin marriage. The distinction between true and functional endogamy has no other relevance to his analysis of marriage.

The premise that the primary purpose of marriage is to integrate different descent groups in a society is a limited one. In spite of Lévi-Strauss's semantic attempt to generalize cross-cousin marriage to both exogamy and endogamy, alliance theory fails to take into account parallel-cousin unions. It fails to account for societies in which members of the same descent group intermarry. Yet this is a prominent cultural feature for many peoples. Of 487 societies in which marriage data are available, 210 (43.12 percent) permit or prefer marriage between cousins. Of these 210 societies, 57 (27.14 percent) permit or prefer marriage with parallel-cousins (Pasternak 1976:68). In spite of this, Lévi-Strauss said nothing further about parallel-cousin marriage.

One of the most widespread types of endogamous marriage is the preferred union between a son and his father's brother's daughter. This is a significant feature of life in the Islamic world, and it is associated with patrilineal descent. Patrilateral parallel-cousin marriage in societies with patrilineal descent is not exogamous. It unites in marriage members of the same descent group. Furthermore, it normally occurs along with all forms of cousin marriage, each of which is also likely to be between partners from the same descent group (Ottenheimer 1986).

The theory that marriage is primarily an exogamous sociopolitical institution, while providing a rationale for those unions between members of different descent groups, ignores parallel-cousin marriage and does not explain systems of marriage in which people marry within their descent groups. It has been previously criticized as an inadequate explanation of cousin marriage (Bourdieu 1977; Dumont 1971; Ottenheimer 1986). Testimony to its failure is also provided by supposedly comprehensive discussions of systems of marriage in which structural analyses of cousin marriage are plentiful but omit any discussion of parallel-cousin marriage or data from societies with marriage between members of the same descent group (see, for example, Buchler and Selby 1968; Fox 1983; and Lévi-Strauss 1969).

Tylor's premises have attained the status of a general theory of marriage over the past century by disregarding those societies with marriages involving endogamy. In particular, the systematic marriage of cousins from the same descent group, usually parallel-cousin marriage, is ignored. When parallel-cousin and other endogamous marriages are included, alliance theory clearly fails to offer an adequate theory of marriage. An adequate theory of cousin marriage must account for both parallel- and cross-cousins. This can be achieved if social theory is willing to move beyond the ancient proposition that exogamy is the standard by which cousin marriage is to be measured. That is, it should be understood that cousin marriage should not be valued only insofar as it is exogamous.

For over a century, discussion of cousin marriage has been dominated by the tenets of either Morgan's or Tylor's writings. Although there are major differences between the two, both view endogamy negatively and exogamy positively. The American view of marriage treats cousin marriage as a singular entity that is a matter of inbreeding, and states have legislated against it. Since, in Morgan's terms, cousin marriage inhibits outbreeding, affects the well-being of offspring, and threatens the civilized status of the nation, it has been prohibited in a large majority of states. In contrast, Tylor's analytical distinction between cross- and parallel-cousin marriage and Lévi-Strauss's brilliant analysis of how cross-cousin marriage acts as an exogamous mechanism to create social unity enabled cousin marriage to continue to be valued in Europe. Europeans have a scientific rationale for allowing cousin marriage through a theory in which cousin marriage is exogamous and has made a positive contribution to society. But only by ignoring parallel-cousins has cousin marriage been viewed as an exogamous mechanism that functioned to create alliances, enhance social development, and maintain group cohesiveness. These beliefs, plus the fact that the scientific evidence has not supported the fears raised in the nineteenth century about the physical dangers to the offspring of cousin unions, are the reason no civil cousin marriage prohibitions exist today in Europe.

By comparing Morgan's bioevolutionary theory and Tylor's alliance theory of cousin marriage, we can see that their differences correspond to the pattern of laws concerning cousin marriage in the United States and Europe. In the United States prohibitions against cousins' marrying were instituted because cousin relationships were considered endogamous, thought to promote inbreeding, and believed to be evolutionarily dangerous. In Europe cousin marriage has been treated as exogamous, thought to provide political alliances or social solidarity, and considered evolutionarily advantageous. Although some evidence suggests that recently in Europe the idea of "natural kinship had been biologised" (Strathern 1992:19), it is unlikely that cousin marriage will be prohibited there anytime in the near future.

Neither Morgan's nor Tylor's approach, however, provides an adequate understanding of the phenomenon. The American view, with its fears about inbreeding, has not been substantiated by modern biological research. It also ignores the sociocultural dimension of cousin marriage. The European view, while in accordance with the results of modern genetic research, fails to take into account parallel-cousin marriage, a widespread and substantive form of endogamy. Both positions fail to provide an adequate understanding of cousin marriage. This is because both value cousin marriage only insofar as it seems to promote exogamy or outbreeding. I suggest that a fresh approach to understanding cousin marriage is necessary, one in which neither Morgan's breeding nor Tylor's alliances provides the framework for understanding cousin marriage.

An alternative to American bioevolutionary and European alliance theories of cousin marriage was proposed by Ottenheimer (1984). It approached the subject from a cultural, not a biological, point of view, but its analysis of the structural-functional aspects of marriage differed from alliance theory. Instead of assuming marriage is a mechanism for establishing alliances between groups, it treated marriage as a social contract that established family units within which cultural continuity is maintained. The family is viewed as the primary mechanism for transmitting key cultural information from generation to generation. Cousin marriage plays an important part in enculturation by ensuring cultural continuity. This approach recognizes that rules of cousin marriage in unilineal descent groups "foster *inbreeding,* not outbreeding," as Berghe (1981:649) pointed out.

By focusing on cultural continuity and seeing both endogamy and exogamy as advancing this end, this approach brings together Morgan's view that cousin marriage is a form of endogamy and Tylor's view that cousin marriage serves a useful purpose. At the same time, the pitfalls of Morgan's argument—that cousin marriage is a dangerous form of biological inbreeding—and of Tylor's argument—which ignores parallel-cousin marriage because it does not serve as an exchange mechanism creating alliances between groups—are avoided. Cousin marriage is viewed as a mechanism with positive functions that can be achieved by both endogamous and exogamous marriages. Both forms can structurally enhance the maintenance of cultural continuity.

Various authors over the past twenty centuries have decried the marriage of cousins for reducing the range of social relationships and for threatening societal development through isolation. The underlying supposition of these critics—that cousin marriage induces isolation or restricts relationships—has proven to be untrue. Tylor realized there were forms of cousin marriage that do not imply isolation, and Lévi-Strauss followed this insight with his exploration of the structural ways cross-cousin marriage operated to establish alliances between different descent groups. As a consequence, anthropologists today recognize that cross-cousin marriage in unilineal societies does not act as an isolating factor but as a means of creating connections between subgroups. Now it is important to go beyond Tylor's insight that certain forms of cousin marriage do not restrict intergroup relationships and to recognize that even when there is endogamy it does not follow that there will be social isolation. It is important to recognize that intergroup relationships are not simply dependent on marriage. Even when descent groups play no important role in a society or when parallel-cousin marriage is practiced, close kin marriage does not necessarily result in social or genetic isolation. Marriages within a group may lessen the number of affinal connections between that group and others, but there are many other ways for alliances between groups to be established: trade, exchanges, agreements, treaties, adoptions, and the like. The significance of cousin marriage as a mechanism for establishing alliances between groups has been questioned by others (Homans and Schneider 1955), and even the contention that exogamy establishes alliances between social units has been contradicted by the results of cross-cultural research (Kang 1979:272). But even if alliances between groups can be established or enhanced by marriage, that does not necessarily imply that endogamous marriage results in isolation. If there is endogamy, there are still other means available to establish alliances between groups. The notion that social interaction is simply a function of marriage connections is a gross oversimplification of social processes.

Another consideration that should be kept in mind about cousin marriage is that wherever and whenever it has occurred, the majority of the married couples in the society have not adopted it. It usually occurs only in a small minority of cases. In Islamic societies, for example, parallel-cousin marriage is highly valued and strongly promoted, but such marriages have rarely exceeded 20 percent (Dodd and Prothro 1985:133). One reason for this low percentage may have been the lack of potential spouses. Another may have been the expectation that only the eldest child should marry a preferred cousin, while the younger siblings are less constrained to have such spouses and can marry individuals who are not, or are only distantly, related. Whatever

the reason for the relatively small number of such marriages, one might conclude that the overall effect of introducing a rule prohibiting parallel-cousin
marriage would be hardly noticeable. Nonetheless, its impact would be felt,
perhaps directly only among the leading or ruling families of the group but
indirectly throughout the society.

The centuries-old discussions of cousin marriage have exaggerated the
negative effects of cousin marriage and have paid little attention to its advantages, although several positive aspects of cousin marriage have been
noted in the literature. Research has almost always been undertaken simply to discover the possible negative effects of consanguinity, even though
cousin marriage may lessen the risk of antigen factors (affecting the health
of the pregnant mother and her child), ensure compatibility between spouses (providing a benefit to a married couple in an alien environment), sup-
ply knowledge of the ancestry of the spouse (helping to avoid genetic risks),
and maintain the family estate (Bittles et al. 1991).

Only occasionally has the importance of the positive aspects of marrying within the group been taken into account. As discussed in chapter 6,
Darr and Modell (1988) recognized that cousin marriage provided extensive support and friendship to Pakistani couples in England. In spite of the
high incidence of genetic disorders among these immigrants, Darr and
Modell recommended against discouraging the Pakistani from marrying
their cousins because they feared that its prohibition would do more harm
than good. Darr and Modell are unusual in recognizing that a prohibition
against cousin marriage may have a profound negative effect on intragroup
relationships.

The importance of endogamy for enhancing cultural communication
between spouses, as Darr and Modell noted, should not be ignored, but
there is an even more important relationship in which cousin marriage
enhances cultural communication. That is the one between parents and
children. First cousin marriages are advantageous in both small, relatively
homogeneous societies and multicultural societies. In centers of communication and trade and in complex societies, parents not closely related are
less likely to share a set of similar cultural values than couples who are first
cousins. The marriage of cousins thus offers a significant advantage. Parents with a common set of cultural values are likely to be more effective
in transmitting a coherent set of cultural values to their children. Since
siblings learn their parents' values and transmit them to their children, if
these children are permitted to marry they can pass on their parents' and
grandparents' values to their children. If the parents are unrelated, there is

a greater probability that they will not share the same set of cultural values and that their children will not receive a coherent set of cultural traits. Marriage between cousins helps ensure the effective transmission of the culture of a group from generation to generation.

If cousin marriage serves to ensure cultural continuity, its prohibition can interfere with the process of cultural transmission. A prohibition may directly affect only a minority of members of the community, but it may have a large overall social impact. For one thing, it is not necessary for every married couple in a community to transmit the complete set of cultural values. What is essential is that a few key members of a community transmit a coherent set of values. The leaders of a community serve as paradigms, as models for others to emulate, or at least as symbols of the cultural values so that others may clearly understand what is expected of members of the culture. While individuals may deviate from the norm, they should at least understand what is expected of them. That is why it is more important for community leaders—royalty, the priesthood, or the wealthy—to follow the norm than it is for commoners. It is also why it is often more scandalous when community leaders fail to follow the expected patterns of behavior. Their behavior is a symbol, a paradigm, or a signpost of the culture, and when it disrupts or contradicts the expected norms of the society, it can be a significant threat to the culture. Likewise, an eldest child may be required or expected to follow the family traditions as an exemplar for the family, while younger siblings are under less pressure to do so and are given more latitude to explore options. If members of the royalty practice cousin marriage, they can maintain a coherent set of cultural values and serve as a model for the community. Even if they are only a small minority, the culture may be significantly affected if they are forbidden to marry their cousins. Although a prohibition may directly affect only the leaders of the community, it can disturb their cultural continuity and thus threaten the culture as a whole.

The transmission of a coherent set of values from one generation to the next is an important part of social life, and it provides a useful framework for analyzing cousin marriage. A prominent feature of social life throughout the world's cultures has been the division of labor by sex. Men have focused their activities on specific functions, while women have focused theirs on others. Specific tasks assigned to one or the other sex vary; almost every task performed by one in some society is performed by the other in a different society. This variation, however, does not alter the fact that societies have divided labor and assigned specific tasks to each sex. Training is accomplished efficiently by having the younger generation in contact with their same-sex elders. In societies with unilineal descent groups, the elder males of the descent group educate the younger men of the group, and the elder females of the descent group educate the younger women. The most efficient way for this to occur, of course, is by having members of the descent group reside together. When there is exogamy in marriage, this is partially accomplished simply in the society with a rule of residence. Patrilocality in societies with patrilineal descent ensures that males of different generations in the same descent group reside together. Similarly, amitalocality ensures that females from different generations of the same patrilineal descent group reside together. Matrilocality and avunculocality serve the same purpose in matrilineal societies. Vital roles are played by both men and women in many of these societies, and the division of labor by sex requires that both the men and the women of the descent group reside with their same-sex members from the younger generation for proper training. A residence rule, however, brings together only one or the other of the sexes. In matrilineal societies, for example, matrilocality brings only the females of the descent group together, while avunculocality brings only the males together. What is required is the simultaneous application of the two residence rules. This can be accomplished in a structured way and thus bring both males and females together through cousin marriage (Ottenheimer 1984).

The simplest way to have males and females of a descent group reside together is by endogamous marriages. In communities with endogamous marriages and unilineal descent, kinsmen and kinswomen are kept together simply by a rule of residence. In these cases, all forms of cousin marriage can serve the same function and can be expected to occur. Even when the dominant ideology calls for only parallel-cousin marriage, the other forms of cousin marriage are also found in these communities (Ottenheimer 1986:938). In a society with unilineal descent that does not permit endogamy, however, only certain forms of cousin marriage maintain the coresidence of same-sex descent group members. The coresidence of the males and of the females can be maintained by marriage between a man and his mother's brother's daughter. Matrilateral cross-cousin marriage combined with residence and descent rules of the society brings together the males of the descent group in one residence, and the females of the descent group also reside together (Ottenheimer 1984). For example, if a society with patrilineal descent groups follows a practice of patrilocality, the fathers and sons of each descent group will reside together. Adding marriage to the mother's brother's daughter to this combination of practices brings a woman of the same patrilineal descent group as her husband's mother into the household. A woman and her father's sister or, conversely, a woman and her brother's daughter are from the same descent group in a society with patrilineal descent. When a man marries his mother's brother's daughter and follows the practice of patrilocal residence, he brings his wife to his father's household, where his mother, of the same descent group as his wife's, also resides. Thus, after marriage a man will be living with his father and a woman with her father's sister. Both the husband and the wife will be living with members from the previous generation of their own unilineal descent group. Matrilateral cross-cousin marriage combines patrilocal and amitalocal rules of residence into one. (See figure 4.)

In societies with matrilineal descent, matrilateral cross-cousin marriage has the same effect on matrilocality and avunculocality. It allows both men and women of their own matrilineal descent group to reside together. At marriage, the bride is brought to the household of the groom's mother's brother. The husband and his uncle belong to the same matrilineal descent group, while the women—related as mother and daughter—are also members of a matrilineal descent unit (Ottenheimer 1984:356).

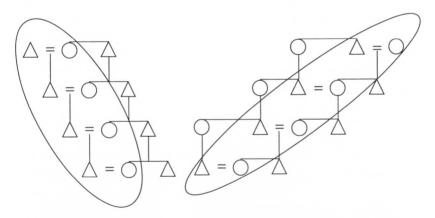

Simultaneous patrilocal and amitalocal residence. Both husbands and wives reside with their own patrilineage members.

Simultaneous matrilocal and avunculocal residence. Both husbands and wives reside with their own matrilineage members.

Figure 4. The Impact of Matrilateral Cross-Cousin Marriage

This analysis demonstrates how matrilateral cross-cousin marriage functions to bring males and females from different generations and the same unilineal descent groups together. With the division of labor in a society, this ensures effective transmission of the culture. The analysis also provides an alternative to Lévi-Strauss's explanation for the disproportionate number of societies with matrilateral, as opposed to patrilateral, cross-cousin marriage. Matrilateral cross-cousin marriage maintains the unity of the same-sex members of the descent group in societies with any number of descent groups. Patrilateral cross-cousin marriage does not. Thus, as a mechanism for the preservation of a culture, cousin marriage in societies with unilineal descent groups will be found in the form of matrilateral cross-cousin marriage when there is exogamy or primarily in the form of parallel-cousin marriage when there is endogamy. Both types of cousin marriage enhance enculturation.

Recognizing that endogamy serves a useful purpose in society and that cousin marriage enhances enculturation allows both parallel- and cross-cousin marriage to be seen as similar social mechanisms performing the same cultural function. They can both be seen as mechanisms for maintaining cultural continuity. Furthermore, first cousin marriage in societies with unilineal descent and exogamous prescriptions can be seen to serve the same purpose as first cousin marriage in societies without unilineal descent. The marriages in both cases serve the same essential function. They bring people with similar cultural values together in a domestic residence that can effectively preserve their culture over generations. Cousin marriage, whether it is endogamous or exogamous, can serve as a social mechanism that helps maintain a culture.

This new view of cousin marriage contrasts sharply with the American myth of cousin marriage. Cousin marriage is primarily seen as a sociocultural institution rather than as a breeding mechanism whose primary purpose is reproduction. Furthermore, cousin marriage is viewed as performing a positive social function in maintaining the culture over generations rather than threatening the development of the society by producing less fit offspring. It has moved the analysis of cousin marriage from the outdated evolutionary theories of the nineteenth century and the unsupported claims of biological risk that still linger in the folklore and law of American society.

Samuel Coleridge thought that the long duration of a belief "is at least proof of an adaption in it to some portion or other of the human mind; and if, on digging down to the root, we do not find, as is generally the case, some truth, we shall find some natural want or requirement of human nature which the doctrine in question is fitted to satisfy . . ." (quoted in Leavis 1980:100). Digging down to the root of the American myth of cousin marriage has revealed that the biological fears on which its legal expression is based are unsubstantiated. The fears of genetic and social dangers that gave rise to the laws in the United States against cousin marriage are not supported by either modern genetics or contemporary social science. Cousin marriage does not threaten the civilized status of a society by reducing the fitness of offspring. Although consanguineal mating does carry a degree of biological risk, this danger is nowhere near the perils supposed by the American myth of cousin marriage or feared by the evolutionists of the nineteenth century.

This biological, sociocultural, historical, and theoretical study of the forbidden relatives in American culture and law has made it clear that an ancient aversion to marriage between close consanguineal relatives emerged in U.S. civil law during the nineteenth century because of a myth. This myth—cousin marriage is a form of inbreeding that threatens the well-being of offspring and the civilized status of the country—led to the passage of laws against the marriage of first cousins in a majority of states. Thirty-one states still maintain injunctions against cousin marriage today in spite of the fact that empirical data do not support the need for any prohibition. In contrast, no European country has civil laws prohibiting cousin marriage. Europeans have viewed cousin marriage as a sociocultural institution that engendered social evolution through the formation of alliances. This European view, however, is rather limited. It is applicable only to cross-cousin marriage in unilineal societies with exogamy. The new view proposed here posits cousin marriage as a means of maintaining cultural continuity. This offers new insights and incorporates fresh developments in social research of kinship, law, and the family.

During the period in which the American myth of cousin marriage emerged—from the 1840s through the 1920s—most states passed their laws against the marriage of first cousins, just as the United States was witnessing large waves of immigrations. The new immigrants threatened the Anglo-Saxon cultural domination of the country (Mann 1979). Reactions to this threat included the virulent anti-Catholicism of the Know Nothing party of the 1850s, the emergence of the Anglo-Saxonist Ku Klux Klan, and the Johnson-Reed Act of 1924, which reduced immigration to a trickle and gave preferential treatment to northern Europeans, especially people from Northern Ireland and Britain. In the last quarter of the nineteenth century, in particular, a breed of Anglo-Saxonists emerged that saw immigration as a threat to the country's social progress. They sought to meet this threat through a process of assimilation or Americanization (Mann 1979:126–35). These Anglo-Saxonists called for the dissolution of the immigrants' cultures and an acceptance of the Anglo-Saxon language and customs to achieve cultural homogeneity in American life. Mann (1979) argues that this could be accomplished by encouraging intermarriage: "Intermarriage, by breaking up ethnic communities, would reinforce the already existing and 'one American nationality'"(130, citing Mayo-Smith 1890:53–78). The cultural analysis of cousin marriage presented here supports this thesis. Intermarriage and the breakdown of traditional culture are encouraged by laws against the marriage of cousins.

That laws against cousin marriage encourage the disruption of cultural tradition and continuity may also explain the spread of the prohibitions in medieval Europe. The Roman Catholic church spread cousin marriage prohibitions as it extended Christianity throughout pagan Europe. The prohibition might have been one of its mechanisms for combating the continuation of the traditional cultures. In the United States it was not a church that wished to make traditional cultures conform to a dominant religion but a dominant group that wanted to make immigrants conform to the dominant culture. Although religion was the specific target in Europe and the immigrants's language and nonreligious culture were the primary targets in the United States, in both cases the prohibitions against cousin marriage served these ends.

Contemporary marital law must also be critically examined in the context of the emerging variety of social relationships of today's society. The large number of adoptions in this country and the increasing use of the new reproductive technologies—artificial insemination, in vitro fertilization, and surrogacy—bring forth issues that did not exist when the laws prohibiting close kin marriage were first introduced. These issues now force one to question the propriety of the laws. Increasing numbers of children today do not know their biological fathers, and some do not even know their biological mothers. It is no longer unusual for a child or the sociological family not to know the child's biological ancestry. This has increased the possibility that individuals may meet, fall in love, and marry without being aware of their consanguineal relationship. In the United States individuals unaware of their close consanguineal ties can not marry under current laws prohibiting consanguinity in marriage without the threat that their marriage could be declared void or dissolved.

American marital laws are a potential disruptive factor in modern family life. They come into conflict with the desire to keep adopted children or children born through new reproductive technologies from knowing their direct genetic forebears. In California, for example, where one male may have provided some two hundred women with his genetic material through a sperm bank, the number of possible situations in which a couple may meet, fall in love, and marry although they are half siblings is clearly increasing. The growing use of sperm banks, plus the high number of adoptions in which the child's pedigree is unknown to the child or the new family, makes the problem more than simply a theoretical issue or an inconsequential matter in today's society.

In Scotland the Human Fertilisation and Embryology Act of 1990 defined the mother of a child as the woman who carried it, irrespective of a genetic link. This has made it possible legally to ignore the relationship between a male child and his genetic mother in the matter of mating. As Mcknorrie (1992) puts it, "So a male born to one woman can legally have sexual intercourse, as fecund as he pleases, with his genetic mother" (218). European laws, in general, reflect an understanding of the sociocultural nature of marriage and the family and modern genetics. European countries have recognized that "current knowledge of genetic inheritance does not justify the persistence of incest statutes in contemporary society" (Bratt 1984:281) and have taken the lead in modernizing their marital and incest codes. Throughout the Continent, the range of injunctions against the marriage of relatives has been reduced, and the laws on incest have correspondingly changed. Glendon (1989) points out that "Sweden, in reaction to a case which had aroused wide public sympathy, changed its law in the 1970s to provide that the marriage prohibition between half-brother and sister could be dispensed" (57). She also notes that France has "eliminated the crime of incest as such and now penalizes only those sexual relations between relatives that involve a person who, by virtue of his position with respect to the minor, is in a position to abuse his or her authority" (58).

We should not, however, overlook the fact that there is a risk, albeit minimal, to the offspring of close consanguineal relatives because of the possibility of homozygosity of detrimental recessive genes. Cousins wishing to marry should have genetic counseling (see Reilly 1977 for a cogent discussion of the issue). The crucial factor, however, is the couple's genetic history, not an archaic concern with the marriage of close kin. Maine acted wisely in 1987 in permitting cousins who have had genetic counseling to marry. As environmental factors influencing health become better controlled and the proportion of health problems due to genetic factors rises, it will be even more prudent for potential marriage partners to obtain genetic counseling and become aware of any potential risks. Forbidding cousin marriage works against this by providing a false sense of security and camouflaging the real issue that genes can be lethal or produce debilitating effects in offspring.

We should be concerned with the real issues of the transmission of genetic material and have laws that reflect a modern understanding of biological and cultural inheritance and evolution. The new sociocultural analysis of cousin marriage presented here, the recognition of the potential benefits of endogamy, the symbolic nature of the prohibitions against first cousin marriage, and the results of recent scientific research into the potential physical dangers to the offspring of cousins that recognizes the risk has been much exaggerated (Bittles and Makov 1988) suggest that the laws against the marriage of first cousins in the United States should be reconsidered. They symbolize an archaic view of the sociocultural aspects of marriage, reflect mistaken notions about the genetic impact of consanguineal marriage, and work against society's best interests. The prohibitions against cousin marriage appear to be counterproductive. Unfortunately, the American myth of cousin marriage is deeply ingrained in the United States. Changing the laws will therefore not be easy. It is a challenge requiring vision beyond the myth.

Bibliography

Adam, William. 1865. "Consanguinity in Marriage." *Fortnightly Review* 2:710–30; 3:74–88.

Allen, Nathan. 1869. "The Intermarriage of Relations." *Quarterly Journal of Psychological Medicine and Medical Jurisprudence* 3(1):244–97.

Alleyne, John. [1775] 1985. *The Legal Degrees of Marriage Stated and Considered, in a Series of Letters to a Friend.* Reprint. New York: Garland.

Alström, Carl Henry. 1958. "First-Cousin Marriages in Sweden 1750–1844 and a Study of the Population Movement in Some Swedish Subpopulations from the Genetic-Statistical Viewpoint." *Acta genetica et statistica medica* 8:295–369.

Anderson, Nancy Fix. 1982. "The 'Marriage with a Deceased Wife's Sister Bill' Controversy: Incest Anxiety and the Defense of Family Purity in Victorian England." *Journal of British Studies* 21(2):67–86.

———. 1986. "Cousin Marriage in Victorian England." *Journal of Family History* 11(3):285–301.

Argonne National Laboratory. 1957. "Recessive Genes in Man." In *Argonne National Laboratory Annual Report,* 29–30. Lemont: Argonne National Laboratory.

Arner, George B. Louis. 1908. "Consanguineous Marriages in the American Population." In *Studies in History Economics and Public Law.* vol. 31, ed. Faculty of Political Science of Columbia University, 347–440. New York: Columbia University.

Augustine, Saint. [c. 420] 1950. *The City of God.* Translated by M. Dods. New York: Random House.

Bachofen, Johann Jakob. 1861. *Das Mutterrecht.* Basel: Benno Schwabe.

Barash, David. 1979. *The Whisperings Within.* New York: Harper and Row.

Barton, Chris. 1987. "Incest and the Prohibited Degrees." *New Law Journal* 137:502–4.

Beckstrom, John H. 1985. *Sociobiology and the Law.* Urbana: University of Illinois Press.

Bell, John. 1859. "The Effects of the Consanguinity of Parents upon the Mental

Constitution of the Offspring." *Boston Medical and Surgical Journal* 60:473–84.

Bemiss, S. M. 1857. "On Marriages of Consanguinity." *Journal of Psychological Medicine and Mental Pathology* 10:369–79 (originally published in the *North American Medico-Chirurgical Review,* January 1857).

———. 1858. "Report on the Influence of Marriages of Consanguinity upon Offspring." *Transactions of the American Medical Association* 11:319–425.

Berghe, Pierre van den. 1981. "Comment on Bisler's Incest Avoidance as a Function of Environment *and* Heredity." *Current Anthropology* 22(6):649.

Bishop, Joel. 1852. *Commentaries on the Law of Marriage and Divorce.* Boston: Little, Brown.

Bittles, Alan H. 1993. "Preferential Inbreeding in Major Populations and Immigrant Communities." Paper presented at the Annual Meeting of the American Association for the Advancement of Science, Boston.

Bittles, A. H., J. M. Coble, and N. Appaji Rao. 1993. "Trends in Consanguineous Marriage in Karnataka, South India, 1980–89." *Journal of Biosocial Science* 25:111–16.

Bittles, A. H., and E. Makov. 1988. "Inbreeding in Human Populations: An Assessment of the Costs." In *Human Mating Patterns,* ed. C. G. N. Mascie-Taylor and A. J. Boyce, 153–67. Cambridge: Cambridge University Press.

Bittles, Alan H., William M. Mason, Jennifer Greene, and N. Appaji Rao. 1991. "Reproductive Behavior and Health in Consanguineous Marriages." *Science* 252:789–94.

Bittles, A. H., and D. F. Roberts, eds. 1992. *Minority Populations.* Proceedings of the Twenty-Seventh Annual Symposium of the Galton Institute, London, 1990. London: Macmillan.

Bixler, Ray H. 1982. "Sibling Incest in the Royal Families of Egypt, Peru, and Hawaii." *Journal of Sex Research* 18:264–81.

Blackstone, William. 1750. *An Essay on Collateral Consanguinity.* London: W. Owen

Bloom, S. S. 1881. *Popular Edition of the Laws of Ohio.* Cincinnati: Robert Clarke.

Bouchard, Constance B. 1981. "Consanguinity and Noble Marriages in the Tenth and Eleventh Centuries." *Speculum* 56:268–87.

Bourdieu, Pierre. 1977. *Outline of a Theory of Practice.* Translated by Richard Nice. Cambridge: Cambridge University Press.

Bramwell, George William Wilshire. 1886. "Marriage with a Deceased Wife's Sister." *Nineteenth Century* 20(115):403–15.

Bratt, Carolyn S. 1984. "Incest Statutes and the Fundamental Right of Marriage: Is Oedipus Free to Marry?" *Family Law Quarterly* 18:257–309.

British Medical Journal. 1981. "Children Born as a Result of Incest." 282:250.

Brooks, C. 1856. "Laws of Reproduction, Considered with Particular Reference to the Intermarriage of First-Cousins." In *Proceedings of the American Association for the Advancement of Science,* 236–46. Cambridge, Mass.: Lovering.

Brundage, James A. 1987. *Law, Sex, and Christian Society in Medieval Europe.* Chicago: University of Chicago Press.

Buchler, Ira R., and Henry A. Selby. 1968. *Kinship and Social Organization.* New York: Macmillan.

Buck, Trevor. 1987. "The Marriage (Prohibited Degrees of Relationship) Act 1986." *New Law Journal* 17:68–70.

Bundey, Sarah. 1992. "A Prospective Study on the Health of Birmingham Babies in Different Ethnic Groups: Interim Findings." In *Minority Populations,* ed. A. H. Bittles and D. F. Roberts, 143–55. London: Macmillan.

Calhoun, Arthur W. [1917] 1960. *A Social History of the American Family.* 3 vols. New York: Barnes and Noble.

Carneiro, Robert L., ed. 1967. *The Evolution of Society.* Chicago: University of Chicago Press.

Censer, Jane Jurner. 1984. *North Carolina Planters and Their Children, 1800–1860.* Baton Rouge: Louisiana State University Press.

Černy, Jaroslav. 1954. "Consanguineous Marriages in Pharaonic Egypt." *Journal of Egyptian Archaeology* 40:23–29.

Chase, Salmon P., ed. 1833. *The Statutes of Ohio and of the Northwestern Territory, Adopted or Enacted from 1788 to 1833 Inclusive.* Cincinnati: Corey and Farbank.

Chavez, Fray Angelico. 1982. "New Mexico Roots: Diligencias Matrimoniales (Pre-Nuptial Investigations 1678–1869) of the Archives of the Archdiocese of Santa Fe." History Library, Museum of New Mexico, Santa Fe.

Chester, Robert, and Martin Parry. 1983. "Reform of the Prohibitions on Marriage of Related Persons." *New Law Journal* 13:237–42.

Child, Gilbert W. 1862. "On Marriages of Consanguinity." *British and Foreign Medico-Chirurgical Review* 461–71.

Chotiner, Renee D. 1974. *Marriage and the Supreme Court.* Law and Women Series, No. 2. Washington, D.C.: Today Publications and New Service.

Clark, Homer H., Jr. 1968. *The Law of Domestic Relations in the United States.* St. Paul, Minn.: West Publishing.

Clarke, Helen I. 1957. *Social Legislation.* 2d ed. New York: Appleton-Century-Crofts.

Clericus. 1827. *Reasons in Favour of the Erasure of the Law Which Forbids a Man to Marry His Deceased Wife's Sister: In a Second Letter to a Clergyman of the Reformed Dutch Church.* New York: G. and C. Carvill.

Commission Appointed by the Archbishop of Canterbury. 1940. *Kindred and*

Affinity as Impediments to Marriage. London: Society for Promoting Christian Knowledge.

Commissioners on Uniform State Laws. 1970. *Handbook of the National Conference of Commissioners on Uniform State Laws and Proceedings.* Baltimore: Port City Press.

Cooke, Parsons. 1842. *The Marriage Question; or the Lawfulness of Marrying the Sister of a Deceased Wife, Considered.* Boston: Samuel N. Dickinson.

Crossman, Edward. 1861. "On Intermarriage of Relations as a Cause of Degeneracy of Offspring." *British Medical Journal* 1:401–2.

Danby, H. 1940. "The Scriptural Background." Appendix 4 in *Kindred and Affinity as Impediments to Marriage.* London: Society for Promoting Christian Knowledge.

Darlington, C. D. 1958. "Cousin Marriages." *Triangle* 3:277–80.

———. 1960. "Cousin Marriage and the Evolution of the Breeding System in Man." *Heredity* 14(3,4):297–332.

Darr, A., and B. Modell. 1988. "The Frequency of Consanguineous Marriage among British Pakistanis." *Journal of Medical Genetics* 25(3):186–90.

Darwin, Charles. [1874] 1901. *The Descent of Man.* Rev. ed. 2 vols. Reprint. New York: P. F. Collier and Son.

———. 1877a. *The Effects of Cross and Self Fertilization in the Vegetable Kingdom.* New York: Appleton.

———. 1877b. *Various Contrivances by Which Orchids Are Fertilized.* 2d ed. New York: Appleton.

Darwin, George H. 1875. "Marriages between First Cousins in England and Their Effects." *Journal of the Statistical Society of London* 38(2):153–82.

Davis, Natalie. 1985. "Review of *The Development of the Family and Marriage in Europe,* by Jack Goody." *American Ethnologist* 12:149–51.

Dodd, Peter C., and E. Terry Prothro. 1985. "Comment on FBD Marriage." *American Anthropologist* 87:133–35.

Domesticus. 1827. *The Doctrine of Incest Stated, with an Examination of the Question, Whether a Man May Marry His Deceased Wife's Sister, in a Letter to a Clergyman of the Presbyterian Church.* 2d ed. New York: G. and C. Carvill.

Dominguez, Virginia R. 1986. *White by Definition.* New Brunswick, N.J.: Rutgers University Press.

Duby, Georges. 1978. *Medieval Marriage.* Baltimore: Johns Hopkins University Press.

———. 1983. *The Knight, the Lady, and the Priest.* New York: Pantheon Books.

Dugard, Samuel. 1673. *The Marriages of Cousin Germans, Vindicated from the Censures of Unlawfullnesse, and Inexpediency.* Oxford: Thomas Bowman.

Dumont, Louis. 1971. *Introduction à deux théories d'anthropologie sociale.* Paris: Mouton.

Ember, Melvin, and Carol R. Ember. 1983. *Marriage, Family, and Kinship: Comparative Studies of Social Organization.* New Haven, Conn.: HRAF Press.

Esmein, A. [1891] 1968. *Le mariage en droit canonique.* 2 vols. Reprint. New York: Burt Franklin.

Farber, Bernard. 1968. *Comparative Kinship Systems.* New York: John Wiley and Sons.

Farrow, Michael G., and Richard C. Juberg. 1969. "Genetics and Laws Prohibiting Marriage in the United States." *Journal of the American Medical Association* 209(4):534–38.

Fleming, Patricia H. 1973. "The Politics of Marriage among Non-Catholic European Royalty." *Current Anthropology* 14(3):231–49.

Forte, A. D. M. 1984. "Some Aspects of the Law of Marriage in Scotland: 1500–1700." In *Marriage and Property,* ed. Elizabeth M. Craik, 104–18. Aberdeen: Aberdeen University Press.

Fox, Robin. 1983. *Kinship and Marriage.* 2d ed. Cambridge: Cambridge University Press.

Fraccaro, Marco. 1957. "Consanguineous Marriages in Italy: A Note." *Eugenics Quarterly* 4(1):36–39.

Frazer, James George. 1919. *Folk-Lore in the Old Testament.* 3 vols. London: Macmillan.

Freire-Maia, Newton. 1957. "Inbreeding Levels in Different Countries." *Eugenics Quarterly* 4(3):127–38.

Frost, J. William. 1973. *The Quaker Family in Colonial America.* New York: St. Martin's Press.

Fry, John. 1756. *The Case of Marriages between Near Kindred.* London: J. Whiston and B. White.

Fustel de Coulanges, Numa Denis. [1864] 1980. *The Ancient City.* Translated by Willard Small. Baltimore: Johns Hopkins University Press.

Gardner, James. 1861. "On Intermarriage of Relations as the Cause of Degeneracy of Offspring." *British Medical Journal* 1:290–91.

Gies, Frances, and Joseph Gies. 1987. *Marriage and the Family in the Middle Ages.* New York: Harper and Row.

Gilman, Charles. 1869. "Bonham et al. v. Badgley et al." In *Reports of Cases Argued and Determined in the Supreme Court of the State of Illinois,* vol. 7, 622–28. St. Louis: W. J. Gilbert.

Glendon, Mary Ann. 1989. *The Transformation of Family Law: State, Law, and Family in the United States and Western Europe.* Chicago: University of Chicago Press.

Goody, Jack. 1962. *Death, Property and the Ancestors.* Stanford, Calif.: Stanford University Press.

———. 1983. *The Development of the Family and Marriage in Europe.* Cambridge: Cambridge University Press.

Gough, Robert J. 1989. "Close-Kin Marriage and Upper-Class Formation in Late-Eighteenth-Century Philadelphia." *Journal of Family History* 14(2):119–36.

Green, M. M. 1975. *Human Genetics Notes.* Reading, Mass.: Addison-Wesley.

Grossberg, Michael. 1985. *Governing the Hearth.* Chapel Hill: University of North Carolina Press.

Group Appointed by the Archbishop of Canterbury. 1984. *No Just Cause.* London: CIO Publishing.

Hafen, Bruce C. 1983. "The Constitutional Status of Marriage, Kinship, and Sexual Privacy—Balancing the Individual and Social Interests." *Michigan Law Review* 81:463.

Hall, Peter Dobkin. 1977. "Family Structure and Economic Organization: Massachusetts Merchants, 1700–1850." In *Family and Kin in Urban Communities, 1700–1930,* ed. Tamara K. Hareven, 39–61. New York: New Viewpoints.

———. 1978. "Marital Selection and Business in Massachusetts Families, 1700–1900." In *The American Family in Socio-Historical Perspective,* ed. Michael Gordon, 101–14. New York: St. Martin's Press.

Hammick, James T. 1887. *The Marriage Law of England.* 2d ed. London: Shaw and Sons.

Hammond, David T., and Charles E. Jackson. 1958. "Consanguinity in a Midwestern United States Isolate." *American Journal of Human Genetics* 10(1):61–63.

Harper, P., and D. F. Roberts. 1988. "Mating Patterns and Genetic Disease." In *Human Mating Patterns,* ed. C. G. N. Mascie-Taylor and A. J. Boyce, 169–81. Cambridge: Cambridge University Press.

Herlihy, David. 1985. *Medieval Households.* Cambridge, Mass.: Harvard University Press.

———. 1990. "Making Sense of Incest: Women and the Marriage Rules of the Early Middle Ages." In *Law, Custom, and the Social Fabric in Medieval Europe,* ed. B. S. Bachrach and D. Nicholas, 1–16. Kalamazoo, Mich.: Medieval Institute Publications.

Homans, George, and David Schneider. 1955. *Marriage, Authority and Final Causes.* New York: Free Press.

Hopkins, Keith. 1980. "Brother-Sister Marriage in Roman Egypt." *Comparative Studies in Society and History* 22(3):303–54.

Howard, G. E. 1904. *A History of Matrimonial Institutions.* 3 vols. Chicago: University of Chicago Press.

Huth, Alfred H. 1875. *The Marriage of Near Kin.* London: J. and A. Churchill.

Imaizumi, Yoko. 1987. "Reasons for Consanguineous Marriages in Japan." *Journal of Biosocial Science* 19:97–106.

Indovina, Frank J., and John E. Dalton. 1945. *Statutes of All States and Terri-*

tories on Marriage, Annulment, Divorce (with 1956 supplement). Santa Monica: Law Publishing.

Ingram, Martin. 1988. *Church Courts, Sex and Marriage in England, 1570–1640.* Cambridge: Cambridge University Press.

Jevons, Frank Byron, ed. 1892. *Plutarch's Romane Questions.* London: David Nutt.

Johnstoun, James. [1734] 1985. *A Juridical Dissertation concerning the Scripture Doctrine of Marriage Contracts, and the Marriages of Cousin-Germans.* Reprint. New York: Garland.

Jorde, L. B. 1991. "Inbreeding in Human Populations." In the *Encyclopedia of Human Biology,* vol. 4, 431–41.

Jorde, L. B., and K. J. Pitkänen. 1991. "Inbreeding in Finland." *American Journal of Physical Anthropology* 84:127–38.

Jorde, L. B., K. J. Pitkänen, E. O'Brien, and A. W. Eriksson. 1992. "Consanguinity and Genetic Disease in Finland's Swedish-Speaking Minority." In *Minority Populations,* ed. A. H. Bittles and D. F. Roberts, 14–34. London: Macmillan.

Kang, Gay Elizabeth. 1979. "The Nature of Exogamy in Relation to Cross-Allegiance/Alliance of Social Units." *Behavior Science Research* 14:255–76.

Kent, James. 1848. *Commentaries on American Law.* Vol. 2. New York: William Kent.

Kevles, D. J. 1985. *In the Name of Eugenics.* New York: Alfred A. Knopf.

Khoury, Muin J., Bernice H. Cohen, Gary A. Chase, and Earl L. Diamond. 1987. "An Epidemiologic Approach to the Evaluation of the Effect of Inbreeding on Prereproductive Mortality." *American Journal of Epidemiology* 125(2):251–62.

Köhler, Josef. [1897] 1975. *On the Prehistory of Marriage: Totemism, Group Marriage, Mother Right.* Translated by R. H. Barnes and Ruth Barnes; edited by R. H. Barnes. Chicago: University of Chicago Press.

Lasley, John F. 1970. *Genetics of Livestock Improvement.* 4th ed. Englewood Cliffs, N.J.: Prentice Hall.

Leavis, Frank Raymond. 1980. *Mill on Bentham and Coleridge.* London: Cambridge University Press.

Leavitt, Gregory C. 1990. "Sociobiological Explanations of Incest Avoidance: A Critical Review of Evidential Claims." *American Anthropologist* 92:971–93.

———. 1992. "Inbreeding Fitness: A Reply to Uhlmann." *American Anthropologist* 94:448–49.

Lebel, Robert Roger. 1983. "Consanguinity Studies in Wisconsin I: Secular Trends in Consanguineous Marriage, 1843–1981." *American Journal of Medical Genetics* 15:543–60.

Lévi-Strauss, Claude. 1966. "The Future of Kinship Studies." *Proceedings of the Royal Anthropological Institute of Great Britain and Ireland* 1965:13–22.

———. 1969. *The Elementary Structures of Kinship*. Translated by J. H. Bell and I. R. von Sturmer; edited by Rodney Needham. Boston: Beacon.

Levitan, Max, and Ashley Montagu. 1977. *Textbook of Human Genetics*. 2d ed. New York: Oxford University Press.

Lewin, Linda. 1979. "Some Historical Implications of Kinship Organization for Family-based Politics in the Brazilian Northeast." *Comparative Studies in Society and History* 21(2):262–92.

"Literature, Art and Science." 1886. *Menorah* 1(2):132–34.

Lubbock, John. 1870. *The Origin of Civilization and the Primitive Condition of Man; Mental and Social Condition of Savages*. London: Longmans, Green.

Luckock, H. M. 1894. *History of Marriage*. London: Longmans, Green.

Ludmerer, Kenneth M. 1972. *Genetics and American Society*. Baltimore: Johns Hopkins University Press.

Lyman, Stanford M. 1978. *The Seven Deadly Sins: Society and Evil*. New York: St. Martin's Press.

Lynch, Joseph H. 1986. *Godparents and Kinship in Early Medieval Europe*. Princeton, N.J.: Princeton University Press.

Mackay, Richard V. 1957. *Law of Marriage and Divorce Simplified*. New York: Oceana Publications.

Maine, Henry Sumner. 1861. *Ancient Law*. London: John Murray.

———. 1883. *Dissertations on Early Law and Custom*. London: J. Murray.

Malinowski, Bronislaw. 1927. *Sex and Repression in Savage Society*. London: Kegan Paul, Trench, Trubner.

Mann, Arthur. 1979. *The One and the Many*. Chicago: University of Chicago Press.

Martindale-Hubbell. 1995. *Martindale-Hubbell International Law Digest*. New Providence, N.J.: Martindale-Hubbell.

Mascie-Taylor, C. G. N., and A. J. Boyce. 1988. *Human Mating Patterns*. Cambridge: Cambridge University Press.

McCulloch, O. C. 1888. *Tribe of Ishmael: A Study in Social Degradation*. Indianapolis: Charity Organization Society.

McCullough, J. M., and D. H. O'Rourke. 1986. "Geographic Distribution of Consanguinity in Europe." *Annals of Human Biology* 13(4):359–67.

McGrath, Mike. 1993. *Organic Gardening*. September/October:5.

Mcknorrie, Kenneth. 1992. "Incest and the Forbidden Degrees of Marriage in Scots Law." *Journal of the Law Society of Scotland* 37:216–19.

McKusick, Victor A., ed. 1978. *Medical Genetic Studies of the Amish*. Baltimore: Johns Hopkins University Press.

McLennan, John Ferguson. [1865] 1970. *Primitive Marriage.* Reprint. Edinburgh: A. C. Black.

McNamara, Jo-Ann, and Suzanne F. Wemple. 1976. "Marriage and Divorce in the Frankish Kingdom." In *Women in Medieval Society,* ed. Susan Mosher Stuard, 95–124. Philadelphia: University of Pennsylvania Press.

Mielziner, M. 1901. *The Jewish Law of Marriage and Divorce.* New York: Bloch.

Milledoler, Philip. 1843. *Dissertation on Incestuous Marriage.* New York: H. Ludwig.

Mitchell, Arthur. 1866. "Blood-Relationship in Marriage Considered in Its Influence upon the Offspring." In *Memoirs Read before the Anthropological Society of London,* vol. 2, 402–56. London: Trübner.

Mogey, John. 1976. "Residence, Family, Kinship: Some Recent Research." *Journal of Family History* 1(1):95–105.

Morel, B. A. 1857. "On the Degeneracy of the Human Race." *Journal of Psychological Medicine and Mental Pathology* 10:159–208.

Morgan, Lewis Henry. 1871. *Systems of Consanguinity and Affinity of the Human Family.* Washington, D.C.: Smithsonian Institution.

———. [1877] 1958. *Ancient Society.* Reprint. Calcutta: J. C. Saha Roy.

Morland, John W. 1946. *Keezer on the Law of Marriage and Divorce.* 3d ed. Indianapolis: Bobbs-Merrill.

Morris, Polly. 1992. "Incest or Survival Strategy? Plebeian Marriage within the Prohibited Degrees in Somerset, 1730–1835." In *Forbidden History,* ed. H. Faust, 139–69. Chicago: University of Chicago Press. (Originally published in 1991 in the *Journal of the History of Sexuality* 2[2]:235–65).

Morton, James. 1988. "The Incest Act 1909—Was it Ever Relevant?" *New Law Journal* 138:59–60.

Morton, Newton E. 1961. "Morbidity of Children from Consanguineous Marriages." In *Progress in Medical Genetics,* vol. 1, ed. Arthur G. Steinberg, 261–91. New York: Grune and Stratton.

Needham, Rodney. 1976. Editor's Introduction. In *The Primitive Family in Its Origin and Development,* by Carl Starcke, ix–xxxi. Chicago: University of Chicago Press.

Newman, Robert. 1869. *Report of the Committee on the Result of Consanguineous Marriages.* Albany: Weed, Parsons.

O'Brien, Elizabeth, Lynn B. Jorde, Björn Rönnlöf, Johan O. Fellman, and Aldur W. Eriksson. 1988. "Inbreeding and Genetic Disease in Sottunga, Finland." *American Journal of Physical Anthropology* 75:477–86.

O'Donnell, William, and David A. Jones. 1982. *The Law of Marriage and Marital Alternatives.* Lexington: Books.

Ottenheimer, Martin. 1984. "Some Problems and Prospects in Kinship and Marriage." *American Anthropologist* 86:351–58.

———. 1985. *Marriage in Domoni*. Prospect Heights, Ill.: Waveland.

———. 1986. "Complementarity and the Structures of Parallel-Cousin Marriage." *American Anthropologist* 88:934–39.

———. 1990. "Lewis Henry Morgan and the Prohibition of Cousin Marriage in the United States." *Journal of Family History* 15(3):325–34.

———. 1992. *Modeling Systems of Kinship 3.0*. Dubuque, Iowa: William C. Brown.

Oxon, J. F. 1886. "Sisters-in-Law." *Nineteenth Century* 20(117):667–77.

Pasternak, Burton. 1976. *Introduction to Kinship and Social Organization*. Englewood Cliffs, N.J.: Prentice Hall.

Peel, J. D. Y. 1972. *Herbert Spencer on Social Evolution*. Chicago: University of Chicago Press.

Pendleton, Hester. 1863. *Husband and Wife; or, the Science of Human Development through Inherited Tendencies*. New York: Carleton.

Peschel, Oscar. 1876. *The Races of Man and Their Geographical Distribution*. New York: D. Appleton.

Pettener, David. 1985. "Consanguineous Marriages in the Upper Bologna Appennine (1565–1980): Micrographic Variations, Pedigree Structure and Correlation of Inbreeding Secular Trend with Changes in Population Size." *Human Biology* 577(2):267–88.

Pryce, Huw. 1993. *Native Law and the Church in Medieval Wales*. Oxford: Clarendon.

Quale, G. Robina. 1988. *A History of Marriage Systems*. Westport, Colo.: Greenwood.

Quick, John. [1703] 1985. *A Serious Inquiry into That Weighty Case of Conscience, Whether a Man May Lawfully Marry His Deceased Wife's Sister.* Reprint. New York: Garland.

Ramesh, A., C. R. Srikumari, and S. Sukumar. 1990. "Parallel Cousin Marriages in Madras, Tamil Nadu: New Trends in Dravidian Kinship." *Social Biology* 36:248–54.

Reddy, P. Govinda. 1985. "Effects of Inbreeding on Mortality: A Study among Three South Indian Communities." *Human Biology* 57(1):47–59.

Reed v. Reed. 1893. *Northeastern Reporter* 32:750.

Reid, Russell M. 1976. "Effects of Consanguineous Marriage and Inbreeding on Couple Fertility and Offspring Mortality in Rural Sri Lanka." *Human Biology* 48(1):139–46.

———. 1988. "Church Membership, Consanguineous Marriage, and Migration in a Scotch-Irish Frontier Population. *Journal of Family History* 13(4):397–414.

Reilly, Philip. 1977. *Genetics, Law, and Social Policy*. Cambridge, Mass.: Harvard University Press.

Resek, Carl. 1960. *Lewis Henry Morgan: American Scholar*. Chicago: University of Chicago Press.

Roberts, D. F. 1992. "The Galton Lecture for 1990: The Price of Isolation." In *Minority Populations,* ed. A. H. Bittles and D. F. Roberts, 35–67. London: Macmillan.

Rosenberg, Charles E. 1976. *No Other Gods.* Baltimore: Johns Hopkins University Press.

Ross, Douglas B. 1987. "Forbidden Degrees of Matrimony." *Journal of the Law Society of Scotland* 32(3):20–22.

Sacks, Karen. 1979. *Sisters and Wives.* Westport, Colo.: Greenwood.

Salmon, Thomas. [1724] 1985. *A Critical Essay concerning Marriage.* Reprint. New York: Garland.

Schneider, David M. 1968. *American Kinship: A Cultural Account.* Englewood Cliffs, N.J.: Prentice Hall.

Schraer, William D., and Herbert J. Stoltze. 1983. *Biology: The Study of Life.* Fairfield, N.J.: Cebco Standard.

Schull, William J., and James V. Neel. 1965. *The Effects of Inbreeding on Japanese Children.* New York: Harper and Row.

Segalen, Martine. 1986. *Historical Anthropology of the Family.* Translated by J. C. Whitehouse and Sarah Matthews. Cambridge: Cambridge University Press.

Semonche, John E. 1965. "Common-Law Marriage in North Carolina: A Study in Legal History." *American Journal of Legal History* 9(4):320–49.

Shami, S. A., R. Qaisar, and A. H. Bittles. 1991. "Consanguinity and Adult Morbidity in Pakistan." *Lancet* 338:954–55.

Shaw, Brent D. 1992. "Explaining Incest: Brother-Sister Marriage in Graeco-Roman Egypt." *Man* (n.s.) 27:267–99.

Shaw, Brent D., and Richard P. Saller. 1984. "Close-Kin Marriage in Roman Society?" *Man* (n.s.) 19:432–44.

Shields, William M. 1982. *Philopatry, Inbreeding, and the Evolution of Sex.* Albany: State University of New York Press

———. 1993. "The Natural and Unnatural History of Inbreeding and Outbreeding." In *The Natural History of Inbreeding and Outbreeding,* ed. Nancy W. Thornhill, 143–69. Chicago: University of Chicago Press.

Sickels, Robert. 1972. *Race, Marriage, and the Law.* Alberquerque: University of New Mexico Press.

Siegle, Bernard Andrew. 1979. *Marriage Today.* New York: Alba House.

Slatis, Herman M., and Robert E. Hoene. 1961. "The Effect of Consanguinity in the Distribution of Continuously Variable Characteristics." *American Journal of Human Genetics* 13(1):28–31.

Slatis, Herman M., Raymond H. Reis, and Robert E. Hoene. 1958. "Consanguineous Marriages in the Chicago Region." *American Journal of Human Genetics* 10(4):446–64.

Spencer, Herbert. 1851. *Social Statics.* London: John Chapman.

———. 1897. *The Principles of Sociology.* 3 vols. New York: D. Appleton.

————. 1900. *The Principles of Psychology.* 3d ed. New York: D. Appleton.

Spuhler, J. N., and Clyde Kluckholn. 1953. "Inbreeding Coefficients of the Ramah Navaho Population." *Human Biology* 25(4):295–317.

Starcke, Carl Nicolai. [1889] 1976. *The Primitive Family in Its Origin and Development.* Reprint. Chicago: University of Chicago Press.

Steger, F. E. H. 1855. "Hereditary Transmission of Disease." *Nashville Journal of Medicine and Surgery* 8(3):177–91.

Steinberg, Arthur G., ed. 1961. *Progress in Medical Genetics.* Vol. 1. New York: Grune and Stratton.

Stern, Heinrich. 1891. "Consanguineous Marriages." *Menorah* 10(6):311–20.

Strathern, Marilyn. 1992. *Reproducing the Future: Anthropology, Kinship and the New Reproductive Technologies.* New York: Routledge.

Stuard, Susan Mosher, ed. 1976. *Women in Medieval Society.* Philadelphia: University of Pennsylvania Press.

Taylor, Jeremy. 1660. *Ductor Dubitantium, or the Rule of Conscience in All Her Generall Measures; Serving as a Great Instrument for the Determination of Cases of Conscience.* 2 vols. London: James Flesher for Richard Royston.

Trautmann, Thomas R. 1987. *Lewis Henry Morgan and the Invention of Kinship.* Berkeley: University of California Press.

Trumbach, Randolph. 1978. *The Rise of the Egalitarian Family.* New York: Academic Press.

————, ed. 1985. *The Marriage Prohibitions Controversy.* New York: Garland.

Tylor, Edward B. 1878. *Researches into the Early History of Mankind and the Development of Civilization.* 3d ed. London: John Murray.

————. 1881. "J. F. McLennan." *The Academy* 20:9–10.

————. 1889. "On a Method of Investigating the Development of Institutions; Applied to Laws of Marriage and Descent." *Journal of the Royal Anthropological Institute* 18:245–69.

Uhlmann, Allon J. 1992. "A Critique of Leavitt's Review of Sociobiological Explanations of Incest Avoidance." *American Anthropologist* 94:446–48.

Veillette, Suzanne, Michel Perron, Jean Mathieu, Claude Prévost, and Gilles Hébert. 1992. "Sociocultural Factors Influencing the Spread of Myotonic Dystrophy in the Saguenay-Lac-Saint-Jean Region of the Province of Quebec." In *Minority Populations,* ed. A. H. Bittles and D. F. Roberts, 83–101. London: Macmillan.

Verdery, Katherine. 1988. "A Comment on Goody's *Development of the Family and Marriage in Europe.*" *Journal of Family History* 13(2):265–70.

Wadlington, Walter. 1984. *Cases and Other Materials on Domestic Relations.* Mineola, N.Y.: Foundation Press.

Wake, C. Staniland. 1874. "Marriage among Primitive Peoples." *Anthropologia* 1874:197–207.

Watson, Alan. 1967. *The Law of Persons in the Later Roman Republic.* Oxford: Oxford University Press.

Webster, Noah. 1790. "Explanation of the Reezons Why Marriage Iz Prohibited between Natural Relations." In *Collection of Essays and Fugitiv Writings on Moral, Historical, Political and Religious Subjects,* 322–24. Boston: Thomas and Andrews.

Westermarck, Edward. 1922. *The History of Human Marriage.* 3 vols. New York: Allerton.

White, Leslie. 1949. *The Science of Culture.* New York: Grove.

Wise, Stuart M. 1983. "An Act of Love." *National Law Journal* 5:47.

Withington, Charles. 1885. *Consanguineous Marriages: Their Effect upon Offspring.* Boston: n.p.

Wolfram, Sybil. 1983. "Eugenics and the Punishment of Incest Act 1908." *Criminal Law Review* May:308–16.

———. 1987. *In-laws and Outlaws: Kinship and Marriage in England.* New York: St. Martin's Press.

Woolf, C. M., F. E. Stephens, D. D. Mulaik, and R. E. Gilbert. 1956. "An Investigation of the Frequency of Consanguineous Marriages among the Mormons and Their Relatives in the United States." *American Journal of Human Genetics* 8(4):236–52.

Wright, Carroll D. 1889. *A Report on Marriage and Divorce in the United States, 1867–1886.* Washington, D.C.: Government Printing Office.

CASES AND OPINIONS CITED

Maynard v. Hill 125 U.S. 190
[Michigan] Op. Atty. Gen. 1939–40, 177
Miller's Estate (1927) 214 N.W. 428, 239 Mich. 455
[Minnesota] Op. Atty. Gen., 300–G, Feb. 26, 1953
[Ohio] Mazzolini v. Mazzolini, 155 N.E. 2d 206
[Ohio] Mazzolini v. Mazzolini, 155 N.E. 2d 208
Reynolds v. United States 98 U.S. 145
State v. Tucker 174 Ind. 715
Toth v. Toth (1973) 212 N.W. 2d 812, 50 Mich. App. 150

STATE SOURCE BOOKS CITED

Acts of the State of Ohio 1803
Illinois Annotated Statutes 1972
Indiana Acts 1873
Indiana Acts 1907
Indiana Code 1982
Louisiana Civil Code 1804
Maine Revised Statutes Annotated 1985

New Mexico Actions of the Legislative Assembly 1876–78
New Mexico Statutes 1986 Replacement
Statutes of Kansas Territory 1855

Index

Abraham: in Old Testament, 61, 101

Adoption: in Texas, 29; reviewed for consanguinity in West Virginia, 41

Adultery: and harmful effects on offspring, 84

Affinal relatives: diminish in prohibitions, 3, 8, 44, 45, 49; omitted from Archbishop Parker's table, 36, 73; and role confusion, 45: distinguished from consanguineal relatives, 48; marry in England, 75; marriage of, threatens society, 79; in evolutionary perspective, 80; marriage of, increases divorce rates, 88; marriage of, encourages illicit sex, 88; of lineal relatives cannot marry, 92; prohibition extends relationships, 97

—marriage of, permitted in: Maine, 25; New York, 26; Ohio, 30; Iowa, 35; U.S., 37; Australia, 87; Scotland, 89

—marriage of, prohibited in: U.S., 19, 23, 31, 35, 36, 41, 42; Massachusetts, 23–24; Connecticut, 24; New England, 25; Pennsylvania, 26; Maryland, 27; North Carolina, 27; Virginia, 27; Georgia, 28; Louisiana, 28; Kansas, 31; West Virginia, 34; Georgia, 36; Tennessee, 36; Roman Catholic church, 63; Leviticus, 66

Affinity: decreased concern about, in U.S., 44; distinguished from consanguinity, 80; in terminology, 109

Alabama, 15, 35, 36, 37, 40

Åland Islands, 96, 128, 130

Alaric I (leader of Visigoths), 99

Alaska, 31, 33–34, 37, 40

Alexander II, Pope, 63

Alexander III of Macedonia, 62

Alexandra Feodorovna (tsarina of Russia), 117

Alexis Nikolaevich (son of Nicholas II and Alexandra), 117

Allele, 121

Alliances: as basis of prohibitions, 51, 95; in Saint Augustine's writings, 95; as mechanism of cohesion, 138

—established by: cousin marriage, 136; exogamy, 137; marriage, 143

Alliance theory, 13, 14, 139, 142, 144

American Association for the Advancement of Science, 53

American Bar Association, 2

American Indian: degraded because of cousin marriage, 50, 110; reduced range of prohibitions, 67; family practices of, 109; data on cousin marriage of, 119; and married cousins, 120

Americanization, 152

American Medical Association, 54, 55

American myth of cousin marriage, 2–4, 16, 46, 116, 118, 151, 154

Amish. See Old Order Amish

Amitalocal residence, 148, 149

Analysis: of cross-cousin systems, 14; of worldwide data, 102

Anastasia Nikolaievna Romanova (daughter of Nicholas II and Alexandra), 117

Ancestors, 34

Anglican church. *See* Church: Anglican
Anglo-Saxon, 152
Antigenic incompatibility, 127
Aquinas, Thomas, 98
Archbishop of Canterbury, 72, 73, 77, 87, 88
Archbishop Parker. *See* Parker, Matthew
Argonne National Laboratory, 126
Aristocracy, 81
Arizona, 11, 35, 37, 40, 60
Arkansas, 30, 35, 37
Arner, George B., 58
Arsinoe Philadelphus (wife of Ptolemy II), 62
Ascendants, 26, 27, 28, 29, 92
Assimilation, 152
Asylums: consanguinity of inmates' parents in, 103
Athenians, 62
Atomic Energy Commission, 83, 125
Attorney general: opinion in Michigan, 40
Augustine, Saint, 95, 96, 101, 108, 135
Aunt: in U.S., 19, 24–29 passim, 31, 34, 41; in Bible, 22, 73, 94; in Europe, 22, 90, 92; third degree of relationship, 33; and confusion of roles, 45. *See also* Mother's sister; Uncle's wife
Australia, 87
Austria, 5, 90
Autosomal disorders: recessive, 128, 131; dominant, 130
Avunculocal residence, 148, 149

Bachofen, Johann, 7
Baptism, 67
Bemiss, S. M., 53–57
Benedict XV, Pope, 67
Bible, 48, 87, 101, 103, 136. *See also* Leviticus; Old Testament; Scripture
Bioevolutionary framework, 79, 92, 115
Biogenetics: basis of U.S. marital law, 11
Biologists: on cousin marriage, 1
Biology: and cousin proscriptions, 4
Birmingham, England, 131
Blacks, 67
Blindness: as result of consanguinity, 53

Boleyn, Anne, 70
Bologna Appenine, 91
Boniface, Saint, 97
Book of Common Prayer, 72
Breeding: and marriage, 13, 46, 80
Brighton Beach Memoirs (film), 116
British, 43
Brother: in U.S., 27, 28, 33, 34, 50; in Europe, 90, 92
Brother's daughter, 24, 27, 34, 69, 73
Brother's son's wife, 34, 73
Brother's widow. *See* Brother's wife
Brother's wife: in U.S., 22, 24, 25, 27, 34; in Bible, 66, 94; in Europe, 73, 87
Bureau of Labor, 37

California, 29, 35, 37, 40, 43, 153
Calvin, John, 69
Canada, 128
Canon law: Roman Catholic, 5, 6, 9
Carrier: of hemophilia, 117; and gene frequency, 122
Cartilage-hair hypoplasia, 129
Caste, 58, 103
Catherine of Aragon, 69
Catholics, 70, 72
Census, 61
Census Act of 1871, 87
Chaos, 45
Chicago, 59, 126
Children: prohibitions against marrying, in U.S., 41; adopted, 90; stepchildren, 90
China, 11
Christianity, 63, 99, 152
Church: Roman Catholic, 5–6, 9, 29, 63, 64, 66, 68, 69, 71, 72, 87, 90, 94, 126, 152; Dutch Reformed, 15; Anglican, 20, 22, 26, 72, 87; Presbyterian, 46; Greek Orthodox, 64, 100; Swedish, 91; Mormon, 114
Church of England. *See* Church: Anglican
Church of Jesus Christ of Latter-day Saints. *See* Church: Mormon
Civil Code Project, 28
Civilization: as result of heterogeneity, 105; as result of exogamy, 108

Clan: significance of, to McClennan, 103; and exogamy, 104, 111, 138

Classes: impact on consanguinity, 83

Cleopatra, 62

Clericus (pseudonym for nineteenth-century minister), 48

Close breeding. *See* Inbreeding

Coefficient of inbreeding, 124

Cohesion. *See* Solidarity

Coleridge, Samuel, 150

Colonists, 20

Colorado, 5, 31, 34, 37, 40, 43

Comet (prize bull), 82

Commission Appointed by the Archbishop of Canterbury, 87, 88

Communities: Islamic, 10

Compaternity, 67

Concubine, 66

Conflict: reduced by exogamy, 137

Connecticut, 24, 35, 37, 40

Consanguineal kin. *See* Relatives

Consanguinity: dangers of, to offspring, 16–17, 44–45, 56, 57, 84, 98, 124, 126, 130; within fourth degree prohibited in Alaska, 33; increased importance of, in U.S., 44, 45; threatens society, 53; violates the laws of nature, 53; excuse to break marriage, 66; distinguished from affinity, 80; and socioeconomic factors, 83, 121; European concerns about, 90; in small groups, 96; prohibition extends relations, 97; characteristic of early humans, 108; in terminology, 109; among Japanese, 124; and fertility, 127; not significant physical threat to offspring, 131; negative effects of, 146

Constantine I (Roman emperor), 63

Continent. *See* Europe

Council of Agde, 63

Counseling: genetic, 3, 25, 40, 131, 132, 153

County clerks, 13

Couples: minimum number for noncousin marriage, 96

Cousin, Cousine (film), 116

Cousins: different kinds of, 4; defined, 10;

sexual relations between, in Ohio, 30. *See also* Cross-cousins; First cousins; Parallel-cousins; Second cousins; Third cousins

Cousins (film), 116

Cretinism: consanguinity blamed for, 86

Crossbreeding: advantageous, 47, 50

Cross-cousins: defined, 12; and alliance theory, 14; distinguished from parallel-cousins, 138, 139; as marriageable, 141. *See also* Cousins

Cultural continuity: and marriage, 14, 144; and endogamy, 15

Culture: and marital law, 10, 12; as basis for theory, 13; and family, 15, 43, 152; and marriage, 16; Hispanic, 29; shift in U.S., 44; Mediterranean (Oriental), 99; European (Occidental), 99; and inbreeding, 132; enhanced by cousin marriage, 146

Darwin, Charles, 3, 85–86, 118

Darwin, George, 84–85

Data: cross-cultural, 7; ethnographic, 47

Daughter: consanguineal, men prohibited from marrying, 24, 25, 27, 28, 29, 34, 61, 69, 73; adopted, men prohibited from marrying, 35; omitted in Leviticus, 101

Daughter-in-law: men prohibited from marrying, 36, 61; men permitted to marry, 37

Daughter's daughter, 73

Daughter's husband, 24, 26, 37

Daughter's son's widow. *See* Daughter's son's wife

Daughter's son's wife, 35, 73

Deaf and Dumb Asylum, 53

Deaf-mutes: proportion of, in families with and without consanguinity, 84

Deaf-mutism: as result of consanguinity, 53, 83, 86

Degrees. *See* Distance

Delaware, 35, 37

Descendants: prohibited from marrying, 26, 27, 28, 29, 34, 92; spouse of, prohibited from marrying, 36

Descent group: and exogamy, 11; marital
    prohibition in, 14; patrilineal, 138, 139;
    matrilineal, 139, 148, 149. *See also*
    Double descent
Disease: as basis for marital regulation,
    51; reduces population, 95
Disorders: caused by consanguineous mar-
    riage, 52
Dispensation: criticized, 9, 68; introduced,
    63; range increased, 65; range reduced,
    67; removed, 71; available from govern-
    ments, 90, 92; relaxation of, increases
    cousin marriages, 91; financial gain in,
    98; result of Visigoth invasion, 99; as
    political ploy, 100; in different churches,
    101; in Chicago area, 126
Distance: diverse relatives prohibited, 4;
    Roman (Civil) method of calculating,
    33, 63, 64–65, 73, 100; German
    (Canonic) system of reckoning, 63, 64–
    65, 67, 100
District of Columbia, 5, 36, 40
Diversity: associated with cousin prohibi-
    tions, 43
Divorce, 62, 66, 77, 90
Doctors. *See* Physicians
Domesticus (pseudonym for nineteenth-
    century minister), 46–48
Double descent, 140
Double first cousins, 26, 34, 54
Dowries, 62
Dutch Reformed Church. *See* Church:
    Dutch Reformed
Dwarfism, 86, 128

Edward VI (king of England), 71
Egypt, 61, 62
Elizabeth I (queen of England), 72, 81
Elizabeth II (queen of England), 117
Ellis van Creveld syndrome, 128, 129
Endogamy: ensures cultural continuity,
    14–15, 150, 154; in U.S., 15; defined,
    103–4; and early humans, 105–6; and
    homogeneity, 108; distinguished from
    inbreeding, 111; and early social life,
    134, 136; and social evolution, 135;

dangerous to society, 141; two types of,
    141, 142; ignored, 143; and parallel-
    cousin marriage, 144
England: cousin marriage in, 3, 81, 74, 86,
    87; marriage act of King Henry VIII,
    25; debate over marrying wife's sister
    in, 45, 75; family trees in, 65; marriage
    prohibitions in, 69–73, 89, 80; opposi-
    tion to Mitchell's thesis in, 85; commis-
    sion to investigate marriage law in, 88;
    family social order in, 88; royal family
    and hemophilia in, 117; Pakistani immi-
    grants in, 146
Epilepsy: consanguinity blamed for, 86
Ethnicity: and cousin marriage, 43
Eugenics, 51, 58, 114
Europe: cousin marriage in, 2, 3, 16, 90,
    91, 117, 118; debate over nature of the
    family in, 6; development of marriage
    regulations in, 9; debate about marrying
    wife's sister in, 79; secularization of
    marriage in, 89, 90; concern with con-
    sanguinity in, 90; and worldwide infor-
    mation, 102; range of prohibitions re-
    duced in, 153
Evolution: framework for marriage analy-
    sis, 7; Darwinian, 7; Spencerian, 7–8,
    107; and close kin marriage, 105; en-
    gendered by exogamy, 141; modern un-
    derstanding of, 154
Evolutionists: and early human behavior,
    105; reject biblical interpretation of hu-
    man history, 106; on homogeneity of
    early humans, 107; on primitive peo-
    ples, 119
Exchange: of women in alliance theory, 14
Exogamy: and cross-cousin marriage, 14,
    139; and circulation of women, 97;
    defined, 103–4; in early human society,
    105–6, 136, 137; and civilization, 108,
    135; as positive mechanism of change,
    111, 112, 134, 135, 141; between sub-
    groups, 138; and social cohesion, 139;
    advances cultural continuity, 144; does
    not establish alliances, 145; with resi-
    dence rules, 148

Family: as institution to maintain order and morality, 6, 79; as breeding unit, 7, 8; regulation of, 12, 14, 97; nuclear, 42; impact of prohibitions on, 45, 65, 75, 77, 98, 102; and cousin marriage, 57, 60; Scotch-Irish American, 58; estate, 98; emerges in evolutionary stage, 108; consanguineal, 109, 126; established through marriage, 144

Farber, Bernard, 42–44

Father, 28, 89

Father-daughter marriage, 19

Father's brother's daughter, 24, 138, 140, 142

Father's brother's wife, 22, 25, 73, 94

Father's sister, 22, 24, 25, 69, 73, 94

Father's sister's daughter, 14, 24

Father's widow, 29, 35, 36, 87. *See also* Father's wife

Father's wife: in U.S., 22, 26, 29, 35, 36; in Europe, 87, 88, 92

Fayetteville, North Carolina, 46

Fees: reduction of, leads to cousin marriage, 91

Fertility: and consanguinity, 85, 127

Fictive kin, 67, 97

Finland, 4, 96, 132

First cousins: marital prohibitions for, 5, 24–35 passim, 37, 54, 67; permitted to marry, 6, 26, 34, 40; defined, 10; different types of, 11; once removed, 11, 30, 37, 40, 67, 124; degree of relationship of, 33; married by Lewis Henry Morgan, 50; in Bemiss report, 54; inconsistent statistics on, 56; not mentioned in Leviticus, 94; with recessive genes, 123; and genetic risk, 124. *See also* Cousins

Fitness: and natural ends, 45, 46, 47, 74, 102; evolutionary, 45, 49, 51; affected by consanguinity, 98; and endogamy, 135

Florida, 29, 35, 37, 40

Fornication: and harmful effects on offspring, 84

Founder effect, 128–31

Fourth Lateran Council, 67

France, 90, 92, 153

Franks, 97

Frazer, James, 119–20

French law, 5

Fry, John, 74, 102

Gene: precursor, 56; mutation and hemophilia, 117; homozygosity, 121, 124, 153; frequency, 122, 123–24; autosomal recessive, 129

Genesis, 79, 101, 106

Genetic drift, 128–31

Genetics: Mendelian, 3; and population, 3, 13; and inherited defects, 56; as basis for prohibitions, 118; poorly understood, 120; modern theory of, 121; and cousin prohibitions, 151; and European laws, 153

Gens. *See* Clan

Georgia, 5, 19, 28, 35, 36, 37, 40

Germany, 92

Godchildren, 63, 67

Godmother, 45, 67

Godparent, 63, 67

Godrelatives, 97

Godson, 45

Goody, Jack, 68

Goths. *See* Visigoths

Grandchild, 28

Grandchild-in-law, 89

Granddaughter, 22, 24, 25, 27, 29, 34, 94

Grandfather's wife, 23, 25, 36, 73, 88

Grandmother, 24, 25, 27, 34, 73

Grandparent, 28

Grandparent-in-law, 89

Grandson's widow. *See* Grandson's wife

Grandson's wife, 23, 24, 25, 36

Gravity, 108

Great Britain, 60, 128, 132. *See also* England and Scotland

Great Northern War, 130

Greece, 62

Gregory I, Pope, 100

Half sister, 22, 25, 27, 34, 94. *See also* Siblings

Hammurabi's Code, 61
Harmony, 50
Hawaii, 31, 37, 40
Health: and marital regulation, 51, 52, 57, 102; antigen effect on mother-child, 146
Hebrews, 45, 48
Hemophilia, 3, 117, 118
Henry I (king of England), 65
Henry VIII (king of England), 25, 69, 70, 71, 81
Herd-book, 82
Heterogeneity: and civilization, 105–6; and evolution, 107
Homogeneity: associated with cousin marriage, 43; and early humans, 105–6; and evolution, 107
Homozygosity, 122
Horde: as lowest form of human social group, 108
Howard, George, 8
Human Fertilisation and Embryology Act, 153
Hungary, 90
Husband's father, 37
Husband's grandfather, 24
Husband's grandson, 24, 26
Husband's son, 26
Huth, Alfred, 86

Idaho, 34, 37
Idiocy: as result of consanguinity, 52, 53, 55, 56
Illinois, 11, 30, 37, 40, 59, 60, 118
Immigrants, 42, 146, 151
Inbreeding: genetic risks of, 1; in Finland, 4; as reason for marital prohibitions, 51; of domesticated animals, 81; and degeneration, 82, 118; and small groups, 96; and early humans, 106, 115, 119; distinguished from endogamy, 111; effect of, on Japanese, 121, 125; and IQ, 131; and cultural factors, 132; defined, 134; and cousin marriage, 144, 151
Incest: with deceased wife's sister, 15, 20, 75; and scarlet letter I, 19–20; between father and daughter, 20; with wife's

daughter, 20; of consanguineal and affinal kin, 20; avoidance of, 47; taboos against, 47, 139; between spiritual kin, 67; and inheritance of physical characteristics, 80; prohibition serves no useful purpose, 92; examination of code, in Illinois, 118
India, 103
Indiana, 11, 29–30, 35, 37, 60
Individualism, 42–43
Infertility: and unequal age marriages, 47
Injunctions. See Prohibitions
In-laws. See Affinal relatives
Inmates: parentage of, investigated, 54, 83
Insanity: consanguinity blamed for, 51, 86
Interbreeding: and social progress, 112
Intercourse: and prohibitions, 71, 75; causes physiological change in partners, 79–80; between relatives, 92; in horde, 108
Iowa, 35, 37, 43
IQ: and inbreeding, 131
Iroquois, 111
Israel, 62
Italian Kingdom, 91
Italy, 91, 92, 99

James I (king of England), 75
Japan, 125, 126, 128
Jehovah, 79
Jesus Christ, 62
Jews: exempt from Rhode Island uncle-niece marital prohibition, 19

Kansas, 31, 35, 36, 37, 43, 54
Kant-Laplace theory, 106
Kentucky, 35, 37, 53
Know Nothing party, 151
Köhler, Josef, 7
Korea, 10, 11
Ku Klux Klan, 151

Law. See Canon law; French law; Miscegenation laws; Natural law; Statutes
Lawrence, Kansas, 54
Leopold (duke of Albany), 117
Leprosy: consanguinity blamed for, 86

Lévi-Strauss, Claude, 14, 139, 140, 142, 145
Leviticus, 22–23, 68, 69, 72, 79, 94, 101, 102. *See also* Bible; Old Testament; Scripture
Lewis, Jerry Lee, 116
Lewis Island, Scotland, 83
Licentiousness, 98
Lineages, 138
Liverpool, England, 82
Local custom: marital prohibitions a reaction to, 99
London, England, 81
Lord Lyndhurst's Act, 15, 75–77, 80, 81
Lothair II (king of Lorraine), 66
Louisiana, 28–29, 35, 37
Louisville, Kentucky, 53
Lubbock, John, 87
Lucre, 6, 68, 71, 82, 98
Lunatics: parents of, investigated, 82
Lust, 98
Luther, Martin, 68

Maine, Henry Sumner, 7
Maine, 3, 5, 11, 24, 25, 35, 37, 40, 43, 60, 100, 153
Malinowski, Bronislaw, 98
Mann, Horace, 49
Marriage: characteristics of, 4, 46, 50, 102, 132, 142; systems of, 7; and evolution, 8, 46, 106, 107, 114; prohabitions against, in U.S., 42, 44; American view of, 135, 143, 144, 150
—affinal: risks of, 47–49, 88
—consanguineal: risks of, 3, 52, 53, 57, 66, 97, 119; prohibitions against, 26, 41, 44, 49, 54, 82; with close kin, 54, 55, 61, 62, 94, 95
—cousin, 2, 9, 58; and culture, 6, 7, 43, 79, 83, 99, 132, 146, 150; prohibited, 9, 26, 41, 44, 54, 63, 66, 99; theory of, 12, 13, 44; permitted, 23, 27, 34, 37, 40, 43, 50, 56, 62, 72; positive effects of, 43, 57; and inbreeding, 56, 86, 113, 151; with endogamy, 58, 111; and demography, 60, 96; result of limited possibilities, 95–96; and evolution, 113, 114
—cross-cousin, 111, 140, 142–45, 148, 149, 150; and alliances, 14, 139
—first cousin: risks of, 1, 46, 49, 126, 128; permitted, 5, 20, 37, 40; prohibited, 6, 7, 15, 24, 26, 28, 41; rates of, 58, 59, 65–66, 90, 91
—parallel-cousin, 141–45, 148
—regulations, 2, 8, 14, 15, 16, 25; and evolution, 52, 80
Marriage Act of 1986, 88
Marriage bond, 27
Maryland, 28, 35, 36, 37, 40
Massachusetts, 5, 20, 22, 23, 24, 25, 35, 36, 37, 40
Matrilocal residence, 148, 149
Maynard v. Hill, 114
McClennan, John Ferguson, 7, 103–5
McGrath, Mike, 116
McIlvaine, Joshua H., 50, 110
McQueen, Archibald: married to wife's sister, 46, 49
Mediterranean, 61, 62, 91, 95, 96
Mexico, 34
Michigan, 35, 36, 37, 40
Middle Ages, 81, 95
Middle Kingdom (Ancient Egypt), 61
Milledoler, Philip, 48–49
Minnesota, 35, 37, 40
Miscegenation laws, 4, 13, 19, 51
Mississippi, 13, 35, 36, 37
Missouri, 35, 37
Mitchell, Arthur, 82–84, 119
Monogamy, 23, 114–15
Montana, 35, 37
Morality: as basis for marital regulations, 6, 22, 51, 79, 80; concern for, replaced by health of offspring, 7
Morbidity: and consanguinity, 127
Morgan, Lewis Henry: and analysis of marriage, 7; and inbreeding, 8, 119; married first cousin, 50; and bioevolutionary view of marriage, 106, 108–12, 131, 134
Mormons: frequency of consanguineous marriage, 59. *See also* Church: Mormon
Mortality: and consanguinity, 85, 124, 126, 127; and offspring of cousins, 126

Mother: in U.S., 22, 24, 25, 27, 28, 29, 34; in Hammurabi's Code, 61; in Bible, 73, 94
Mother-in-law, 36
Mother's brother's daughter, 4, 14, 24
Mother's brother's wife, 73
Mother's husband, 26
Mother's sister, 22, 24, 25, 69, 73, 94. *See also* Aunt
Mother's sister's daughter, 4, 24
Mother-son marriage, 19
Mountbatten, Prince Philip (duke of Edinburgh), 117
Murphy, Frank, 115
Muscular dystrophy, 130
Mutual support: as purpose of marriage, 102
Myotonic dystrophy, 130
Myth: and marital regulation, 16; in Genesis, 95; of cousin marriage as inbreeding, 151; requires vision, 154. *See also* American myth of cousin marriage

National Conference of Commissioners on Uniform State Laws, 2
Natural law: as basis for marital prohibitions, 6, 7, 119
Natural selection, 7, 80, 137
Nature: violated by consanguinity, 53
Nebraska, 34, 37
Nephew: in U.S., 19, 26, 27, 28, 31, 34, 41; third degree relative, 33; and confusion of roles, 45; in Europe, 90, 92
Nephew's widow, 34
Nephew's wife, 28
Netherlands, 15, 92
Nevada, 35, 37
New England, 19, 24
New Hampshire, 24, 29, 35, 36, 37
New Jersey, 35, 37, 40
Newman, Robert, 56
New Mexico, 31, 37, 40
New York, 26, 35, 37, 40, 43, 50, 56
Nicholas II (czar of Russia), 117
Niece: prohibitions against marriage to, 22–29 passim, 31, 34, 41, 90, 92; third degree relative, 33

Nobles: and family trees, 65
North America, 103
North American Indian. *See* American Indian
North Carolina, 2, 11, 26–27, 35, 37, 46
North Dakota, 35, 36, 37
Norway, 92

Offspring: health of, affected by consanguinity, 2–3, 56, 82–84, 102, 116, 118, 129, 143, 154; and evolutionary fitness, 46, 51, 98, 113; degeneracy of, due to unequal age of parents, 47; investigated, 54, 119; dangers of consanguinity exaggerated, 56, 58, 86, 131; of Japanese, 125
Ogelthorpe, James, 28
Ohio, 29–30, 35, 37, 53, 56
Ohio State Medical Society, 56
Oklahoma, 5, 10, 34–35, 36, 37
Old Order Amish, 128, 129
Old Testament, 22–23, 45, 48, 61, 70, 72, 95, 101. *See also* Bible; Leviticus; Scripture
Oregon, 35, 37
Osiander, Andreas, 69
Outbreeding, 135, 143
Outer Hebrides, 83

Pakistan, 126, 128
Palestine, 62
Papal authority, 101
Parallel-cousins, 12, 138, 139, 141
Parents: prohibited from marrying children, 41, 90
Parents-in-law, 90
Parent's sibling, 92
Parent's spouse, 36
Parker, Matthew, 20, 45, 72
Parliament, 15, 22, 70–81 passim
Patrilocal residence, 138, 148, 149
Penitential of Theodore, 63
Pennsylvania, 25–26, 35, 37, 129
Pentecost Sunday, 67
Pepin III (Frankish king), 97
Phenotype, 121

Physical debilities: as basis for prohibiting cousin marriage, 40

Physicians: investigate consanguinity, 16, 46, 51, 53, 81, 103; as protagonists in marriage debates, 45; address to Ohio State Medical Society, 56; support Mitchell's thesis, 85

Plutarch, 95

Polygamy: outlawed, 19, 23, 144; and U.S. Supreme Court, 114–15; as barbaric practice, 115

Population: and genetics, 1, 129, 130; size and cousin marriage, 91, 96

Primogeniture rights, 91

Procreation: as purpose of marriage, 102

Profit: as motive for prohibitions, 6

Progeny. *See* Offspring

Progress: in evolution, 8; and marriage, 46, 50, 51, 80, 111, 135; threatened by consanguinity, 120

Prohibitions: basis for, 1, 4, 6, 9, 10, 12, 13, 17, 42, 44, 45, 47, 48, 51, 68, 80, 94–100 passim, 102, 103; history of, 2, 4, 5, 9, 29, 60, 62–64, 152; in states, 2, 20, 22, 23, 24, 28; of spiritual and adoptive kin, 3, 34, 66, 67, 68; and scarlet letter *I,* 19; inferred, 22, 23, 69; in Bible, 22, 45, 48, 70, 94, 100; for a woman, 24, 34, 36, 37; in Europe, 66–73 passim, 88, 89, 93, 101, 153; established through intercourse, 71; of polygamy, 114, 115; of incest, 139

—affinal: in states, 19, 25, 27, 28, 29, 31, 35, 36, 37, 41, 42, 78; of wife's sister in Europe, 22, 45, 75, 76, 77, 79, 80, 102; of wife's sister in U.S., 24, 27, 28, 45, 47, 48, 50; in Europe, 43, 75, 76, 77, 87; in Australia, 87

—consanguineal: in states, 3, 19, 27, 29, 30, 31, 34, 35, 37, 40, 41, 43, 44, 54, 100, 115; and biology, 3, 59, 84, 98, 116, 118, 132, 143; and social progress, 8, 52, 105; and culture, 12, 14, 15, 42, 43, 64, 65, 111, 133, 146, 152, 154; in Europe, 74, 91, 143; and minimum population, 96

Promiscuity: characteristic of early humans, 107, 109–10; and kinship terminology, 110

Proscriptions. *See* Prohibitions

Protestant Reformation: and change in prohibitions, 5, 69, 70, 91, 101, 102; and opposition to dispensations, 9, 68; and explanation of prohibitions, 98, 102

Protestants: 5, 69, 70, 72, 73, 101

Providence, Rhode Island, 53

Ptolemy II (Egyptian ruler), 62

Public good, 47

Pundit Club of Rochester, New York, 50

Punishment of Incest Act, 80

Puritans, 6, 28, 73, 74

Pyruvate kinase deficiency, 129

Quakers, 6, 25–26, 73–74

Quebec, 130

Range: of forbidden relatives, 64–66

Reckoning. *See* Distance

Reformation. *See* Protestant Reformation

Reformer: legal, 1

Reforms: in Roman Catholic marriage law, 68

Regulation. *See* Prohibitions

Relatives: marriage of, forbidden in U.S., 19, 24, 31, 41; lineal, 29, 31, 47, 50; adopted, 40, 97; consanguinity important to, 44; consanguineal distinguished from affinal, 48; marriage of, not dangerous, 56; marriage of, forbidden in Europe, 92. *See also* Affinal relatives

Report of the Committee on the Result of Consanguineous Marriages, 56

Revolutionary War, 28

Reynolds v. United States, 114

Rhode Island, 19, 24, 25, 35, 36, 37, 40

Rickets: consanguinity of parents blamed for, 86

Rochester, New York, 50, 110

Roman Empire, 62, 63, 99, 100

Rome, 63

Royal commission, 76–77

Rules. *See* Marriage: regulations
Russia, 90

Saguenay-Lac-Jean, Quebec, Canada, 130
Sarah, 61, 101
Savagery: and close kin marriage, 106
Scarlet letter: *A,* 19; *I,* 19–20
Scotland, 82, 83, 84, 89, 153
Scripture, 71, 74, 79. *See also* Bible; Lev-
    iticus; Old Testament
Second Act of Supremacy, 72
Second cousins: marriage of, prohibited, 5,
    33, 34–35; defined, 10; marriage of, 27,
    29–30, 37–38, 53; and risk to offspring,
    54, 56, 124
Second cousins once removed, 67
Sewall, Samuel, 23
Seymour, Jane, 70
Shakespeare, William, 62
Shaw, George Bernard, 62
Siblings: as ancestors of cousins, 10, 12,
    29; adopted, 40; marriage of, 55, 61, 62
—full: prohibited from marrying, 19, 26,
    29, 31, 41
—half: permitted to marry, 5, 41, 92, 153;
    prohibited from marrying, 26, 29. *See
    also* Brother; Half sister; Sister
Sister: in Bible, 22, 73, 94; in U.S., 24, 25,
    27, 28, 29, 94; as second degree rela-
    tive, 33; in Europe, 73, 90, 92
Sister-in-law. *See* Wife's sister
Sister's daughter, 24, 27, 34, 69, 73
Sister's son's wife, 34, 73
Smith, Mike, 116
Social evolution: and marriage, 50; stages
    of, 135
Social order: maintained by proper mar-
    riage, 46, 47, 51, 79
Society: marriage rules as expression of,
    16; multiethnic, 16; and consanguinity
    in marriage, 47, 53, 97
Society of Friends in England, 74
Solar system, 108
Solidarity: produced by cousin marriage,
    140, 143
Son, 28
Son-in-law, 88

Son's daughter, 73
Son's son's widow. *See* Son's son's wife
Son's son's wife, 35, 73
Son's widow. *See* Son's wife
Son's wife: in Bible, 22, 66, 73, 94; in
    U.S., 23, 24, 25, 26, 27, 29, 34, 35, 36,
    37; in Europe, 88, 89, 92
Sororal polygyny, 45
Sottunga Island, Finland, 128
South America, 67
South American Indians. *See* American In-
    dians
South Carolina, 28, 35, 36, 37, 40
South Dakota, 35, 36, 37
Soviet Union, 92
Spain, 90, 99
Spartans, 62
Spencer, Herbert, 105, 106–7, 113
Sperm bank, 153
Spiritual kin: marriage of, prohibited, 14,
    63, 66, 67; and role confusion, 45
Spouse: descendant of, 36. *See also* Affinal
    relatives
Spouse's sibling, 92
Sri Lanka, 126
Statutes: rational basis for, 6; in U.S., 9,
    12–13, 25, 27–28, 30, 31, 40, 44; and
    interracial marriage, 13; in Europe, 70–
    71. *See also* Miscegenation laws
Stepchild, 26, 29, 90
Stepdaughter, 24, 28, 35, 36
Stepdaughter's daughter, 22, 25, 94
Stepfather, 31, 35
Stepmother: in U.S., 23, 24, 25, 27, 34, 35,
    36; in Europe, 66, 73, 94
Stepparent, 26, 29, 90
Steprelatives, 26, 31, 36
Stepsister, 35
Stepson, 24, 28, 35
Stepson's daughter, 22, 25, 94
Sterility: as result of consanguinity, 40, 86
St. Kilda Island, Scotland, 83
Succession, 70
Supreme Court: of U.S., 19, 23, 114; of
    Indiana, 98
Survival: of the fittest, 8, 52, 136; of soci-
    ety and marriage, 46, 50

Sweden, 41, 91, 92
Switzerland, 5, 90
Systems: of kinship terminology, 110

Table of Kindred and Affinity, 20–22, 24,
    28, 36, 72–73, 87
Taporetinal disease, 128
Taylor, Elizabeth, 62
Taylor, Jeremy, 99
Tennessee, 35, 36, 37, 40
Texas, 29, 35, 36, 37, 40
Textbooks, 117
Theory: as revealing culture, 13; lack of,
    13; alliance, 13, 14, 139; bioevolution-
    ary, 13, 119; genetic, 13, 121
Theutberga (queen of Lorraine), 66
Third cousins: defined, 10; and genetic
    risk, 54, 56, 124
Thomas Aquinas. See Aquinas, Thomas
Tower of London, 70
Traditions. See Culture
Tranquility: and marriage to wife's sister,
    48
Treason, 70
Tribe: and exogamy, 104
Tristan da Cunha, 96, 128
Troyer syndrome, 129
Tudor, Mary, 69, 71, 72
Tylor, Edward, 7, 14, 134, 136–39, 145

Uncle: in U.S., 19, 26, 27, 28, 31, 34, 41;
    as third degree relative, 33; in Europe,
    90, 92
Uncle's widow. See Uncle's wife
Uncle's wife, 23, 28, 34, 36, 66. See also
    Aunt
Uniform Marriage and Divorce Act, 2
Unilineal descent, 111, 139, 140, 148,
    150
Unions. See Marriage
United States: cousin marriage in, 1–3, 10,
    41, 42, 58, 60; marital law in, 5, 8, 12;
    affinal marriage in, 6, 45, 49, 73, 79;
    and evolution, 8, 113; cousin terminolo-
    gy in, 10; endogamy in, 13, 15; individ-
    ual freedom in, 16; consanguinity in,
    19, 31, 45, 46, 50–51, 57, 58, 59, 85,

152; monogamy in, 115, and immigra-
    tion, 151
Utah, 34, 37, 59

Vermont, 25, 35, 37, 40, 49
Victoria (queen of England), 3, 117
Victorian God of Science, 79, 80
Virginia, 27, 34, 35, 37, 40, 49
Visigoths, 99, 100

Wake, C. Staniland, 7
Waldrada (consort of King Lothair), 66
Washington, 35, 36, 37
Webster, Noah, 45, 46
West Virginia, 34, 37, 40
Widow, 24
Wife's aunt, 28
Wife's brother's daughter, 73
Wife's child's daughter, 26
Wife's cousin, 26
Wife's daughter: in U.S., 22–27 passim,
    29, 31, 34, 35, 36; in Europe, 73, 87,
    88, 94
Wife's daughter's daughter, 73
Wife's father, 88
Wife's father's sister, 73
Wife's granddaughter: in U.S., 23, 25–29
    passim, 34, 35, 36; in Mississippi, 35; in
    Europe, 88
Wife's grandmother, 23, 25, 36, 73
Wife's mother: in U.S., 22–25 passim, 35,
    36, 37; in Europe, 73, 88, 94
Wife's mother's sister, 73
Wife's niece, 28
Wife's sibling's daughter, 24
Wife's sister: controversy over, 6, 15, 45–
    47, 49, 75, 77, 102; in U.S., 22–24, 27,
    28; in Bible, 25, 48, 94; in Europe, 73,
    80, 87
Wife's sister's daughter, 73
Wife's son's daughter, 73
Wife's stepdaughter, 27, 34
Wisconsin, 35, 37, 40, 59, 60
World War II, 83, 121, 125
Wyoming, 35, 37

Zoologists: on advantages to inbreeding, 1

MARTIN OTTENHEIMER, who received his Ph.D. in anthropology from Tulane University in 1971, is a professor of anthropology at Kansas State University. In 1994–95 he was president of the Central States Anthropological Society. He is the author of *Marriage in Domoni: Husbands and Wives in an Indian Ocean Community* (1985) and *Modeling Systems of Kinship and Marriage* (1992) and the coauthor of *Historical Dictionary of the Comoro Islands* (1994).

DATE DUE

GAYLORD			PRINTED IN U.S.A.